The Catholic Guide to Depression

The Catholic Guide to Depression

How the Saints, the Sacraments, and
Psychiatry Can Help You Break Its Grip
and Find Happiness Again

Aaron Kheriaty, MD

with Fr. John Cihak, STD

SOPHIA INSTITUTE PRESS
Manchester, New Hampshire

Sophia Institute Press
Box 5284, Manchester, NH 03108
1-800-888-9344

www.SophiaInstitute.com

Sophia Institute Press® is a registered trademark of Sophia Institute.

Library of Congress Cataloging-in-Publication Data

Kheriaty, Aaron.
    The Catholic guide to depression : how the saints, the sacraments, and psychiatry can help you break its grip and find happiness again / Aaron Kheriaty with Fr. John Cihak, STD.
      p. ; cm.
    Includes bibliographical references.
    ISBN 978-1-933184-76-0 (pbk. : alk. paper)
    I. Cihak, John R. II. Sophia Institute (New York, N.Y.) III. Title.
    [DNLM: 1. Depression. 2. Catholicism—psychology. 3. Spiritual
      Therapies. WM 171.5]

616.85'27— dc23

2012029992

For Matt Allen and Gabriel Scheller:

Requiescant in pace.

Contents

Foreword ix

Introduction xvii

Part I
Understanding Depression

1. Types of Depression and Their Causes 5

2. Depression and the Spiritual Life 35

3. Depression and Related Disorders 79

4. Depression and the Tragedy of Suicide 89

Part II
Overcoming Depression

5. Medication and Other Biological Treatments 113

6. Psychotherapy: Its Benefits and Limitations. 135

7. Spiritual Help for Depression 167

8. Divine Filiation and the Virtue of Hope. 203

Appendices

1. Resources for Further Reading 227

2. Prayers in Times of Distress 231

3. Address of Pope John Paul II
    on the Theme of Depression 243

About the Authors 247

Foreword

by J. David Franks, Ph.D.

Now that His heart is opened and His hands with wounds are lit,
There is no cross of our living where His body will not fit,
There is no sin of ours for which He has not a wound.
Oh, then, from Thine altar, Savior, come where Thy sheep are found!
See how Thy creature is pierced to depths profound!

Paul Claudel, Coronal

The pain of history piles up, and depression seizes more and more. The advantages of the modern world are there to see, but an immense psychic cost is incurred. Constant innovation and movement have wrought dislocation and alienation, amplifying the anxiety of mortal existence. The book in your hands is essential reading for our time. Depression is the modern affliction, and Dr. Kheriaty, with help from Fr. Cihak, has attained to the profundity of this complex reality, which ultimately must be understood under the sign of solidarity.

Descent into Darkness

Life bears such simple and nourishing joy: the delicious air of evening, the radiance of natures under our questioning, the love of family and friends, generosity between strangers, the virtually infinite condensation of abundance in great literature and art and music, a good run when the air is dry, the vivifying spontaneity of children. To be sure, suffering intrudes in every life, but the sun rises, and most of us are able to start again. Even in the darkness, we yet see the glimmerings of exuberant life.

But some there are for whom darkness comes, and all light, and all memory of light, is obliterated. Every inhalation is a premonition of suffocation; possibility fails; time encases them in unbreakable concrete that stretches endlessly. A blackness closer and more invasive of marrow than the ninth plague envelops. A night falls in which dawn is incredible. Depression means englobement in a world without hope, even more unrelenting and unrelieved than Dante's passage through hell or the post-apocalyptic world of Cormac McCarthy's *The Road*.

Some simple human hope is necessary or one cannot do anything. All of us get out of bed in the morning because there is something to be done, some desire to fulfill, requiring a basic expectation that our powers can have effect in the world, that there are purposes worth pursuing. Depression means losing grip on simple human hope. It means losing the basic tendency or appetite to expand, to rise. It is to be trapped, and sinking.

Wisdom in Darkness

What Dr. Kheriaty offers here is an elegant work of Christian wisdom, synthesizing science, philosophy, and theology. No dramatic aspect of life, and certainly not depression, can be adequately accounted for without the Christian revelation of the human person as created in the image of God, redeemed in Christ, and called to Trinitarian communion. These are the plot points that alone render meaningful the trajectory of life.

God the Father's plan of loving goodness, the set of providential stratagems to raise to eternal happiness every single human person, is completely concentrated in Jesus Christ, the Word of God, through whom all things were made, who descends without reserve into the sin-conditioned flesh of human existence, loving us to the end in total self-expenditure, pouring out the blood and water of his Sacred Heart into the channels of the world. Jesus, in the mysteries of his life, consummated in the Paschal Mystery, becomes the very fluid dynamics of all our staying and moving, of all our breaking and healing.

And the mystery of the Cross reveals even the meaning of darkness, depression included.

Christian anthropology secures a fact knowable by reason without sanctifying grace, but which often goes unrecognized without that grace: that the human person is a body-soul unity (integral humanism). And faith sees that this unity finds its measure only in the gracious initiatives of providence. This book shows the fruitfulness of the Catholic integration of faith and reason for engaging mental illness, eschewing, on the one hand, the supernaturalism/fideism/moralism that fails to see how the gracious life of God reassumes into itself all the schemes of recurrence of nature and history and, on the other hand, the materialism that misses the whole dramatic context of human life.

On the one hand, Christians often fail explicitly to maintain what belongs to their faith; in the religion of the Incarnation, integral humanism is central. There is a temptation among Catholics to explain away depression as if there were no medical issue involved—simply a spiritual failure on the part of the sufferer. There is a powerful spiritual reality at play in depression, but the insinuation that the sufferer is somehow at fault gets things exactly backward: it is the innocence of the depressed one that is the key. This book descends into crucial details about mental illness, but it also, and even more impressively, descends into the mystery at the heart of this, as of all, suffering.

On the other hand, the dominant way of missing the unity of the human person is to reduce everything to material processes. Depressed? Take the right medication, and that's that.

The great medical progress of the modern world is dogged by the ambiguity introduced by a materialistic reduction of the human person. For instance, in medicalization, there is often segregation. We do not want to see suffering; as a society, we hide it away. We construct public spaces that have been sanitized, in which the question of suffering and death is tamed, made less urgent, less demanding of an impassioned quest on our part to seek the answer why. There is in fact no answer without true love, but that, most inconveniently for our consumerist desire, always means we must suffer along with the suffering.

The bourgeoisifying marginalization of suffering is a flight from solidarity; it is the pretense that life is really about being healthy, successful, beautiful, rich, young, independent. Suffering exposes this as a fatuous delusion. It interrupts the ideology of libertarian autonomy. It insists that there is no authentic exercise of autonomy not rooted in givenness, and therefore that there is no human life without a crying need for love. We depend radically on each other.

Solidarity in Darkness

Mortal existence is a bleeding. Amid the immense joys, there is the fact that vanity and futility pervade all our projects, for we will surely die. Then there is the spiritual laceration that love entails, the surrendering of mere self-will so as to be one in spirit with another. And there is never enough time for the ones we love. Love means exposure to the pain of separation. Loved ones decline and die. We never love well enough. We are never loved well enough.

And the slaughter! The savagery everywhere found in history, the diabolical fury unleashed against the weak and innocent: the sex trade, the culture of death, the sexualization of children, the abuse and murder of children, the domestic barbarity of aggressive domination, the extermination of peoples, the extermination of one person after another in nihilist bloodlust—all the victims, victims, piled up, piled high.

We must all be present to the victims, to the extent we can: "Blessed are they who mourn" (Matt. 5:4). But some are dragged entire into the vortex of the world's pain. To be depressed is to be a wound open to the stinging air of reality. Pretending that depression is "all in the head" or that it is just a matter of neurochemistry is false consciousness. The depressed stand on the marches of the world, where the waters of chaos threaten to overwhelm the bright little circle of life we enjoy. They feel all the deficiencies of love.

And depression is a remembering, in the strong Augustinian sense: memory as presence. The depressed one remembers the victims, absorbing their psychic pain in every member of his or her body, into the deep places of the spirit.

Jesus absorbs all the horror of selfishness and suffering and sin, draining the dregs of the chalice of finitude bleeding. However, this remarkable book, in its profound spiritual wisdom, indicates that people suffering depression participate in this saving darkness of Christ. Certainly, baptismal grace renders suffering a mode of direct configuration to Christ crucified. But I would argue, in accord with the strong tendency of this book, that even for the unbaptized person, depression is an objective mode of union with Christ. The depressed person is an innocent in hell; Christ descends without reserve into the hell of suffering. When there is someone suffering, there is Christ suffering.

Abandonment Is a Mode of Union

True love costs everything and gives everything, burns right through and joins the extremes of ecstasy and pain in its astonishing synthesis of all things. Self-sacrificial love stands surety for the impossible paradox of mortal existence: a vertiginous drama of anguish and hope, blood and joy—astonishing in its sweetness, appalling in its brutality. And the crossing of the poles occurs in Christ crucified, for God so loved the world ...

Johann Christoph Arnold recounts words from his father, Heinrich, who lost his first child at three months:

> Children are closer than anyone else to the heart of Jesus, and he points to them as an example for us. The fact that children have to suffer is very strange. It is as if they are bearing someone else's guilt, as if they are suffering because of the fall of creation. In a way they seem to be paying the wages of sin....

This mystery of substitutionary suffering, the mystery at the heart of salvation, the mystery of a solidarity forsaking safe boundaries: this is the mystery without which depression cannot really be understood.

Only in the total context of a love that spans the world in its total dramatic amplitude can one dare approach the mystery of depression. Only in the light of the descent of Jesus into the darkness of human existence can the darkness of depression take on light. The ultimate Word of response to the cry of human agony is the Word spoken by the Father into the hell of human hopelessness, unto the silence of death.

In loving us to the end, even into the depths of godforsakenness, the Son is paradoxically unfolding his infinite love for his Father, carrying out his loving will to save every single one of us. Jesus simply is the reception of the Father's will. Therefore, as the Swiss theologian Hans Urs von Balthasar insists, the abandonment of Jesus on the Cross is the absolute revelation of the unbreakable, eternal union of Father and Son, and from that love alone do all the loves of the world flow. Jesus' becoming our despair (without himself despairing!); his being made to be sin, who knew no sin: this is the utter obedience of the one who is our leader in faith. To trust the Father even when all light is extinguished, all signs of his presence are gone: this is Christian faith, and that faith—mysteriously—hopes and loves without limit.

Will You Watch with Me One Hour?

Should the depressed person, then, not seek medical help? Heaven forbid such a supernaturalist misreading of Christian solidarity! "Deliver us from evil," Jesus commands us to pray to his Father. Trouble will find us; we need not court it. And any bout of depression inserts a person into the dark infinity of hell; there is no need to multiply infinities.

It is from the West, with its Christian humanism, that medical technology has gained its decisive impetus to mitigate effectively so much human suffering. The Father does not want to lose anyone in the darkness; he does not want suicide. Yes, we must stay with Jesus, we must seek to be with him (even when he goes into the garden of agony), we must endure the darkness—but we do not need to be depressed to be in union with Jesus.

By the transfusion of the Cross, there now courses through this infinitely suffering thing that is the vast system of mortal existence the new medium of the Christian life. We live only by the blood and water flowing from the Sacred Heart of Jesus. But we must never preempt the particular way of being united with Jesus that our Father has in mind for us. Healed of depression, let us continue to watch with the Lord. Let us do so under the mantle of the Blessed Virgin Mary, at the foot of the Cross.

In our vigil, we have in this remarkable book an indispensable guide, a great gift of providence for our time. The same God who so elegantly designs the patterns of nature so that medical remedies might be found for depression is the same God who enters our drama so that we might be liberated into a kingdom of unending light and life and love: this book unfolds in that intersection of nature and grace. And we can live in that intersection far more wisely because of this book.

The Catholic Guide to Depression

And God himself will be with them; he will wipe away every tear from their eyes, and death shall be no more, neither shall there be mourning nor crying nor pain any more, for the former things have passed away. (Rev. 21: 3-4)

Introduction

*"Depression is a disorder of mood, so mysteriously painful and
elusive in the way it becomes known to the self — to the mediating
intellect — as to verge close to being beyond description."*

William Styron, *Darkness Visible*

The Problem of Depression

Depression is a disturbance — often serious and sometimes life-
threatening — in a person's psychological and physical functioning. This description is only a starting point, however, for
depression is a complex condition that cannot be described
exclusively using a disease-based model alone. The science of
medicine has taught us much about depression, but the full story
of this affliction is more complicated. Depression is often caused
and influenced by, in addition to biological and psychological
factors, various social, cultural, and spiritual factors, some quite
complex. Because it is multifaceted, depression requires several
complementary perspectives to understand, address, and cure it
adequately. We will return to these factors throughout the course
of this book.

Regardless of how we understand depression's causes and cures,
it is clear that the burden of depression worldwide is tremendous.
Among the serious and chronic mental illnesses, depression is

the most frequently occurring. Research strongly suggests, moreover, that depression exerts the greatest societal burden of all the psychiatric disorders. The World Health Organization ranks depression fourth among the ten leading causes of disease burden globally; it is expected to rise to second on that list in the next twenty years. As one psychiatric researcher and clinician put it, we now live in an "age of melancholy."[1]

For someone who has not experienced it firsthand, the suffering associated with depression is difficult to appreciate. I recall a patient, a woman in her seventies, who had suffered bouts of severe depression and also suffered from a cancer that had nearly killed her. The cancer was eventually cured after a long period of physical pain and grueling chemotherapy. She told me, however, that if she could choose between going through the cancer or enduring another episode of clinical depression, she would choose the cancer in an instant. "The suffering caused by depression was far, far worse," she explained. A few years after she stopped coming to me for treatment, I heard from another colleague that while in the midst of another serious depressive episode, this patient had taken her own life. She was a practicing Catholic. She left behind a husband, five children, and several grandchildren.

The very word *depression* probably does not do justice to the reality of this affliction. The term suggests a slight dip on a flat surface, like a "depression" in the road. The experience of depression, by contrast, is not just a dip, but a dark and miserable pit. It is an intense and serious cause of mental, physical, and spiritual suffering.

Many of us who have not been visited by this affliction might mistakenly believe that we know what depression feels like. After all, everyone feels down and dejected from time to time. We all have experiences of sadness, fear, or mental fatigue. Depression,

[1] Dan Blazer, *The Age of Melancholy: Major Depression and Its Social Origins* (New York: Routledge, 2005), 3.

we might assume, must be more or less like the common everyday blues—perhaps more intense or longer in duration, but not qualitatively different. This assumption is mistaken. While there is a sort of pale analogy between depression and ordinary experiences of feeling down, depression is really another animal altogether.

If what psychiatrists and psychologists call depression is not just a more intense form of sadness, although it can certainly involve intense sadness, then what is it? Furthermore, what causes depression? Is it a biological problem, with roots in our genetic constitution? Is it a psychological problem, stemming from troubles in our thinking or behavior, or perhaps from adverse life experiences? Is it a social problem caused by unhealthy relationships, or by problems in the wider culture in which we live? Or perhaps it is a spiritual problem, related to difficulties with faith, personal sins, or problems in our relationship with God. Perhaps the more important question for some readers is not what causes depression, but what can be done about it? I hope, in the course of this book, to shed some light on these questions.

The Purpose of This Book

I am a psychiatrist and medical educator who has treated, both in the hospital and in the clinic, many patients who suffer from depression and related disorders. Catholics and other Christians sometimes seek me out as their physician because they want to see a mental-health professional who shares their faith. As a result, I have treated many Catholics, including priests and religious, who suffer from depression.

In the course of this clinical work, I have been asked many questions about depression and its relationship to the spiritual life. Some patients have family members and friends, or even pastors and spiritual directors, who have given them unhelpful and untrue advice for dealing with depression. "If you only had more faith, you would not suffer like this"; or "All you need to do is

ıd read the Bible more—not take medications or see a
ɲnerapist"; or "This is simply a biological malady and has
ıl bearing on the life of faith." This sort of counsel often does
ıɩ. ɩe to worsen depression than to relieve it. It betrays an igno-
rance of depression as an illness and fails to appreciate the impact
of depression on a person's spiritual life and faith.

This book is primarily for people who suffer from depression,
as well as those close to them—family members or friends—who
want to understand better what their loved one is going through.
It may also prove helpful to priests, pastors, spiritual directors,
and catechists. Finally, it may be of interest to mental-health
practitioners who want to understand their Christian patients
better. This book is intended for educational purposes only: it
is not a treatment manual and cannot serve as a substitute for
psychiatric care or spiritual direction. For a depressed individual, this book can profitably be used in conjunction with treatment methods such as psychotherapy and medications, when
these are recommended by a competent physician or mental-
health professional. Likewise, this book should be seen as a complement to, and not a substitute for, personal spiritual direction
and pastoral care.

Too often, people avoid seeking professional medical help
when they are suffering from an illness, particularly a mental illness. They do themselves a disservice by trying, without proper
expertise or training, to self-diagnose and self-treat. Long hours
searching the Internet for explanations of symptoms, and many
failed trials of self-help strategies, often precede a visit to the doctor. In the meantime, the person's condition may have worsened,
and valuable opportunities to treat early in the course of the illness are lost.

If this book does anything, I hope it convinces those suffering
from depression to obtain a clinical consultation with a competent psychiatrist sooner rather than later.

Introduction

The Catholic Perspective of This Book

This book is written by a Catholic and is especially intended for Catholics and other Christians. On matters of faith and morals, this book remains faithful to the teachings of the Catholic Church. Yet I am convinced that Protestant and Orthodox Christians will find the theological perspectives in this book congruent with their beliefs, perhaps with the exception of a few sections that discuss distinctively Catholic practices, such as the sacrament of Confession, which is not part of most Protestant denominations. The common doctrines that unite all Christians are greater than those that still separate us, and so I believe that this book can be profitably appreciated by anyone who confesses that "Jesus is Lord" (Rom. 10:9).

This book is also informed by a philosophical understanding of the human person consistent with the Christian faith. Throughout these pages, I attempt to integrate perspectives from the modern psychological and medical sciences with the teachings of Sacred Scripture and Tradition, with special attention given to the insights from the Church Fathers and saints. This book is grounded in the conviction that to know ourselves fully as human beings, we must know Jesus Christ. As the Second Vatican Council taught, "The truth is that only in the mystery of the incarnate Word [Jesus Christ] does the mystery of man take on light."[2]

Some readers might wonder: what do psychiatry or psychology have to do with religion or spirituality? Would it make sense for a dermatologist to write about skin disorders from a Christian perspective? If not, then why the need for a psychiatrist to write about depression from a Christian perspective? John Paul II gave an excellent answer to this question when he said the following to a gathering of psychiatrists:

[2] *Gaudium et spes*, no. 22.

By its very nature your work often brings you to the threshold of human mystery. It involves sensitivity to the tangled workings of the human mind and heart, and openness to the ultimate concerns that give meaning to people's lives. These areas are of the utmost importance to the Church, and they call to mind the urgent need for a constructive dialogue between science and religion for the sake of shedding greater light on the mystery of man in his fullness.[3]

This last sentence encapsulates one of the central purposes of this book. It seeks to be a constructive dialogue between science and religion for the sake of shedding greater light on the mystery of man in his fullness. More specifically, this dialogue can shed greater light on the mystery of this affliction that we call depression, so that those who suffer may seek and find more effective relief. Dermatology runs only skin deep. Psychiatry delves into the tangled workings of the human mind and heart, where people grapple with problems of self-identity, of meaning and purpose. As a result, psychiatry cannot help but dialogue with philosophy and theology, which must grapple with the same questions about who we are and why we are here.

According to its Greek root, the word *psychiatrist* literally means "doctor of the soul." But in modern psychiatry, this original meaning has largely been abandoned. The philosopher Plato said that the ancient Greek physicians of his day failed to cure diseases because they separated the soul (*psyche*) from the body (*soma*). The same complaint could probably be leveled against contemporary psychiatrists: we focus on the body, especially the brain, to the exclusion of the soul. Others have leveled the opposite complaint against psychiatry and psychology, claiming that

---

[3] John Paul II, Address to the Members of the American Psychiatric Association and the World Psychiatric Association, January 4, 1993.

we overstep our limitations and often tread on territory once occupied by religion. For example, Bishop Fulton Sheen wondered whether the psychoanalyst's couch has replaced the priest's confessional. Philip Rieff wrote about this cultural phenomenon in his classic book, *The Triumph of the Therapeutic*.[4]

Despite the legitimate concerns raised by these complaints, John Paul II reaffirmed the real need for a constructive dialogue between psychiatry and psychology on the one hand and philosophy and theology on the other. A genuine dialogue presupposes that both parties involved have something worthwhile to say to each other. The confessional was never meant to cure neurosis or other mental disturbances, and the couch was never meant to absolve sin. Where there is psychological disorder or mental illness, we need good medicine. The late Pope continues in the same address I quoted earlier:

> The Confessional is not and cannot be an alternative to the psychoanalyst or psychotherapist's office, nor can one expect the Sacrament of Penance to heal truly pathological conditions. The confessor is not a physician or a healer in the technical sense of the term; in fact, if the condition of the penitent seems to require medical care, the confessor should not deal with the matter himself, but should send the penitent to competent and honest professionals.[5]

This book is informed by great respect for the benefits offered by modern science, modern medicine, and the healing methods of psychiatry, including good psychotherapy. Because God created the world, all truth is ultimately one. Therefore, the truths of science, sufficiently verified and rightly interpreted, can never

[4] *The Triumph of the Therapeutic: Uses of Faith After Freud* (New York: Harper & Row, 1966).
[5] John Paul II, Address to the Members of the American Psychiatric Association and the World Psychiatric Association.

contradict the truths of revealed religion, rightly understood. Therefore, I encourage a both-and rather than an either-or approach to healing. When a patient who is a religious believer asks whether he should pray more or take a medication to help with an episode of major depression, my answer is yes to both.

Modern psychiatry has much to offer religious believers in the same sense that modern cardiology has much to offer religious believers: psychiatrists can offer medical remedies for diseases, illnesses, and sufferings that afflict people, including people of devout religious faith. Furthermore, psychiatry and related psychological sciences have gained insights, through research, clinical experience, and careful observation, that can shed light on perennial questions about human beings and human nature. Some of these are questions that have also been explored and addressed for centuries by the great religious and philosophical traditions. The search for answers to these questions can be enriched by insights from modern science and medicine.

Some readers might wonder why this book specifically addresses Christians. Why not broaden the perspective to include religious believers in general?

The reason is that it is difficult to write about "religion" in general. Although we can say that man is religiously oriented by nature, there is no such thing as generic "religion"; there are only particular religions, each proposing different (and not always compatible) answers to questions about suffering and its meaning. I have never met anyone who believes in "religion," but I have met a lot of Christians, Jews, Muslims, Hindus, and Buddhists. These religions may very well have some elements in common, but to lump them all together under the generic heading of "religion" and then try to address this heterogeneous group as if it were a unified reality would be to remain hopelessly abstract. Rather than addressing everyone, I think that such a book would end up speaking directly to almost no one.

Introduction

Consider the different approaches to suffering found in different religions. We can take just one example. For a Buddhist, suffering is actually an illusion; in the last analysis, it is not real. The solution to suffering, according to Buddhism, is to detach oneself in such a way that one frees oneself from the illusion of suffering, the illusion of duality between oneself and everything else in the world. Contrast this with Judaism, which offers, for example, the figure of the suffering man Job, who hopes in God in the midst of his suffering, all the while never denying that his suffering is real. Whether it is Job's suffering, or the suffering expressed by the psalmist, or the suffering of the Israelites while enslaved in Egypt—nowhere in the Hebrew Scriptures is it suggested that this suffering is an illusion. It is real and cannot be ignored. Because it is real, this suffering calls forth hope in God's deliverance, hope in the promises made by God through the prophets, and an expectation of a future Messiah.

If the Buddhist view of suffering contrasts with that of Judaism, it contrasts even more with the view of suffering proposed by Christianity. For Christians, as for Jews, suffering is not illusory. In Christianity, suffering not only calls for hope of future deliverance; suffering actually becomes redemptive. The Christian's suffering takes on meaning when it is united to the redemptive suffering of Jesus Christ on the Cross.

It is precisely in the Cross that our salvation is found. It should be clear from these briefly sketched contrasts that there is no single "religious" answer to coping with suffering, whether we are talking about depression or other forms of mental or physical suffering.

Of all the religions of the world, I would suggest that Christianity offers the most compelling answers to the problem of suffering. While I admire the ancient Stoic philosophers in their stark resolve in the face of suffering, I believe we ultimately need a relationship with the living God to endure most adequately the suffering we face in this world. Consider the approach to suffering currently offered by secular humanism, which proposes to eliminate all pain and suffering someday through purely technological means. Since this is clearly not currently possible (and even in the future it will never be completely possible), the backup plan seems to be to eliminate suffering by eliminating the people who are suffering; for example, through euthanasia or assisted suicide. This strikes me as being a rather primitive and destructive form of denial. If we are looking for pragmatic ways to cope, non-religious answers to suffering appear rather pale and thin compared with religious responses that do not shrink from or ignore the reality of human suffering.

Virtually every saint, teacher, or great mystic of the Church has written on the problem of human suffering, and many have grappled with the suffering rooted in human emotional life. In fact, centuries before the emergence of psychology and psychiatry as scientific disciplines, Christian philosophy and theology devoted considerable attention to human affectivity, including depression. Some notable thinkers in this regard include St. Augustine in the fourth century and St. John Damascene in the eighth century. One of the most perceptive and enduring philosophical and theological accounts of human emotion can be found in the writings of St. Thomas Aquinas. Although he did not advance a theory of repression or other "defense mechanisms" described by modern psychologists, already in the thirteenth century he presented a remarkably thorough and profound account of human emotions, including depression.[6] Also noteworthy in this

---

[6] Cf. St. Thomas Aquinas, *Summa Theologica*, I-II. Contemporary scholars still study St. Thomas's account of human affectivity. Compare, for example, Stephen Loughlin, "*Tristitia et Dolor:* Does Aquinas Have a Robust Understanding of Depression?" (*Nova et vetera* [English edition] 3 [2005]: 761-784) and Paul Gondreau, *The Passions of Christ's Soul in the Theology of St. Thomas Aquinas* (Münster: Aschendorff, 2002).

regard is St. Thomas More's meditation on Christ's agony in the garden, *The Sadness of Christ*, which he wrote during his imprisonment in the Tower of London while awaiting his own execution.[7]

This is not to say, however, that practicing a religious faith (or any belief system) guarantees that a person will remain free from suffering, including depression. Christian faith does not propose any such doctrine. The spiritual realities of life in Christ—the sacraments; prayer; the theological virtues of faith, hope, and love; the natural virtues, including courage and magnanimity; and good works—all play an important role in our mental health. But they do not immunize a person against depression or other mental illnesses. Unfortunately, the mistaken idea that they do circulates among some religious believers. It is a notion we must put to rest because it simply is not true. Of course, oftentimes a person's behaviors, such as overeating or smoking, contribute to causing diseases, such as diabetes or lung cancer. But it certainly does not follow that *all* physical illnesses can be prevented with the right behaviors or the right beliefs. So also with mental illnesses.

Some afflictions currently classified as mental disorders are best understood as "diseases" in the strict sense of the term—that is, they come from disordered biological factors that lie mostly beyond one's control, such as our genes. Disorders such as schizophrenia or bipolar (formerly called manic-depressive) illness, although manifested at the psychological or behavioral level, have very strong genetic and neurobiological causes and cannot be prevented, managed, or cured through psychological means, belief, or willpower alone.

Other mental illnesses result from being at the far end of the spectrum on a normally distributed trait—such as having abnormally low intelligence, or possessing more extreme personality

---

[7] St. Thomas More, *The Complete Works of St. Thomas More*, Vol. XIV: *De Tristitia Christi* (New Haven: Yale University Press, 1976).

traits. These traits are affected by factors such as genetics and early environmental influences, which lie outside one's control or are not dependent upon religious faith. Other mental disorders are the result of trauma, including psychological trauma from devastating life experiences, or physical trauma from injuries to the brain. Obviously, these cannot be prevented by any belief system or moral practice.

Throughout history, many saints and people of heroic virtue suffered from mental illness of one sort or another. If we do not recognize this fact, we run the risk of uncharitably and unjustly stigmatizing those who suffer from depression. If the saints, the men and women *closest* to God who were *exemplary* in their faith and good works, experienced profound sorrow and even periods of depression, then it certainly follows that faith alone does not inoculate the believer against this affliction.

In the Apostles' Creed, Christians profess faith in the "resurrection of the body." We are neither disembodied souls nor simply material bodies. Rather, in each human person there is a substantial unity between soul and body, between spirit and matter. St. Thomas Aquinas explored the implications of this view with regard to human affectivity and emotional life: spirit (that is, reason and love) ought to shape our physical desires and passions, and on the other hand, the passions and emotions influence our intellect and rational capacities. This philosophical perspective, confirmed by Christian revelation, is also consistent with experimental findings from modern medical science. It is clear that there exists a profound connection between the mind and the body: what affects the one has ramifications for the other.

In a manner consistent with this view of the human person, we will approach depression both from "above," examining its psychological, social, and spiritual causes and cures, as well as from "below," examining its genetic and other biological roots and its medical remedies.

Introduction

This notion of the substantial unity of body and soul in the human person constitutes one of the basic philosophical presuppositions that informs the approach in this book. Among the other fundamental presuppositions, drawn from the Catholic philosophical and theological tradition and confirmed by scientific psychology, I include the following: On the natural level, human persons are *rational;* that is, we are able to seek and to grasp the truth. This intelligence gives rise to rational desire (free will), so that we are *volitional,* able to shape our emotional lives and our desires, in order to live in accordance with the truth. That is, we are *free* to choose between good and evil and are therefore *responsible* for our actions before others and before God. Finally, our intelligent freedom empowers us to be *relational* by nature, capable of entering into relationships of love and reciprocity with other human persons and with God. As has been mentioned, because of the unity of body and soul, our thoughts, choices, feelings, and actions are intrinsically related to each other. The Catholic view of the human person, in other words, is *holistic* — open to every aspect of the truth about the human person. In this book, I therefore attempt to take a holistic approach to understanding and treating depression.

Christian doctrine provides a rich and balanced view of our human situation. We are created in the image and likeness of God, and thus fundamentally good and endowed by God with an inherent dignity. At the same time, our nature is wounded, fallen through Original Sin, and thus inescapably flawed, inclined toward evil, and subject to illness and suffering. But more important, we have been redeemed by Christ's Sacrifice on the Cross and called to union with Christ and his Body, the Church. We are being sanctified by the continued work of the Holy Spirit. Therefore, we can receive forgiveness and redemption by contritely turning in faith toward God's love and mercy. Indeed, we are able to find meaning, hope, and redemptive value even in the midst of suffering or illness—perhaps, I would suggest, even in the midst of depression.

These features are central to who we are as human persons: substantially one, bodily and spiritual, rational, relational, free, created good, fallen and therefore wounded, but redeemed and capable of being sanctified by God.[8] These characteristics, unfortunately, are often denied or contradicted by many modern and overly narrow psychological theories. Such incomplete accounts of the human person often amount to flawed philosophies masquerading as valid "scientific" conclusions, which ultimately result in flawed treatments.

Psychiatry and Religion

Some Christians approach psychiatry with a degree of mistrust or suspicion. The historical roots of this go back at least a hundred years, to the beginning of modern psychiatry at the end of the nineteenth century. Perhaps a brief historical detour will help us understand why so many Christians and mental-health professionals seem to have difficulty understanding or appreciating one another. To begin with, the founder of psychoanalysis, and probably the most famous psychiatrist in history, Sigmund Freud, was profoundly antireligious. In fact, he argued that religious belief was not just mistaken; it was pathological. Believers were not simply wrong, according to Freud; they were sick; they had an illness. Religious faith was "neurotic." In his phrase, religion was the "universal obsessive neurosis of mankind."

Furthermore, his strange view of human psychology claimed that man, at his core, was merely a bundle of unconscious sexual and aggressive drives. Freud's biographer Ernest Jones listed the

---

[8] For a fuller account of this framework, see the article by E. Christian Brugger, "Psychology and Christian Anthropology," *Edification: Journal for the Society of Christian Psychology* 3(1) (2009): 5-18.

six most common words Freud used to describe our unconscious mental life: repressed, active, bestial, infantile, alogical, and of course, sexual. Such are the forces bubbling up from the seething cauldron of our unconscious. When the patient (with the expert assistance of the psychoanalyst) looked inward, what he saw was not pretty. This hardly sounds consonant with the Christian view of the dignity of the human person, who is (although fallen and flawed) still rational and free—capable of knowledge and love, created in the image and likeness of God.

The next in the line of famous psychiatrists, Carl Jung, appeared at first glance to be friendlier toward religion. But in some ways his theories were even more subversive of religion than Freud's. While not overtly denying God's existence, Jung argued that God is merely housed in mankind's "collective unconscious." In the last analysis, for Jung, we are God and God is us. No claim could be more contrary to the Judeo-Christian understanding of God. In fact, the temptation to self-divinization was precisely what Satan whispered in the ear of our first parents: "You shall be like God" (Gen. 3:5).

Now, the Freudian and Jungian accounts of religious belief—despite their claims to scientific status—were in fact unscientific, indeed untestable and therefore unfalsifiable and circular in their reasoning. Many who wanted to turn psychology into a legitimate science wanted none of this mumbo jumbo.

The next wave in psychology after psychoanalysis was behaviorism, which dominated the psychological sciences in the middle of the twentieth century. But the behaviorists often went off the rails as well—just in a different direction. According to behaviorism, an objective science of the mind must be restricted to externally observable things. The only things that mattered were measurable environmental inputs and observable behavioral outputs. What transpired in the subjective "mind" was set aside.

Behaviorist experiments produced some interesting scientific findings in psychology. While these experimental findings were one thing, radical behaviorist theory, which was not scientific but ideological, was another. Radical behaviorists claimed that the human being is *nothing but* a wholly determined product of inputs and outputs. The mind functioned like a machine that runs entirely on its prior programming—its history of rewards and punishments. This was all we needed to explain the human person and human psychology. This theory waved farewell to human reason and free will.

It followed from this that, according to radical behaviorism, human beings had no distinctive stature among the animals. The most influential American behaviorist, B. F. Skinner, actually claimed that we could understand humanity completely by studying the behavior of rats and pigeons. Skinner's bestselling manual on childrearing recommended that parents feed their children according to rigidly controlled schedules and give them a minimum of attention and affection. The title of his most famous book on human psychology is telling: *Beyond Freedom and Dignity*. There you have it.

Naturally, this sort of nonsense could continue for only so long. The brain was smuggled back into psychology through scientific advances in neuroimaging techniques such as MRI and PET scans. More refined methods in experimental psychology allowed for advances in studying social and interpersonal relationships. Things began to look much more complex, and much more interesting, than the behaviorists dreamed.

But even today human reason and free will are often still denied by many neuroscientists or scientific popularizers. Their conclusions are in fact bad philosophy masquerading as science. The so-called New Atheist writers, including Richard Dawkins, Daniel Dennett, and Christopher Hitchens, try to convince us that all things distinctively human, including religious faith, can be (or someday will be) shown to be reducible to chemical discharges in the brain. According to this ideology, all that we are, all that we think, and all that we do are completely determined by our biology. (We should note, however, that these writers implicitly appeal to our reason and free will in asking us to rationally consider and freely accept their arguments.)

Today, brain science has made tremendous advances in exploring biological aspects of human behavior and mental illness. Yet for all this scientific progress, psychiatry still often misses what is highest and most noble in its human subject. As one psychiatrist put it, "Today, psychiatry has rejoined mainstream medicine and holds empirical science sacred. Psychiatry focuses on the observable, and at least implicitly, debunks the mysterious. Therefore, psychiatry has lost depth even as it has gained precision."[9]

Is this trade-off necessary? I would suggest that the answer is no. We can gain precision and yet maintain a sense of mystery in the face of our subject—the human person—who, in the end, always remains beyond our complete grasp. The psychiatrist and philosopher Karl Jaspers wrote, "The object of psychiatry is man ... When we know him, we know something about him, rather than himself. Any total knowledge of man will prove to be a delusion brought about by raising one point of view to the status of an only one, one method to the status of a universal method." Jaspers reminds us that, "like every person, every patient is unfathomable."[10]

As mentioned earlier, the word *psychiatrist* literally means "doctor of the soul." But as you can see from this brief history, modern psychiatry and the other psychological sciences have in one fashion or another often lost sight of the human soul. Psychiatry has often ignored man's dignity, his freedom, his rationality,

[9] Blazer, *The Age of Melancholy*, 143.
[10] Karl Jaspers, *Philosophy and the World: Selected Essays*, trans. E. B. Ashton (Washington, DC: Regnery Gateway, 1963), 213.

and his orientation toward God. Recent surveys show that among the various medical specialties, psychiatrists are the least religious physicians. Another study showed that Christian physicians are more likely than non-Christian physicians to refer patients with mental-health problems to a member of the clergy or a religious counselor, and less likely to refer them to a psychiatrist. The researcher Dr. Farr Curlin commented:

> Something about psychiatry, perhaps its historical ties to psychoanalysis and the anti-religious views of the early analysts such as Sigmund Freud, seems to dissuade religious medical students from choosing to specialize in this field. It also seems to discourage religious physicians from referring their patients to psychiatrists. Previous surveys have documented the unusual religious profile of psychiatry but this is the first study to suggest that that profile leads many physicians to look away from psychiatrists for help in responding to patients' psychological and spiritual suffering. Because psychiatrists take care of patients struggling with emotional, personal and relational problems, the gap between the religiousness of the average psychiatrist and her average patient may make it difficult for them to connect on a human level. Patients probably seek out, to some extent, physicians who share their views on life's big questions.[11]

This book attempts to help close this gap by bringing good medical and psychological science into contact with sound philosophy and theology. It is my firm conviction that Catholics need not fear or be suspicious of sound science. For science is simply a set of methods for exploring and discovering truths about the

[11] Quoted in University of Chicago Press Release, September 3, 2007: http://www.uchospitals.edu/news/2007/20070903-psychiatrists.html.

Introduction

natural world—the very world that God created. As St. Thomas Aquinas pointed out, since God is one, all truth—whether natural or supernatural, whether scientific or religious—is also one. Where there appears to be a contradiction between a discovery of science and a truth of faith, this is only an *apparent* conflict, based either upon inaccurate science or upon a misapplication of religious truths. It is important to note in this context that much of what passes for "science" in the popular media, or even in some apparently scientific circles, is not science at all, but theory or ideology masquerading as science.

Many today would have you believe that there has been a long-standing war between science and religion. This is nonsense; it is a myth that has been mindlessly repeated since the Enlightenment with little evidence then or now to support it. Modern science itself developed only in the Christian West. Science as we understand it today emerged in human history within the cultural context of Christian faith. This is not surprising, since the very practice of scientific inquiry presupposes that the world is fundamentally lawful, rationally ordered, and therefore knowable by the human intellect. But this is precisely the sort of world that a God who is *logos*—word, reason, truth, intelligence—would create. Modern science grew from the soil of a Christian culture and flourished among Christian believers. There is no war between science and religion—only misunderstandings, perhaps, or skirmishes among the ill-informed or overzealous on both sides. But these need not detain us.

So also, the historical tensions between psychiatry and religion described earlier were ill conceived and unnecessary. It is time for theologians and scientists, priests and doctors, patients and physicians to learn from one another. It is my hope that by examining depression from a Catholic perspective, this book can make a contribution to that dialogue.

The Catholic Guide to Depression

Part I

Understanding Depression

Chapter 1

Types of Depression and Their Causes

"The Tower of Babel never yielded such confusion of tongues
as this Chaos of Melancholy doth variety of symptoms."
Robert Burton, *The Anatomy of Melancholy* (1621)

∽

Major Depressive Disorder

What is depression, and how should we understand it? Is it a medical illness, like diabetes? Is it a transient emotional state, perhaps more intense than our typical moods, but different only in degree and not in kind? Is it part of some individuals' inborn genetic temperament, endured more frequently by those whose personalities tend toward "melancholic" traits? Is it a spiritual problem?

The current medical understanding of depression as an illness or disorder suggests that it is more than just routine sadness, and different from merely a somber or introverted temperament. But, then, what exactly is it? There is no simple answer to this question.

Before we delve into some of these more theoretical issues regarding the origins and causes of depression, we can begin simply with a description of the symptoms of depression. Regarding these features of depression, there tends to be universal agreement. Only after we have a good description of the "phenomena"—the manifestations and signs—of depression will we discuss various theories about its causes. The different subtypes of depression will be discussed in more detail later in this chapter. For now, please note that the use of the word *depression* here will be equivalent to and interchangeable with the term *major depressive disorder*, which is the official term used by psychiatrists to classify this affliction, or *melancholia*, the older word used to describe this illness. For our purposes, *depression*, *major depression*, and *melancholia* all signify more or less the same thing.

Depression is more than just an emotional state, although it certainly involves changes in a person's emotions and feelings. It is not synonymous with mere sadness, although sadness and fear are the predominant emotions experienced when one is depressed. This disorder affects the whole person: it involves one's emotions, one's perceptions, one's thoughts, and one's physical health. It involves the body as well as the mind; these two aspects of the human person are, after all, inseparably intertwined.

The subjective mental state experienced in depression is elusive and difficult to describe accurately. Some attempts to describe it depict a quality of "mental pain" or "psychic pain," although these terms are not typically found in most lists of symptoms. The novelist William Styron's memoir of depression is entitled *Darkness Visible*, a phrase taken from Milton's description of hell in *Paradise Lost*. Styron describes the experience of mental pain in this way:

> I was feeling in my mind a sensation close to, but indescribably different from, actual pain. This leads me to touch again on the elusive nature of such distress. That the word "indescribable" should present itself is not fortuitous, since it has to be emphasized that if the pain were readily describable most of the countless sufferers from this ancient affliction would have been able to confidently

depict for their friends and loved ones (even their physicians) some of the actual dimensions of their torment, and
perhaps elicit a comprehension that has been generally
lacking; such incomprehension has usually been due not
to a failure of sympathy but to the basic inability of healthy
people to imagine a form of torment so alien to everyday
experience. For myself, the pain is most closely connected
to drowning or suffocation — but even these images are off
the mark. [Psychologist and philosopher] William James,
who battled depression for many years, gave up the search
for an adequate portrayal, implying the near-impossibility
when he wrote in *The Varieties of Religious Experience*: "It is
a positive and active anguish, a sort of psychical neuralgia
wholly unknown to normal life."[12]

Styron goes on to protest the very use of the word *depression* as
a weak and inadequate term to describe this affliction. Again, he
is worth quoting:

When I was aware that I had been laid low by the disease,
I felt a need, among other things, to register a strong protest against the word "depression." Depression, most people know, used to be termed "melancholia," a word which
appears in English as early as the year 1305 and crops up
more than once in Chaucer, who in his usage seemed to
be aware of its pathological nuances. "Melancholia" would
still appear to be a far more apt and evocative word for the
blacker forms of this disorder, but it was usurped by a noun
with a bland tonality and lacking any magisterial presence,
used indifferently to describe an economic decline or a rut
in the ground, a true wimp of a word for such a major illness. It may be that the scientist generally held responsible

[12] William Styron, *Darkness Visible: A Memoir of Madness* (New
York: Vintage, 1990), 36.

for its currency in modern times, a Johns Hopkins Medical School faculty member justly venerated—the Swiss-born Adolf Meyer—had a tin ear for the finer rhythms of English and therefore was unaware of the semantic damage he had inflicted by offering "Depression" as a descriptive noun for such a dreadful and raging disease. Nonetheless, for over seventy-five years the word had slithered innocuously through the language like a slug, leaving little trace of its intrinsic malevolence and preventing, by its very insipidity, a general awareness of the horrible intensity of the disease when out of control.[13]

The first passage quoted from Styron describes depression as an "ancient affliction," and he is correct in this. Depression is not a disorder invented by modern psychiatrists. Clinical descriptions of depression—called melancholia in ancient and medieval times—extend back at least to Hippocrates, the father of Western medicine. Equating what we today call depression with what the Ancients called melancholia somewhat oversimplifies things, since the latter could refer to several different things, including fleeting moods, mental disorders ranging from mild to very severe, normal reactions, or long-standing character or personality traits. However, it seems clear that many references to melancholia in the literature of the West, and the descriptions of this affliction found there, have close affinities to the modern biomedical concept of depression.

According to the foundational medical theory that began with Hippocrates in the fourth century B.C. and his successor, the great Roman physician Galen in the second century A.D., and continuing until roughly the nineteenth century, scientists believed that all physical and mental illnesses were caused by an imbalance in the four bodily "humors," or fluids (black bile,

---

[13] Ibid., p. 43.

yellow bile, phlegm, and blood). The theory was that every person was naturally born with a predominance of one of these four humors—giving us the classical four temperaments: melancholic (introverted and brooding), choleric (intense and extroverted, perhaps irascible), phlegmatic (even-keeled and mild-mannered), and sanguine (optimistic and outgoing). According to this ancient theory, if one of the four humors became out of balance, with either too much or too little present, the result was disease or illness.

As the name *melancholia* implies, the ancient and medieval physicians believed that depression was caused by an abnormal excess of black bile (*melan* = black; *choler* = bile), which could result in a sort of "fevered brain." From this fevered brain sprang all the frightful symptoms of depression. Ironically, we often think of biological explanations for mental illnesses as a particularly modern way of explaining things. But this ancient theory also gives primary importance to a biological cause, paying less attention to psychological factors. It was only at the end of the nineteenth century, with the rise of psychoanalysis, that psychiatrists began paying more attention to the unconscious or other psychological explanations for depression. Today, psychiatrists attempt to understand depression from biological, psychological, and social perspectives. Those who are attentive to the spiritual dimension also perceive the importance of spiritually informed perspectives. We will say much more about this in the next chapter.

• *Inability to focus.* Depression is often understood as an emotional problem, but those who experience it firsthand often describe its ill effects as more cognitive than emotional. That is to say, many experience it more in terms of negative effects on thinking rather than on feeling. In addition to pervasive sadness, fear, dejection, or feelings of hopelessness, a depressed person will often experience significant difficulties in concentrating or paying attention. His mind tends to have problems focusing on any one thing—a sort of mental fog hangs over his conscious awareness. Conversations are hard to follow; books are difficult to comprehend; ordinary tasks are hard to accomplish. The normal flow of the depressed person's thought process becomes sluggish, and the very act of thinking can feel oppressive and burdensome. A depressed person may need to expend great effort just to sit in a room with another person and carry on a normal conversation.

Historians generally believe that Abraham Lincoln suffered recurrent bouts of severe depression. Lincoln wrote once about the terrifying effects that depression had on his thinking. He lamented "that intensity of thought, which will some times wear the sweetest idea thread-bare and turn it into the bitterness of death."[14] He captured the intensity of severe depression's misery in a letter he wrote to his law partner: "I am now the most miserable man living. If what I feel were equally distributed to the whole human family, there would not be one cheerful face on the earth." A strong claim indeed. Many often mistake depression for weakness of will or wrongly understand it to be evidence of a flawed moral character. Yet how many such people would accuse Abraham Lincoln of being weak-willed or deficient in moral character?

• *Changes in sensory perceptions.* A person's sensory perceptions can be altered in a depressed state. A sort of "tunnel vision" takes effect, and the depressed individual tends to notice (or interpret) things in his environment as predominantly negative or threatening. Experiments show, for example, that when presented with pictures of faces with neutral expressions and asked to interpret the emotions expressed there, a depressed person will interpret emotional neutrality instead as sadness, anger, irritability, and so on. Someone who is not depressed, on the other hand,

[14] Joshua Wolf Shenk, "Lincoln's Great Depression," *Atlantic Monthly* (October 2005): 42-47.

will typically interpret these same pictures in more neutral or positive terms.

• *Disruption of sleep.* Sleep is very commonly disrupted when one is depressed. The illness affects a person's circadian rhythm, the biological cycle of sleeping and waking, of tiredness and alertness, which is controlled by the hypothalamus, a structure deep within the brain. Typically, depression results in the inability to get enough sleep. The depressed person might lie in bed for hours with insomnia, exhausted but unable to fall asleep. Or he might initially fall asleep but wake up every hour or two with difficulty getting back to sleep. A classic feature of depression is early-morning awakening: the afflicted person wakes up at four or five a.m., and, try as he might, he cannot fall back asleep. The hypothalamus is out of balance, so to speak, and the individual's sleep is at the mercy of disjointed brain physiology. As one might imagine, the sleep deprivation often found in depression compounds the exhaustion and drained energy that are core features of the disorder.

There is a subtype of depression that psychiatrists call *atypical depression,* in which the sleep disturbance takes the opposite form. Instead of insomnia and sleep deprivation, atypical depression is characterized by too much sleep, in some cases up to sixteen or eighteen hours a day. The person has difficulty staying awake, and during the few hours when he is awake, he feels completely exhausted. According to some theories, this excessive sleep itself tends to contribute to the depression and make an already bad state even worse.

• *Low energy.* Whether the depressed person is getting too much or too little sleep, or even if his sleep is not disturbed, he will also commonly feel physically drained and exhausted when he is awake. Low levels of physical energy are another central feature of major depressive disorder. Exercise and exertion in this state require great, sometimes heroic, efforts of will to maintain. Even the simplest tasks, such as brushing one's teeth or walking downstairs for breakfast, can feel overwhelming. This is often a difficult aspect of depression for others to appreciate and understand. The person does not appear physically impaired or medically compromised—so why is it so difficult for him to get out of bed in the morning or brush his teeth? Others may easily misinterpret the physical exhaustion of depression as laziness or lack of effort. This sometimes results in family conflicts or misunderstandings between the depressed person and others who encourage him just to pull himself up by his bootstraps.

• *Changes in appetite.* Another characteristic physical feature of depression involves changes in appetite, which are sometimes quite pronounced. Typically, the person experiences a lessening or complete loss of appetite; as a result, food intake may be inadequate to maintain healthy nutrition or a normal body weight. Inadvertent weight loss is a common sign of depression. The idea or sight of food may cause the depressed individual to experience nausea or a sense of revulsion. Many people in a depressed state report that food loses its taste altogether. They may eat because they "have to" or because others encourage them to do so, but they derive no sense of pleasure or satisfaction from food intake.

In the less common "atypical" form of depression mentioned earlier, rather than a loss of appetite and lowered food intake, the person experiences the opposite. Along with excessive sleep, the person with atypical depression has an increased appetite and may gain considerable weight. In either case, marked changes in appetite and weight—whether lowered or increased—commonly accompany depression and can have adverse effects on a person's physical as well as mental health.

• *Changes in psychomotor movements.* All of us have some level of physical movement that occurs spontaneously without our thinking about it or willing it. While you are sitting down reading this book, you may shift positions in the chair from time to time, or perhaps tap your foot gently, or cross and uncross your legs. Rarely do we sit completely stone still, even when we are at rest. Psychiatrists refer to this by the rather strange term *psychomotor movements*. With depression, a person's baseline level of psychomotor movement changes. Depressed individuals are usually slowed down and have few spontaneous movements (termed *psychomotor retardation*), or they are shifty and restless, with difficulty sitting still (dubbed *psychomotor agitation*). Psychomotor retardation and agitation are both common features of depression. The depressed person may appear sluggish and slow; or he may appear keyed up and on edge, shifty and restless, as though he is uncomfortable in his own skin.

• *Inappropriate feelings of guilt.* Excessive or inappropriate thoughts or feelings of guilt are often seen during a depressive episode. It is important to clarify that guilt is a normal emotion experienced by a person with a well-working conscience. Not to feel guilt when one has committed evil is a serious problem indicating a grievously deformed conscience, precisely the dreadful state of a sociopathic personality. Feelings of guilt are a normal part of life in this fallen world and are not of themselves a sign of an emotional disorder. Guilt on the psychological or spiritual level is analogous to pain on the physical level. It is normal to feel pain when one is injured. Likewise, it is normal to feel guilty when one has committed evil. But pain becomes pathological when it continues even after the underlying cause has been corrected. Pain is dysregulated in diseases of the nervous system where the body feels pain even though there is no underlying physical damage to the body.

If a person has done wrong, the cure for the resultant grief is confession of the sin and absolution. However, if one has not done anything wrong, then pervasive thoughts or feelings of guilt without due cause, or guilt that is far out of proportion to any offense, may be a symptom of depression. It should be noted that pathological guilt or scrupulosity can be a feature of other mental disorders as well, particularly anxiety disorders such as obsessive-compulsive disorder. A full explanation of these anxiety disorders lies outside the scope of this book and may be the subject of a future volume. We will return to the problem of guilt in Chapter 6.

• *Anhedonia.* Another characteristic feature of depression is the inability to find joy or pleasure in activities that one typically would enjoy. Psychiatrists call this *anhedonia.* Patients will describe having no interest in the activities that they used to enjoy and looked forward to—whether these are hobbies, sports, personal interactions, work, and so on. The depressed person often cannot find joy or gratification in anything. The usual sense of satisfaction or pleasure—whether the physical pleasure of eating or conjugal intercourse, or the spiritual pleasures of contemplative activities or artistic pursuits—seem to be blunted or completely shut down. As a consequence, the anhedonic individual often disengages from his usual activities.

• *Frequent thoughts of death.* Finally, it is common for depressed individuals to experience frequent thoughts of death. In the maelstrom of a depressive episode, suicide may (falsely) appear to be the only way out. In the midst of a severe depressive episode, a person may come to believe that self-annihilation is the sole escape hatch that will end his intolerable suffering. More will be said on the difficult subject of suicide in Chapter 4. Here I simply mention the fact that many who, for moral and religious reasons, would never consider suicide as an option when they are in a normal mental state, and who ordinarily recoil at the thought of taking their own life, nevertheless do consider (and sometimes act upon) suicidal thoughts when they are severely depressed. This is one of the great tragedies of depression.

• *Anxiety.* In a majority of cases, depression is associated with some degree of anxiety. An age-old definition for depression—when it was called melancholia—was "fear and sadness without cause." One might say more accurately, "without *apparent* cause," or "out of proportion to the apparent cause." This definition highlights the prominence not just of the emotion of sadness, but also of fear or anxiety. The underlying biological factors that predispose to depression also seem to play a role in anxiety disorders. So there is overlap between the two at the level of the brain. In our current diagnostic classification schemes, psychiatrists tend to distinguish between depression and anxiety disorders (such as generalized anxiety, obsessive-compulsive disorder, etc.). But it may be more accurate to understand them as *overlapping* disorders existing on a spectrum, with some cases being predominantly depression with associated symptoms of anxiety, and other cases involving predominantly anxiety with associated disturbance of mood.

How long do such symptoms need to last before one is considered "clinically depressed"? Generally, if a person has half or more of the symptoms described—depressed mood, anhedonia, abnormally low energy, disturbed sleep, appetite changes, psychomotor agitation or retardation, impaired concentration, excessive feelings of guilt, or suicidal thinking—for more than a week, it is worthwhile to get an evaluation from a psychiatrist or at least a primary care physician who has experience diagnosing depression. A state that lasts for a day or two and then subsides or remits may be just a normal emotional reaction to stress, setbacks, or other life events. Certainly, if one has been experiencing such symptoms most of the time for weeks or months on end, it is time to seek clinical attention. There are treatments available, and a person should not suffer needlessly in such a state any longer than necessary.

Depressive episodes tend to be recurrent. Each time a person experiences a sustained period of depression, research suggests that the brain becomes "primed" for further episodes, a process termed *kindling*. Someone who has experienced one episode of clinical depression is much more prone to recurrent episodes. After the first episode, a person has about a 60 percent chance of experiencing a second episode at some point in his or her life; after the second, there is a 75 percent chance of having a third; and after a third, there is a 90 percent chance of having a fourth. In brief, the more episodes of depression a person has, the more likely it is that he or she will experience another episode at some point. What is more, subsequent episodes can often last longer and sometimes be more difficult to treat. For this reason, efforts to prevent recurrent episodes before they occur are a key part of treating depression.

Depression in Children and the Elderly

While depression in pre-adolescent children is found more rarely than in teenagers or adults, it does sometimes occur. Rates of depression rise among adolescents compared with younger children and are comparable to rates among adults. In children and adolescents, depression may manifest itself somewhat differently than in adults. Changes in appetite, energy, concentration, and sleep are common, as seen in adult depression. However, in children the emotional expression of a depressed mood may not always be as apparent. An irritable mood (rather than sadness) is commonly seen in depressed children. Because their cognitive development is still in progress, children generally have different ways of expressing their emotional state and may not be able to describe their depressed mood verbally with the same facility as an adult. For this reason, behavioral changes may be an important clue that a child is suffering from depression. If parents suspect that their child is depressed, they should obtain an evaluation from a psychiatrist, preferably a child and adolescent psychiatrist if one is available.

Depression is also commonly found in the elderly. Medical illnesses, loss and loneliness, and physical and mental disabilities are all factors that can predispose elderly individuals to depression. The elderly often have more pronounced cognitive changes in depression than other adults. Their thinking may appear to be more profoundly affected than their emotional state or mood. The symptoms of impaired concentration and inattention can sometimes make depression in the elderly look like dementia. An elderly individual may appear to have impaired memory or recall, but if this is caused by depression, the process is reversible with treatment. This contrasts with memory loss due to dementia, such as Alzheimer's disease, in which the cognitive problems tend to be progressive and irreversible. To complicate matters, these two disorders can sometimes be present at the same time. In fact, depression is more commonly seen in individuals with dementia than in the general population. In such cases, the person will need treatment for both disorders. Therefore, it is important to have an adequate evaluation, preferably from a geriatric psychiatrist, in order to distinguish geriatric depression (sometimes called *pseudo-dementia*) from dementia.

Dysthymia: A Chronic Mildly Depressed State

The line between ordinary periods of sadness, dejection, or demoralization and clinical depression is not always clear. A person may experience a few but not all of the symptoms described earlier. Signs and symptoms may wax and wane over time, perhaps lasting only a few days, and then remit spontaneously.

A common affliction that psychiatrists call *dysthymia* is characterized by some symptoms of depression—feeling down, diminished energy, sleep difficulties, and so forth—that are milder but tend to last longer. If a person experiences a few mild symptoms of depression for more days than not for a year or more, he or she may be suffering from dysthymia. People with dysthymia tend to be prone to episodes of more pronounced depression superimposed on their baseline dysthymia, a so-called "double depression." Although it is less severe than depression, dysthymia can sometimes be more difficult to treat, as it may not respond as well to antidepressant medications.

Rather than thinking of depression or dysthymia as distinct illnesses or separate disorders, it may be more accurate to understand depressive disorders as existing on a spectrum from mild and chronic (dysthymia) to severe and acute (major depressive disorder or "melancholic" depression). Between these extremes there are gradations of moderate depression. There are also gray areas in which the line between "normal" and "pathological" is not always clear.

To help sort through the question of whether a mild depressive state is something that should be treated, it can be helpful to use the benchmark of evaluating whether and to what extent a person's normal daily functioning is impaired by the symptoms. If one's lack of energy or poor concentration rises to the level at which the person can no longer work, go to school, or take care of everyday activities, then it is time to seek clinical attention.

Melancholic Depression and Psychotic Depression

There is a severe and debilitating form of depression that still goes by the older name *melancholia*. Psychiatrists debate whether melancholic depression should be considered a distinct disorder, qualitatively different from other forms of depression, or rather a subtype of depression with some unique features. In any case, this mood disorder seems to involve severe emotional disturbances that appear unrelated to any stressor or external cause. A

person feels very apprehensive and has thoughts of death or fix-
ates on similarly morbid themes. The afflicted person experiences
severely diminished energy and may find it difficult even to get
out of bed. At times, melancholic depression is characterized by
physical agitation, such as hand-wringing or pacing, and mental
bewilderment or confusion. The person's mood and energy are
typically worse in the morning and may improve slightly as the
day goes on. Sleep is severely disturbed in melancholic depression.
Melancholic depression has very high rates of suicide, so symptoms of this kind warrant immediate psychiatric attention.

Research suggests that, in contrast to other types of depression, melancholia does not benefit as much from psychotherapy.
In melancholia, the person's concentration is typically so impaired
that he or she is unable to engage meaningfully in psychotherapy.
This form of depression appears to be deeply rooted in biology
and probably more disconnected from psychological, social, or
spiritual factors. Lab tests may reveal hormonal imbalances. Here,
it is worth briefly mentioning that some studies also suggest that
the ideal medication treatments for melancholia may differ from
those indicated for milder depression. (I discuss medication treatments in Chapter 5.)

In melancholia or other severe forms of depression, the person
can experience psychotic symptoms; that is, mental experiences
that indicate a loss of touch with reality. These include hallucinations (perceptions without external stimuli, such as hearing
or seeing things that are not there) and delusions (fixed false,
idiosyncratic beliefs, such as the belief that the world will be
destroyed if I eat food). In depression with psychotic features, hallucinations and delusions tend to "fit" the person's mood; that is,
the contents of the hallucinations or themes of the delusions tend
to be dark, terrifying, and nihilistic. Obviously, a person in such
a state requires immediate psychiatric attention and may require
hospitalization.

Seasonal Affective Disorder (SAD)

Seasonal affective disorder is a form of depression that is connected to reduced sunlight exposure during the fall and winter. For individuals prone to it, the depressed mood and other symptoms of depression tend to recur in a relatively predictable fashion at a certain time of year, most commonly in the winter months. In addition to the symptoms of depression described earlier, headaches and irritability can also be characteristic features of seasonal affective disorder. Some individuals seem much more genetically predisposed to this problem than others. They may have a difficult time living in certain climates where exposure to sunlight is inadequate. The connection between exposure to ultraviolet sunlight and the brain's proper functioning is direct and profound. Special receptors in the retina receive signals from UV light, which are sent to the hypothalamus, a structure deep within the brain that is involved in mood, regulates the sleep/wake cycle, influences energy and alertness, and helps to direct other bodily and mental functions.

The exact causes of seasonal affective disorder are not entirely clear. We do know that the hypothalamus produces the hormone melatonin, which is important for falling asleep. Fewer hours of sunlight may decrease the production of melatonin when it is needed at night, altering the sleep/wake cycle, and may affect the hypothalamus in other ways. Rates of seasonal affective disorder in the population can vary widely by region, as weather and climate are so closely tied to the clinical syndrome. It is much more common, for example, in Seattle or Fairbanks than in Los Angeles or Miami. Seasonal affective disorder can benefit from many of the treatments for depression described in Part II. In addition, research shows that it can also be lessened or cured by daily exposure to UV light, so-called "light therapy." Where sunlight is scarce, one can use a "light therapy box," which is a machine that emits UV light and is approved for the treatment of seasonal affective disorder. Exposure to UV light in the morning can suppress melatonin production during the waking hours and restore the normal melatonin production at night, which may help treat or prevent seasonal affective disorder.

Depression and Normal Bereavement and Grieving

Someone who is grieving the loss of a loved one, or a lost relationship, may frequently experience some of the symptoms of depression described above. Bereavement is considered a normal rather than a pathological state. Grief, like guilt, is a normal part of human life. Bereavement does share many symptoms with mild or even moderate forms of clinical depression. So it becomes important to distinguish between normal grief and pathological depression.

When making this distinction, the person's recent life history and the reasons for his or her sadness or dejection must be taken into account. However, in practice, this distinction can sometimes be difficult to ascertain. Occasionally, normal grief can, over time, develop into a depressive disorder that requires treatment. Are there features of depression not seen in someone who is grieving? If so, how do we recognize these features?

A seventeenth-century rabbi, Bunam of Pzysha, observed this difference between grief and depression: "A broken heart [grief] prepares man for the service of God, but dejection [depression] corrodes service."[15] Grief, however painful, need not lead to spiritual despair. While it may be a spiritual trial, it does not necessarily corrode the service of God or isolate us from others. Depression, on the other hand, more often impairs our ability to pray and weakens our capacity to connect with and find solace in others.

[15] Perle Besserman, *The Way of the Jewish Mystics* (Boston: Shambhala, 1994), 115-117.

Grief can, of course, involve profound sadness and anguish. A parent grieving the death of a child is a most painful example. But however emotionally wrenching a period of bereavement might be, the grieving person typically does not experience excessive feelings of guilt (beyond, perhaps, some regret about not saying goodbye to the departed, or similar things directly related to the loss). The grieving person also does not typically experience a sense of personal worthlessness or self-loathing, as is commonly found in depression, nor does he focus exclusively on negative memories of the departed. Alienation from others, an inability to be consoled, self-hatred, or suicidal thinking all could be signs that bereavement has morphed into depression.

Although I disagree with Sigmund Freud's theory that the cause of most depression is unconscious sexual conflicts, he did provide a helpful description of the difference between pathological depression and normal grieving in his book *Mourning and Melancholia*. The grief-stricken individual focuses on the loss of the loved one, whereas the depressed individual focuses in an exaggerated or unrealistic way upon his own perceived limitations and inadequacies. The depressed person's thoughts are narrowly self-focused and may involve intense self-hatred. Freud writes that the depressed person describes himself as "worthless, incapable of any achievement and morally despicable; he reproaches himself, vilifies himself and expects to be found out and punished."[16] He adds that the depressed person typically believes this has always been the case.

In periods of mourning or grief, the emotional connection to others who are still living—family members and friends—is preserved; whereas, in depression, the person becomes excessively focused on himself, feeling outcast, alienated from others, and alone in his pain. In the grieving state, some degree of consolation

[16] Sigmund Freud, *Standard Edition Collected Works*, 14:239, 246-247.

can be found in friends, in prayer, and in other activities. The depressed person is typically inconsolable; his or her mood seems quite impervious to the influence of other people, activities, or the environment. The grieving person generally senses that the grief will eventually end or at least become tolerable; even though it may take a long time, those suffering from grief can grasp that life may be better in the future. The depressed individual, by contrast, believes that the depression will never end, which leads to a sense of hopelessness and a feeling that time itself has slowed down or stopped. Even in the thick of intense grief, a sense of personal agency, of confidence in one's own ability to act in the world, is still preserved. By contrast, in depression, with its characteristic self-loathing and irrational or excessive guilt, a person feels quite impotent to act in the world. Finally, suicidal thinking is a clear sign that a person is suffering from depression rather than ordinary bereavement.

In some cases, it might be difficult to distinguish normal bereavement from clinical depression. Some combination of the two states may be present simultaneously. Complicated grief can slowly shade into an ongoing depressed state that gradually takes on dark features. Consultation with a skilled and sensitive psychiatrist may be helpful in distinguishing between the two. An experienced clinician can also assist the suffering individual in deciding whether and when psychotherapy or medications would be indicated. Physicians are, with good reason, typically reluctant to medicate normal grief. However, untreated depression that is mistaken for normal grieving causes unnecessary suffering and may place an individual at risk for suicide.

What Causes Depression?

Now that we have described the characteristic signs and symptoms of depression, we can ask what causes it. There is no simple answer to this question. Is depression due to one's genetic makeup? What about life experiences or the behaviors a person engages in and the choices he makes—do these play a causative role? Is depression a disorder of "nature" or "nurture"? The answer is not either-or, but rather both-and—nature and nurture, genes and environment, temperament and life experiences all contribute. In biology and psychology, we have in recent years come to a greater appreciation of the fact that most of the time, there is no strict dichotomy between nature and nurture.

By "nature" people typically refer to our inborn genetic makeup—what we come into the world with. But even our genetic endowment is not static and fixed: genes themselves can be turned on and off by factors in our environment and experience. Nurture—our life experiences and environmental factors—interacts with our genes to determine which of them are expressed. Genes can be activated or remain dormant during different stages of our development. This is not a predetermined process, but one that is shaped by environmental factors, especially in the early years of life. Even identical twins, who share the very same genes, may have different "gene expressions," depending upon their environment and life experiences. Likewise, our experiences are shaped by the inborn genetic dispositions we bring to them.

So even saying that a particular disease or disorder is all (or mostly) genetic does not mean that it is fixed and unalterable and that "nurture" is irrelevant. Furthermore, the genetics of the disorder are very complex. There is not a single gene responsible for depression. As is the case with other complex medical illnesses such as obesity, diabetes, or various cancers, so also with depression: a complex combination of many genes may predispose an individual to depression. If one parent has depression, his or her child is two or three times more likely to have depression. This risk goes up to four or five times as likely if the parent had early-onset depression—that is, prior to the age of twenty. If both parents suffered from depression, the risk to the child is still greater.

Types of Depression and Their Causes

So family history plays an important role in assessing the risk of depression. The exact inheritance pattern is too complicated to be predicted accurately, due to the fact that there are many genes or combinations of genes that influence the risk for depression. Scientists have already identified and studied some of these genes, such as the serotonin transporter gene. However, we do not currently have clinically available genetic tests that can predict one's risk for depression. The genetics of depression and other mood disorders continues to be a very active area of scientific research.

Genes alone, however, are not the whole story. Life experiences—most especially experiences of loss or deprivation, and any number of other physically or mentally stressful circumstances—also play a significant role in causing depressive episodes or symptoms. Indeed, most of our traits, behaviors, character strengths, and vulnerabilities, and even our illnesses, arise from this complicated interplay between nature and nurture. To describe this nature-and-nurture theory of depression's causes, scientists and physicians use the term *stress-diathesis* (*diathesis* means roughly "predisposition" or "tendency"). According to the stress-diathesis model of depression, some people, through no fault of their own, come into the world with genetic vulnerabilities to depression. If the vulnerability is strong enough, a person might become depressed, regardless of his environment and life circumstances. If the vulnerability is not as strong, it may take significant stress, such as the loss of a job, the death of a loved one, a medical illness, sleep disturbances, a drug or alcohol addiction, a spiritual crisis, or a combination of several factors for the depressive symptoms to develop. Although it may clearly be triggered by stress, the depression is not *only* a result of environmental causes; rather, it results from the interplay of environmental and genetic factors.

Sometimes depressed patients are puzzled when they cannot pinpoint external causes of their depression. "I have no reason to be depressed," they may say, yet the symptoms are clearly present.

It is important to remember that depression can often be present even in the absence of apparent external causes. About thirty or forty years ago, psychiatrists would commonly distinguish between so-called *exogenous* depression (caused by external environmental factors or life circumstances) and *endogenous* depression (which seemed unrelated to life circumstances, and so was thought to be more biologically or genetically caused).

However, further research showed that this distinction between exogenous and endogenous depression was not always clinically useful, since the symptoms and the treatments were the same, and the causes were usually complex. People often assumed that an endogenous depression should be treated with medications, because of its supposed biological origin, whereas an exogenous depression should be treated with psychotherapy or behavioral changes, because of its supposed environmental origin. Research and clinical experience showed, however, that regardless of the combination of causative factors that led to the depression, the final pathway was the same in the end. The patient still experienced the signs and symptoms of depression regardless of whether he or the evaluating physician ascribed its cause to external or internal factors. Research demonstrated that the most effective treatments for depression were the same for so-called exogenous and endogenous depression. Medication alone was helpful for both; psychotherapy alone was helpful for both; and the combination of medications and psychotherapy showed more benefit than either one alone, for both types of depression. (More will be said on treatments for depression in Part II.)

Regardless of the combination of factors that leads to a depressive episode, the nature of the illness and the most effective treatments tend to be similar. For this reason, psychiatrists today often do not consider it very clinically useful to distinguish between exogenous and endogenous depression. In most cases, a complex interplay of several factors and causes—both internal and external—lead to the depression. Accordingly, treatment should be aimed at addressing all of the biological, psychological, social, and spiritual aspects of the illness.

Depression ranks among the more common medical illnesses. Perhaps as many as 13 percent of people will experience an episode of depression at some point during their lifetime. Some researchers have questioned that figure as possibly being too high, since it is unclear how many cases of mild depression are included and precisely how one defines the illness can vary. But all medical epidemiologists agree that depression, even severe depression, is a relatively common affliction. For reasons that are not entirely understood, it is twice as common in women as in men. There is some evidence that female hormone levels, or perhaps rapid shifts in levels of estrogen and progesterone, may play a role in the development of some cases of depression.

Depression can manifest itself at any age, with rare cases even in childhood, although the average age of onset for a first episode of depression is forty. In women, it is common for an episode to be present in the first few months to a year after giving birth, termed *postpartum depression*. The symptoms of postpartum depression are exactly the same as those of major depressive disorder. The postpartum period appears to be a time of particular vulnerability to depression, likely due to dramatic hormonal shifts at delivery and the myriad stresses and sleep disturbance associated with mothering a newborn. In severe cases of postpartum mood disorders, the mother can even experience psychotic symptoms, such as hallucinations, delusions, or obsessive thoughts, often about her baby. This condition requires immediate medical attention for the safety of the mother and her child.

There is no proven correlation between socioeconomic status and depression: it afflicts the rich, the poor, and the middle class alike. Rather than stemming from *economic* poverty, depression occurs more commonly in what could be called *relational* poverty — in those individuals who have impoverished inter-personal relationships and tenuous personal ties. For example, there are higher rates of depression for those who are separated or divorced, and higher rates among single people than among married people.

One of the reasons it is important to get an evaluation from a psychiatrist, or at least a primary care physician, is that several medical illnesses can have signs and symptoms that look a lot like depression. A psychotherapist or counselor who is not medi-cally trained may mistake another medical illness for depression and thus miss the correct diagnosis and approach to treatment. A common example is hypothyroidism (low levels of thyroid hor-mone, which regulates many metabolic functions). This can pre-sent with low energy, weight gain, fatigue, and other symptoms similar to depression. Other medical conditions, such as anemia and vitamin deficiencies, should be ruled out by an appropriate medical evaluation before making a diagnosis of depression. This may sometimes require a physical examination, lab tests, or other medical tests to rule out a general medical condition that mimics depression.

Depression itself can occur in the context of a general medical condition, following upon a heart attack or a stroke, for example. Approximately one in six individuals who have a heart attack develop depression during the recovery period, due to the physio-logical stress on the body and the psychological burdens of recov-ery. In this situation, both the general medical condition and the depression need to be treated. Research shows, for example, that after a heart attack, if the depression is not concurrently treated, the future prognosis for the heart condition is actually worse. Patients with depression are at a higher risk for a repeat heart attack or other negative cardiac outcomes. Similarly, depressive episodes are common after a stroke, particularly those strokes that affect the left frontal lobe of the brain. Depression can also be related to Huntington's disease, AIDS, and several other less common medical conditions. Some prescription medications can cause or contribute to depression and so should be reviewed in the context of a medical evaluation.

Current research suggests that the relationship between depression and other medical illnesses is bidirectional. Depression increases a person's risk for developing a number of medical illnesses and also worsens the prognosis of those medical illnesses; medical illnesses put a patient at higher risk of developing depression. The reasons are complex and involve brain chemicals (neurotransmitters), hormones, and physiological effects of both depression and various medical conditions. In cases where there is both depression and another general medical condition, the best treatment approach is adequately to address both. It is not necessarily the case that treating the general medical condition will also take care of the depression. The depression, even if originally caused by another medical condition, can take on a "life of its own" and require its own treatment. So both conditions should be addressed to ensure the best medical and psychological outcomes.

Alcohol dependence or drug abuse can also contribute to depression. When depression occurs in the context of alcohol or drug addiction, the question often arises, which came first? It can often be difficult to tell. In some cases, the depression comes first, and the person ineffectively attempts to "self-medicate" the depression with alcohol or drugs. In other cases, the chronic abuse of a substance such as alcohol can lead to depression by its effects on the brain and the body, or its negative effects on a person's life and functioning. In most cases of depression where alcohol and drugs are involved, treatment typically needs to address both the addiction and the mood disorder. Even if the mood disorder came first and is successfully treated, the addictive behavior can take on a "life of its own" and will likely require other interventions in order for the person to maintain sobriety. Consultation with a skilled psychiatrist who has clinical experience treating drug and alcohol abuse is warranted in cases in which an addiction is suspected. A thorough discussion of addictions and their effects on mental health would require another book and lies outside the scope of this work. For our purposes, it is important to note that drugs or alcohol often play a role in depression and thus need to be addressed also.

In addition to these biological and medical factors, there are clearly psychological and social factors that play a role in the origins of depression. Theories regarding psychological conflicts, patterns of thinking or behaving, or other developmental or emotional problems abound. It would take many volumes to cover them all. I will briefly mention only a few, keeping in mind that some psychological theories apply to some cases of depression but not to others, so one should not overgeneralize.

One example is Sigmund Freud's theory of the origins of depression. He believed depression to be the result of repressed unconscious anger, turned inward against the self. In my clinical experience, repressed or unresolved anger often does play a significant role in some cases of depression, although not in all. So this theory may have some merit, but we should not assume that it applies in every case. A person should not presume that he must have depression simply because he suffers from this sort of an emotional conflict; conversely, if a person does not have a problem with repressed anger, that does not mean that he cannot become depressed.

The psychologist Aaron Beck developed a theory of depression that locates its origin in unrealistically negative patterns of thinking. Specifically, there are problems in three domains of thinking: thoughts about oneself (a negative self-concept), about the world (a tendency to experience the world as hostile and overly demanding), and about the future (the expectation of inevitable suffering and failure). If these patterns of thinking become fixed and habitual, even if they have no grounding in reality, the individual is liable to develop depressive symptoms. What is especially interesting about this theory is that it shows how our emotions arise from patterns of thinking. Our rational powers have primacy over our affective faculties. Our feelings then reinforce these maladaptive patterns of thought in a vicious circle. Beck developed a method known as "cognitive" therapy for depression (discussed in Part II), which is aimed at systematically and deliberately correcting these problematic patterns of thinking. The idea is that if we can bring our habitual thoughts more in line with objective reality, our moods will follow.

The psychiatrist John Bowlby focused on the role of developmental factors in later emotional and behavioral patterns. He studied ways in which early parent-child attachment could go wrong; for example, when parents were neglectful, overly smothering, or abusive. Research shows that insecure attachment relationships early in life tend to lead to depression later in life. Examples of events that contribute to insecure attachment are abuse, death of a parent or sibling, divorce, war, an alcoholic or addicted parent, or a parent who is mentally ill. Often the emotional wounds from these insecure attachments lie outside the person's awareness, or the person may be dimly aware of them but have limited insight into the role that attachment patterns play in his or her subsequent behaviors or moods. A skilled psychotherapist can help uncover these problems and assist the patient to grow in self-knowledge and awareness. This kind of therapeutic work can be important in the process of psychological healing and recovery from depression.

Individuals who experience physical, sexual, or severe emotional abuse early in life are at three- or fourfold higher risk of depression than the general population. Early emotional neglect or interpersonal loss also places a person at higher risk for depression later in life. As society becomes more fragmented, and divorce and family breakdown continue, we will likely continue to see rates of depression rising as today's children become adults. The theories of depression described here, including the cognitive theory of Beck and the attachment theory of Bowlby, are not mutually exclusive. Good mental-health professionals are aware of all these factors in their approach, even if they maintain certain preferences in terms of what they emphasize.

Other social factors, such as loneliness, isolation, or financial stress, can also play a significant role in depression. Psychiatric researcher Dan Blazer argues that many negative cultural and societal changes have made depression more common in our day.[17] He wisely asks why the incidence of major depression has increased in the past fifty years if human bodies and brains have not changed significantly? While not ignoring biological factors, Blazer argues that the recent historical transition from modernity to postmodernity in Western society is important in understanding the social origins of depression. The early modern period was characterized by an optimistic confidence in the power of autonomous human reason and technological progress to solve all human problems and gradually eliminate human miseries. In our so-called postmodern period, this confidence has been deconstructed and undermined. The consequence is widespread anxiety, along with depression, which can be interpreted as a desire to withdraw from a world that has lost its foundations and its compass.

Western society is now characterized by instability, saturation of media images, social isolation (the "lonely crowd"), and a widespread sense of dislocation. Blazer marshals evidence that the frenetic pace of modern life, social and occupational pressures, disjointed relationships, and social isolation all play a role in the

[17] Blazer, *The Age of Melancholy*, 114-116, 135-159.

rising rates of depression. He also pays close attention to spiritual factors, and the ways in which spiritual values have often been eclipsed in modern life. This marginalization of spiritual values has led to crises of meaning and purpose for many individuals and has contributed to depressive trends on a large scale.

The late novelist Walker Percy, who himself suffered from depression, wrote extensively about these features of our contemporary life, arguing that we feel dislocated in this world precisely because we are wayfarers. Percy was referring to our everyday experience of discontent, our sense that we never seem to be completely at home in this world. In this vein, with his characteristically sarcastic wit, he chided the self-help genre, which attempts to help us adjust more adequately to life as it is:

> You are depressed because you should be. You are entitled to your depression. In fact, you'd be deranged if you were not depressed. Consider the only adults who are never depressed: chuckleheads, California surfers and fundamentalist Christians who believe they have had a personal encounter with Jesus and are saved once and for all. Would you trade your depression to be any one of these?[18]

Our present social and cultural milieu, described by Blazer, as well as our permanent condition of being wayfarers and pilgrims in this world, described by Percy, both contribute to difficulties for many in finding a sense of meaning and purpose. Particularly today, our present cultural climate tends to undermine the faith of many Christians and other believers. This is not to say, however, that every individual suffering from depression is experiencing a crisis of meaning or faith. It is simply to acknowledge that these overarching social and spiritual factors play a role in many cases

---

[18] Walker Percy, *Lost in the Cosmos: The Last Self-Help Book* (New York: Farrar, Straus & Giroux, 1983), 79.

and may be among the important causes contributing to rising rates of depression in already vulnerable individuals.

Pope John Paul II recognized depression's biological and medical aspects, while encouraging us to explore and address the social and cultural forces that appear to be contributing to rising rates of depression worldwide. In an address on the topic to Catholic healthcare workers, he said:

> *The spread of depressive states has become disturbing.* They reveal human, psychological and spiritual frailties which, at least in part, are induced by society. It is important to become aware of the effect on people of messages conveyed by the *media* which exalt consumerism, the immediate satisfaction of desires and the race for ever greater material well-being. It is necessary to propose new ways so that each person may build his or her own personality by cultivating spiritual life, the foundation of a mature existence.[19]

These words from Pope John Paul II help to introduce the theme of the next chapter: how depression and one's spiritual life might be related; how one can affect the other.

---

[19] John Paul II, Address to the Participants in the 18th International Conference Promoted by the Pontifical Council for Health and Pastoral Care on the Theme of "Depression," November 14, 2003, no. 2. See Appendix 3 for the full text of this address.

Chapter 2

Depression and the Spiritual Life

"Depression is always a spiritual trial."
John Paul II

＾

The relationship between mood disorders and our spiritual life is complex. Often it is hard for a person to know whether he or she is simply going through a difficult time—a dry spell in prayer, a period of demoralization in life due to external circumstances—or whether these ordinary trials and challenges may have led to, or may have been caused by, depression. Sorting out such matters may require the help of a knowledgeable spiritual director who is able to work in conjunction with a medical professional. In an ideal situation, the mental-health professional would be a person familiar with or at least respectful of Catholic faith, morals, and spiritual life, and the spiritual director would have some familiarity with medicine and psychology, at least enough to know when referral may be warranted.

Several scientific studies published in the past few years suggest that patients want to be able to speak with their physician or therapist about religious or spiritual issues. A 1995 study of psychiatric patients showed that 80 percent of patients considered themselves "religious" or "spiritual," with 48 percent of patients describing themselves as "deeply religious." Over half attended religious services and prayed daily, and 83 percent believed their spirituality had a positive impact on their lives. A striking and unfortunate finding here was that 38 percent of patients felt uncomfortable mentioning their spiritual or religious beliefs to their therapist. This should give healthcare professionals pause, since therapy is supposed to be the place where all of the patient's thoughts, beliefs, and emotions can be expressed and discussed. Yet a large proportion of patients were uncomfortable in this setting discussing something that they considered a very important — perhaps the most important — aspect of their lives.

Patients' general impression that their religious beliefs and practices have a positive impact on their lives is borne out in other research studies on spirituality and mental health. A review article from the leading research journal in psychiatry looked at all of the quantitative studies on the topic of religious commitment and mental health published over the past ten years.[20] Overall, 72 percent of the studies found a positive association between religious commitment and mental health; only 16 percent found a negative association, and 12 percent found no association. The overall weight of evidence certainly tilts away from Sigmund Freud's dubious claim that religious belief itself is intrinsically neurotic. On the contrary, if there is any effect on mental health, the evidence suggests that it is generally a beneficial one.

Furthermore, studies among adults consistently reveal lower rates of depression among individuals who are more religiously observant. The vast majority of these studies looked at Christian patients (almost no research has been done to compare different denominations or other religions, so we do not yet have good

[20] D. B. Larson, K. A. Sherrill, J. S. Lyons, F. C. Craigie Jr., S. B. Thielman, M. A. Greenwold, and S. S. Larson, "Associations between dimensions of religious commitment and mental health reported in the American Journal of Psychiatry and Archives of General Psychiatry: 1978-1989," *American Journal of Psychiatry*, 149 (1992): 557-559.

data on how Christians compare with Jews, how Catholics compare with Protestants, and so on). Religious factors become more important as a person's life stressors increase. More than a hundred research studies have examined the relationship between religion and depression. Two-thirds of these found fewer depressive symptoms in those who were more religious. Only 5 percent of these studies found that being more religious was associated with more depression. Out of twenty-two long-term studies, fifteen found that greater religious practice (prayer, church attendance, Scripture reading) predicted milder symptoms and a more rapid recovery. Research suggests that feelings of anger toward God, loss of faith, or lack of support from one's religious community are factors that correlate with greater depression symptoms and more difficulty with recovery. One study found that a belief in life after death was consistently related to better mental health. To explain this finding, the authors hypothesized that belief in life after death may help put personal identity, adverse experience, and interpersonal difficulties or struggles into a broader context.[21]

Unfortunately, many psychiatrists or therapists today are uncomfortable discussing spiritual issues with their depressed patients. When they do broach the topic, the patient often feels misunderstood. The therapist may not have taken the trouble to learn enough about the patient's spiritual or religious beliefs and convictions, or may be disrespectful or dismissive of them. Cultural and societal prejudices and biases against religious or moral beliefs have a tendency to work their way into clinical encounters, sometimes tainting the advice offered or harming the therapeutic relationship. And it must be admitted that there are many half-baked therapists out there who really do not know what they are

---

[21] P. S. Mueller, D. J. Plevak, C. J. Ellison, et al., "Belief in life after death and mental health: findings from a national survey," *Journal of Nervous and Mental Disorders*, 194 (2006): 524-529.

doing. They end up doing more harm than good to the patients or clients under their care.

We are, however, seeing some positive developments in medical education and psychiatric residency training. In many medical schools today, a new generation of physicians is being trained to be more attentive to and respectful of religious or spiritual issues that may arise in the clinical setting, in response to the preponderance of evidence in the kind of research studies cited earlier. Fortunately, training in these areas has become a more widely accepted part of mainstream medical-school curricula and is included in the curricula of some psychiatry residency training programs.

It remains true that many psychiatrists and therapists operate with unexamined biases against religious beliefs or spiritual practices. They may uncritically assume without good evidence that a patient's religion is the source of his problem, rather than a potential strength to be encouraged and developed as part of the solution. As mentioned previously, studies show that psychiatrists are, as a whole, less religious than the general population, less religious than their patients, the least religious among physicians, and proportionately less Christian. As a result, they may dismiss or undervalue the role of religious factors in helping patients cope with their illness.[22] The same trends hold for clinical psychologists and other mental-health professionals. It may be a good idea to ask your therapist or physician, during one of the initial visits, whether he or she is comfortable discussing religious matters with you in the course of treatment. The mental-health professional need not be a theologian, but he or she should make every effort to understand and respect your convictions, insofar as these may be relevant to the presenting problems or proposed treatments.

---

[22] J. Nelleman and R. Persaud, "Why do psychiatrists neglect religion?", *British Journal of Medical Psychology* 68 (1995): 169-178.

Depression and the Spiritual Life

I have treated some individuals who refuse to seek help for depression, or other mental afflictions, unless the doctor or therapist is a Christian, or specifically a Catholic Christian. While I understand their reasons, I think in many cases these individuals are missing opportunities to get help from competent and honest professionals who would honor their beliefs, even if they do not share them. It does not generally make sense to avoid getting help simply because one cannot find the practitioner one considers ideal. I am also quick to point out that being a Catholic in no way guarantees that a person is a competent psychiatrist or psychologist.

I know some Catholic psychiatrists to whom I would avoid referring patients because they are not competent in their medical field; on the other hand, I know many non-Catholic psychiatrists and psychologists who are perfectly competent and to whom I would refer a friend or family member. The two crucial factors are that they are skilled and knowledgeable in their field and also aware and respectful of their patient's faith and moral convictions. This does not necessarily require that they share the patient's convictions or beliefs. Particularly in smaller communities or rural areas, it may be difficult to find a skilled Catholic psychiatrist, and it would be a mistake to avoid a necessary consultation simply because the available doctor is Jewish, Buddhist, or a non-believer of good will.

Having briefly mentioned the research on the generally positive relationship between psychiatry and the spiritual life, I want to enter a note of caution. The reader should not misinterpret this research as suggesting that religious faith inoculates one from depression. It is but one protective factor. As described at the end of the previous chapter, the causes of depression are complex, and many individuals come into the world with strong genetic or early environmental causes, which manifest regardless of the individuals' life circumstances or choices and regardless of how much the individuals pray or how virtuous they are. Many religiously devout and even saintly individuals suffered from severe depression.

The Jesuit priest and poet Gerard Manley Hopkins is just one example of a devout Catholic who suffered severe and recurrent bouts of melancholia. Some of his most moving and beautiful poetry grew out of his experience of depression and his struggle to situate this experience in the context of his faith. The following example, which arose from his personal experience with depression, is aptly titled "No worst":

> No worst, there is none. Pitched past pitch of grief,
> More pangs will, schooled at forepange, wilder wring.
> Comforter, where, where is your comforting?
> Mary, mother of us, where is your relief?
> My cries heave, herds-long; huddle in a main, a chief
> Woe, world-sorrow; on an age-old anvil wince and sing—
> Then, lull, then leave off. Fury had shrieked "No lingering! Let me be fell: force I must be brief."

> O the mind, mind has mountains; cliffs of fall
> Frightful, sheer, no-man-fathomed. Hold them cheap
> May who ne'er hung there. Nor does long our small
> Durance deal with that steep or deep. Here! Creep,
> Wretch, under a comfort serves in a whirlwind: all
> Life death does end and each day dies with sleep.[23]

As another example, St. Benedict Joseph Labre, an eighteenth-century homeless man who was beloved by the people of Rome, suffered from a severe and chronic mental illness and was likely psychotic at times. He was turned away from several religious communities because of his evident mental illness. Eventually, he

---

[23] Gerard Manley Hopkins, *The Major Works*, ed. Catherine Phillips (Oxford: Oxford University Press, 2002), 167.

discovered that his vocation was to be a wayfarer, a pilgrim without a home, who lived among and befriended others who were homeless in the city of Rome. Despite his persistent and severe mental illness, the Church recognizes him as a model of holiness. Fr. Benedict Groeschel observed the following about this patron of his: "He may have had only half a mind, but he gave it completely to God."

At this point, we can consider what Christian faith has to contribute to our understanding of depression. Has God said or done anything about this type of suffering? After this consideration, we will turn our attention more specifically to the questions of how to distinguish depression from other spiritual states: negative sinful states such as sloth and lukewarmness, positive mystical states such as the dark nights described by St. John of the Cross, and the movements of desolation described by St. Ignatius of Loyola and other spiritual writers.

The Ultimate Origin of Depression

As we saw in the previous chapter, psychiatry and philosophy can trace depression to various causes, including chemical imbalances in the brain, genetic predispositions, physical or psychological trauma, deficient interpersonal relationships, or other social and cultural factors. While affirming these origins of depression, Christian revelation traces the *ultimate* origin of depression (indeed, of all illness) to something even deeper. In the beginning, God endowed human nature with an emotional life—and it was good; indeed, it was very good. Among other things, our emotional life is essential for us to love and be loved, first by God and then by other rational persons, whether angelic or human. Because human beings were made by Love for love, our emotions help to draw us into loving relationships and vivify these relationships. Christian revelation purports that the Lord did not originally create human beings to be depressed or anxious, compulsive or addicted. He created us for an authentic love, found in and through self-giving relationships.

In the original state, Adam and Eve were not subject to depression. God did not create depression, nor did he insert it into creation. In the Garden of Eden there was no reason to be depressed: man's body and soul were so integrally constituted that depression was not a possibility. Even though man and woman had not yet attained to the perfection of the Beatific Vision of God's Trinitarian life, which is the ultimate goal of human existence, Adam and Eve nonetheless enjoyed intimate communion with him and with each other. Their intellect, will, emotions, appetites, bodies, and relationships all operated in mutual harmony, because they were in harmony with God.

In our present fallen state, it can indeed be difficult to imagine such a situation. Christian revelation shows that depression, while real and present in our fallen state, is not *original* to human nature. This truth of faith reveals that depression, in the last analysis, is foreign to our original nature. It is no more a part of our fundamental human nature than cancer or dementia. The point may seem obvious, but those who suffer from depression may be tempted to believe that it is part and parcel of being human and, as such, cannot really be changed. If divine revelation shows that depression is not original to our nature, then the possibility exists that one can heal from it and be free of it.

So if depression did not come from God and is not original to human nature, then from where did it come? Christian revelation locates its origin in that fateful decision of our first parents to separate themselves from communion with God. The Fall is what we call this event of prideful disobedience rooted in distrust of God the Father's incomprehensible beneficence toward us. This catastrophic fall had terrible consequences for us—for our bodies and souls—and for the world. Human nature became deeply wounded as a result of Original Sin. The intellect was darkened, the will was warped to be inclined to evil, and our emotions were no longer harmoniously integrated with our intellect, will, and bodily health. Sickness, decay, and death came into the world—attacking the body and harming its union with the soul. It is in this primal fracture that depression finds a way into the human body and soul.

Catholic tradition explains this in terms of successive rebellions and sunderings: Adam and Eve rebel against God, separating themselves from the source of life, truth, goodness, and beauty. The "lower parts" of the soul (emotions and appetites) rebel against the "higher parts" (intellect and will). The emotions throw off the wise and gentle guidance of reason that is suffused with divine love. Human thinking, willing, and feeling thereby become fragmented and disordered. This interior fracturing then spills out into fragmented and disordered relationships. The first man, who had called his wife "bone of my bone and flesh of my flesh" (Gen. 2:23) now blames her for his evil choice, while she blames the serpent for hers (Gen. 3:12-13). The world of which they were stewards rebels against them and becomes a dangerous place.

We descendants of Adam and Eve begin our existence, at conception, in a state of *Original Sin*—that is, lacking the intimacy with God that he originally intended for us to enjoy. This lack of the essential element in our lives—friendship with God—has very real effects throughout human history: we become heir to the dysfunctions and ruptures that bedeviled our first parents.

No doubt one of the first things that man and woman felt in their guilt was a profound *sorrow*—indeed, the first experience of human sorrow—because they experienced tremendous loss. Thus, all forms of suffering, including mental infirmities such as depression, trace their ultimate origin to the Fall. Depression (and all other illness) now enters the world of human experience because humanity set itself at enmity with God. Considering this deepest origin of depression, and taking into account a holistic view of the human person, a Catholic approach would not consider overcoming depression apart from the spiritual life. After all, the whole point of human existence since the Fall is to become whole once again, by finding, returning to, and deepening our communion with God—by the operative grace of God given through the Spirit of Jesus Christ.

It is important to clarify here, as I began to discuss in the previous chapter, that the solution for depression is not only a matter of becoming a better Christian. While we may trace the primal origin of depression to the Fall, dealing with depression as it now afflicts the human person is complicated. Healing requires a joint effort between the sciences of medicine, philosophy, and theology. Furthermore, it is important to distinguish between Original Sin (which we all inherit as part of the human condition) and personal sins that we freely commit. While depression might sometimes have roots in sinful personal choices, this is not usually the case. Original Sin simply means that all the children of Adam and Eve are conceived lacking that intimate relationship with God that he desired to have with us all along. Lacking this relationship, our personal powers are out of joint, and we are subject to the consequences of lost spiritual and bodily integrity, including depression. While Baptism removes Original Sin (precisely by causing us to be intimately united to God), the baptized person is still subject to the *effects* of Original Sin—including concupiscence (that misshaping of our desires into a "tinder box" always ready to ignite into sin), physical and mental illness, and, ultimately, death. But fortunately for us, this terrible situation is not the end of the story.

God Cares About Depression

After the Fall, God did not abandon the human race to sin and its consequences; immediately in the wake of that first sin, he promises redemption (Gen. 3:15). God promises that sin, evil, and death will not have the last word in his creation. As the history of salvation unfolds in the relationship between God and the human race, concretized in his chosen people of Israel, God reveals his concern for those who experience sorrow—indeed, for those who experience even the submersion in utter darkness we call depression. God also reveals his divine plan for overcoming and redeeming this sorrow and this darkness.

The example par excellence of this divine concern for those who are sorrowful or in darkness occurs when God sees the affliction of his people and hears Israel's cry in their slavery to the Egyptians (Exod. 3:7). The Old Testament continues to address the theme of sorrow and anguish in the prophetic writings and the Psalms. Take, for example, the prophet Jeremiah. He had a truly difficult mission, and he often saw his attempts to fulfill his mission as an utter failure. In a prayer of total sincerity and brutal honesty, he tells the Lord exactly what he is feeling about his awful situation: "You duped me, O Lord, and I let myself be duped ... I have become a laughingstock all the day, every one mocks me ... For the word of the Lord has become for me a reproach and derision all day long" (Jer. 20:7-8). Although convinced of his divinely mandated mission, he gives voice to his bitterness, going so far as to curse his birth (Jer. 20:14-18). He also cries in abject grief because it appears that evil always seems to have its way (Jer. 12:1).

For the people of Israel, their hopes appear to be completely shattered during their long exile, when their interior distance from the Lord becomes concretized in their geographical exile from the Promised Land. Their collective sorrow is expressed here: "A voice is heard in Ramah, lamentation and bitter weeping. Rachel is weeping for her children; she refuses to be comforted for her children, because they are not" (Jer. 31:15). The Book of Lamentations is a sustained examination and prayer in sorrow and anguish. The Psalms offer a divine vocabulary and grammar to give voice to human sorrow and emotional pain. Psalms 22, 55, 89, and 102 are particularly expressive of this anguish.

What emerges in the Old Covenant is this: there is a sorrow that God approves—the sorrow for sin that moves the sinner to repent. One could call this a sorrow of love. However, the Old Testament also recognizes a sorrow that is destructive (Prov. 15:13; 17:22; 18:14). This is a sorrow bound up with sin.

Joy, by contrast, is linked to repentance and salvation. The faithful are instructed not to give in to sorrow too much (Sir. 30:21-23; 38:18), as it can be an ally of the enemy. The Wisdom books even recommend wine (in moderation, naturally) to ease sorrow (Eccles. 9:7; 10:19). Such counsel points to the unity of body and soul and would appear to lend support to the use of medicinal remedies to help with excessive sorrow or destructive anguish.

The Old Testament understanding of sorrow comes to its culmination in Job, the just man who suffers innocently and whose sorrow and mental anguish are incredibly intense. He experiences tremendous loss: first his property, then all his children in a single tragedy, and then his bodily health. His wife and friends neither understand his suffering nor accurately discern his spiritual situation. The former concepts regarding God and suffering of the past no longer speak to his present dilemma. His friends wrongly insist that his suffering must be the result of his own personal sin. Job feels that God is not simply absent but that he is actually an enemy who hunts him down (Job 3:20; 9:15-18). Like Jeremiah, Job gives voice to his sorrow with savage sincerity: "I will not restrain my mouth ... I will complain in the bitterness of my soul" (Job 7:11). In an even longer lament than Jeremiah's, he curses his birth (Job 3:1-19), he wishes to die but cannot, he feels isolated and misunderstood (Job 6:13), he suffers physically (Job 7:3), and he makes heartrending statements such as, "I loathe my life" (Job 10:1). At the end of the book, we are never given a totally satisfactory answer to the mystery of evil: the Lord has yet to give his full answer to Job's questions about suffering, which will come only when his Son dies on the Cross. Nevertheless, in the encounter with the living God, Job says that he sees something that overwhelms him, and he abandons himself to this mystery (Job 42:2-6).

One noticeable aspect of all treatment of sorrow in the Old Testament is that it takes place in the context of the covenant, a unique relationship with God. As such, it is always accompanied by faith, hope, and love, no matter how obscure. The Lord instructs Israel to continue to hope: "For I know the plans I have for you, says the Lord, plans for welfare and not for evil, to give you a future and a hope" (Jer. 29:11). In the end, sorrow, anguish, and mental pain will be overcome (Isa. 35:10; 51:11).

From this brief and far-from-exhaustive glance at the Old Testament, we can draw some themes for our consideration. The anguish of intense sorrow is not denied or dismissed, but neither is it something to be treated as a good in itself. It is real and is acknowledged as part of living in a fallen world with a fallen human nature (Prov. 14:13; Eccles. 3:4). The faithful believer is not exempt from experiencing it, or even the prophets who are on a divinely conferred mission and those not conscious of any sin. Furthermore, we are given permission, as it were, to acknowledge our sorrow, to put words to it, and to bring it into our relationship with the Lord and into the mystery of his presence and plan. But we should avoid giving in to sadness or grief too much, if we can help it, as it can be an ally of the enemy.

God, for his part, recognizes sadness and is concerned about it, even expressing his own sorrow in the face of the fracture and disfigurement of his creation and the continued sinfulness of his people. What emerges clearly is that, even in the Old Covenant, this affliction is taken up into salvation history, which means

God is doing something about it. He has accounted for it in his plan — a plan for a future full of hope.

Jesus Redeems Depression

Divine concern for human sorrow and mental anguish takes a quantum leap in the New Testament. The utter uniqueness of the Christian revelation, which definitively distinguishes it from every other religion, is that the almighty God — the Second Person of the Blessed Trinity — became one of us in the Incarnation, a man like us in all things but sin. God the Son, without loss of his divinity, took on a full and integral human nature in the womb of the Blessed Virgin Mary. As Catholic teaching explains it in the early ecumenical councils (especially the Council of Chalcedon), Jesus is one Divine Person who unites in himself two complete natures, divine and human.

The person of Jesus of Nazareth, therefore, has profound implications for all human afflictions, including depression. Because he now possesses for all eternity a full and integral human nature, Jesus has the full range of human emotional life. Human intellectual, volitional, and emotional life has been united to God the Son's own person and brought into the Trinitarian life of Father, Son, and Holy Spirit.

Our Lord's thinking, willing, and feeling work a bit differently from ours: they are neither darkened nor disordered because his human nature is without sin. Although Jesus was never clinically depressed, we need not think that this distances him from those who are depressed. His ordered interior life does not make him less human than we are, but actually *more* human. Indeed, his divine and human perfection makes him capable of entering into the depths of human darkness more profoundly than anyone else.

Even a cursory walk through the Gospels shows that the Lord experienced the range of human emotions, including profound sorrow and anguish of soul. This can be of great solace for those suffering depression. God is no distant figure. He enters fully into human life and redeems human nature *from the inside*. For the sake of brevity, let us just look at a few moments when Jesus encounters profound sorrow. We can see his reaction to people who are sorrowful, such as the widow of Nain, who was accompanying her dead son on his way to be buried. The plight of this woman moves the Incarnate Son to profound compassion; he raises her son from the dead right then and there (Luke 7:13-15). When Jairus is informed that his daughter has died, in the very moment when sorrow would be crashing in upon him, Jesus tells him to have faith; then he raises her too (Luke 8:50-55).

Not only is he compassionate with those who are sorrowful, but Jesus himself experiences and expresses deep sorrow. More than once, he is grieved by the hardness of heart of the Pharisees. For example, when Jesus saw a man with a withered hand, he asked whether it was lawful to do good on the Sabbath or not. When his interlocutors were silent, Jesus "looked around at them with anger, *grieved* at their hardness of heart, and said to the man, 'Stretch out your hand.' He stretched it out, and his hand was restored" (Mark 3:5).

Our Lord's sorrow is such that he even weeps. As he draws near to Jerusalem amid the shouts of "Hosanna," Jesus weeps over the city because of its rejection of the Messiah and its coming destruction (Luke 19:41). He is moved by the sorrow and grief of those he loves, such as Martha and Mary after the death of their brother Lazarus; he himself, troubled in spirit, weeps (John 11:35). As he approaches the tomb of Lazarus, he is overcome once again with sadness and grief (John 11:38). His sorrow is such that the people around him exclaim, "See how he loved him!" (John 11:36). Later in the Garden of Gethsemane, he says, "My soul is very sorrowful, even to death," and he pleads with his friends not to abandon him in that moment of anguish: "Remain here, and watch" (Mark 14:34).

These events in the life of Jesus take up the Old Testament themes about sorrow and anguish, expanding and concretizing them in the sorrow of the Incarnate God. Jesus willingly takes this suffering unto himself. Sorrow and mental pain are no longer something foreign to the life of God. The heart of the depressed person can find a connection with the profound sorrow found in the Heart of Jesus. When human suffering encounters the Sacred Heart of Christ, the result is life and hope: a withered hand is restored; an only son, a precious daughter, and a good friend are raised from the dead. Jesus points us to a future full of hope.

Our Lord not only experiences sorrow but also teaches about it. He solemnly declares in the second Beatitude: "Blessed are those who mourn, for they shall be comforted" (Matt. 5:4). He indicates, paradoxically, that the sorrowful are *makarios*—that is, "blessed" or "fortunate." Erasmo Leiva-Merikakis, a Catholic scholar and linguist, comments that this Greek word for "blessed" conveys the state of the person's life as good.[24] This is a state not everyone obtains; and it is a state not dependent on how one feels. The Jewish biblical translator Andre Chouraqui suggests that the Hebrew equivalent *ashrei* "indicates the thrill of the wayfarer who is about to reach his goal ... the joy of the pilgrim who never halts in his movement toward the sanctuary of the heavenly homeland." Chouraqui thus translates *makarios* ("blessed") "as 'underway' or 'forward,' thus keynoting movement toward the good goal and the rejoicing that fills the pilgrim at being sure that he will reach God by this road and no other."[25]

How can Jesus say that those who mourn are fortunate? What does he mean? Leiva-Merikakis suggests that the disciple of Jesus who mourns is blessed because he is viewing death, the ultimate

---

[24] Cf. Erasmo Leiva-Merikakis, *Fire of Mercy, Heart of the Word: Meditations on the Gospel according to St. Matthew*, vol. 1 (San Francisco: Ignatius Press, 1996), 189-193.

[25] Ibid., 185.

cause for sorrow, from God's point of view. In a way, precisely on the path of mourning, he is stepping in to share God's vision and life. The one who mourns is being faithful to a particular love and expressing the conviction that life is stronger than death and that death should not be. The mourner who perseveres in his non-acceptance of death as the ultimate reality becomes *makarios* — blessed. In other words, the follower of Jesus in the Beatitudes is hopeful within sorrow and grief, even if he is tempted to despair. He is hopeful because Jesus is there with him. The phrase "shall be comforted" literally means, "to be called to someone's side." The sorrowful are called close to Jesus' side; they are not abandoned. Leiva-Merikakis comments, "God does not console us by abolishing our solitude but by entering it and sharing it."[26] The disciple of Christ has a hopeful sorrow because Jesus is with him. And this hopeful sorrow — this sorrow of love — is indeed a Christian virtue.

The disciples of Jesus experience sorrow and anguish in their walk with the Master. One prospective disciple, a rich young man, sorrowfully leaves Jesus when he is invited to sell all he has and follow Jesus (Matt. 19:16-22). His sorrow stems from a disordered attachment to material goods and prevents him from responding fully to the call of Jesus. Jesus acknowledges the sorrow of the apostles at the Last Supper: "Because I have said these things to you, sorrow has filled your hearts" (John 16:6). While in the Garden of Gethsemane, the disciples themselves are so weighed down by sorrow, confusion, and grief that they cannot stay awake (Luke 22:45).

Most of all, our Lady experiences moments of intense sorrow, even anguish, as she accompanies her divine Son in his mission of salvation. Catholics have a centuries-old devotion to the Seven Sorrows of Mary. They are indicated in Scripture: in Simeon's

[26] Ibid., 191.

prophecy when Jesus is presented as an infant in the Temple (Luke 2:34-35), when Mary and Joseph have to flee to Egypt to escape King Herod's murderous plot (Matt. 2:14-15), when they lose Jesus for three days when he is twelve years old (Luke 2:45-48), when Mary meets Jesus while he carries his Cross (Luke 23:27), while she stands at the foot of the Cross watching him die (John 19:25-27), when she holds the body of her dead Son after he is taken down from the Cross, and finally, when, along with Joseph of Arimathea, Mary places his body in the tomb and sees the stone rolled over the opening and sealed (Luke 23:55-56).

Jesus' sorrow culminates on the Cross, where he painfully and mysteriously cries out, "My God, my God, why have you abandoned me?" (Mark 15:34). This cry of anguish occurs as he hands himself over to the One who appears to have forsaken him. This brings together in a single event all human sorrow and depression from the Fall to the consummation of the world. All the world's sufferings are taken up into the death of Jesus and transformed in the revelation of his infinite and unconditional love for man. Sorrow and anguish, which used to indicate man's *separation* from God, is now paradoxically made into an expression of God's love for man and thus an indication of *union* with God. The Cross and Resurrection irrevocably and fundamentally alter sorrow and its meaning. Brought through the fires of the Paschal Mystery, neither man nor his mental suffering are the same, because the individual who is united to Christ now finds himself in a previously unforeseeable communion with God: he is made a member of Christ's Mystical Body; he is brought to share in the Trinitarian life of God. Christ has redeemed depression.

Christ's redemption of depression brings with it some compelling implications. The Old Testament revelation of divine concern for sorrow is affirmed, concretized, and infinitely expanded in the New Covenant. Mental anguish has been taken into the very life of God and has been redeemed and transformed. Indeed, our entire interior life has been taken into the Paschal Mystery of Jesus' life, death, and Resurrection and, therefore, into the Trinitarian life itself. Faithful to his promise after the Fall, God does not allow sorrow or anguish to have the last word on human life. All suffering is relativized by his love. Suffering is compelled by Christ to become a grammar of his love. No suffering or misery is greater than God; depression need not utterly overwhelm those who are united to him. Instead of indicating separation from God, suffering can become a vehicle by which one is brought into deep intimacy with him. Human suffering can have sanctifying value when united to the sufferings of Christ. For the first time since the Fall, the human race does not have to be irredeemably sad. We need not give in to despair.

One of the first consequences of the Cross and Resurrection is that the disciple is freed from oppressive sorrow. Sin and death have been conquered and their power destroyed by Christ. Indeed, the accounts of the disciples' contact with the Risen Lord are filled with awe and joy. Upon hearing the news of the Resurrection, Peter and John run to the tomb to see the truth for themselves. And after receiving the Holy Spirit at Pentecost, it seems that sorrow is greatly diminished in the lives of the disciples. Jesus promised at the Last Supper: "You will be sorrowful, but your sorrow will turn to joy" (John 16:20). The reality of the Resurrection extends so far into the interior life of the disciple that St. Paul can say that he even rejoices in his suffering (Col. 1:24).

But note that St. Paul's statement indicates also the persistence of sorrow in the Christian's life. The Cross and Resurrection do not abolish sorrow from Christian experience. Sorrow will be present in the life of every believer, but it is something that is used by God to bring the disciple into closer union with him.

So the Christian will inevitably experience sorrow. Peter wept bitterly after his denial of Jesus (Matt. 26:75), and he was deeply grieved after the Resurrection when Jesus asked him a third consecutive time whether Peter loved him (John 21:17). St. Peter's sorrow served a greater purpose of repentance and healing, which made him capable of fulfilling his own divinely conferred mission and brought him into deeper union with Jesus. The Lord is at work in and through the disciple's sorrow. Peter is not relegated permanently to feel sad or be depressed about his denial. On the contrary, in the Acts of the Apostles, we see him with the grace of God moving forward with great confidence and joy in preaching and healing. In his letters he is again confident and eager as he acknowledges the trials of the early Christians, encourages and affirms their joy even in the midst of these trials, admonishes against sin, and exhorts them to hope and love.

We see sorrow afflicting other disciples. The disciples on the way to Emmaus were sad and disillusioned about Jesus' death before their encounter with him as risen (Luke 24:17), as was Mary Magdalene (John 20:11). Paul expressed his sorrow over the unbelief of the Jews (Rom. 9:2) and the rebellion at Corinth (2 Cor. 2:1). He also picked up the Old Testament thread referring to the sorrow that God approves—namely, the sorrow of repentance that produces good fruit (2 Cor. 7:10).

Christ's disciples were not spared sorrow simply by following him. Indeed, the experience of a disciple of Christ can be precisely the reverse. The thirteenth-century Dominican mystic John Tauler wrote:

Since God draws men to him by means of joy and others by means of sorrow, by which of these did he draw the disciples? The answer is found in considering their life. It was passed in our Savior's company in much hardship, ending in great shame and distress. So they were drawn to God more by sorrow than by joy. And especially after their master's cruel death were they in a state of bitter suffering, until they had become entirely detached. And thus, by the special favor of their heavenly Father, they were made fit to receive the Holy Spirit by the way of suffering. The drawing through sorrow is a safer way than that through joy.[27]

Union with Christ cannot occur without a sharing in his Cross. In Christ, one has existential joy even amid the darkest hours of life. Our Lady's sorrow reveals this most fully. Because she is without sin, she has no need for repentance. In fact, we could say that her sinless state has *led* her into a special participation in her Son's sorrow. All her sorrow has to do with him. Her sorrow begins to show forth what we could perhaps call a uniquely *Christian* experience of sorrow. It is a sorrow born of love, a mystical participation in our Lord's sorrow. It is a state in which sorrow and joy are not mutually exclusive. It is a sorrow that is redemptive. We will examine this more closely later. As always, here Mary shows the way to union with her Son. The paradox of the Christian life is this: walking through sorrow, with Christ and in Christ, we truly become *makarios*, blessed.

The person suffering from depression needs to know and to recall this deepest of truths: he or she is not alone. Christ is there in the darkness; in our pain, as in our joy, we can be united to Christ. Christian revelation, therefore, leads to freedom from the sorrow of total despair and dejection, and yet acknowledges a salutary sorrow producing repentance and union with God. Indeed, at advanced stages of the spiritual life, one may experience a mystical, participatory, redemptive sorrow indicating deep union with God—a solidarity in the suffering of Christ on the Cross, wherein Jesus really undergoes all the human suffering of all times.

What I would like to suggest here is that the person suffering from depression may also be experiencing a participation in the agony of the Cross. Scripture teaches that whatever its source,

---

[27] John Tauler, *The Sermons and Conferences of John Tauler* (Washington, DC: Apostolic Mission House, 1910), 29.

all our sorrow should be brought into our relationship with the Lord, in order to become subject to his saving plan for a future of hope. More will be said later in this chapter to help us distinguish between two types of sorrow: a sorrow of desolation (depression) that does not produce spiritual fruits of repentance and from which we should be freed by means of healing; and a salutary spiritual sorrow in a person who has repented and is in deep union with Christ.

Having briefly sketched theologically the origin of sorrow in the Fall and Original Sin, and described its definitive redemption and transformation in Jesus Christ, we can now turn our attention to how sorrow operates in the spiritual life. In the next section we will distinguish depression from (1) the spiritual disorder of acedia (or sloth), from (2) the dark night of the senses and of the spirit, and from (3) the spiritual trials of desolation.

Depression Does Not
Always Have a Spiritual Cause

Depression should *not* be simplistically equated with feelings of guilt following upon an awareness of personal sins, nor should it be equated with sloth, spiritual laziness, or lukewarmness, a precise spiritual condition that tradition has analyzed under the term *acedia*.

Christians who suffer from depression, or those close to them, can make the incorrect assumption that their lack of energy and dejected mood are caused exclusively by a spiritual problem. If only the depressed person would engage in the right spiritual exercises, such as reading the Bible or praying more often, or going to Mass or to confession more frequently, he could find a cure for his dark mood and get back on the right spiritual path. If we are dealing with a true case of depression, with roots on the natural level, we should not automatically presume exclusively upon a supernatural cause or cure. It would be unintelligent, for example, for someone with diabetes to rely on divine grace to manage his blood sugar, when the Lord himself placed in the natural order the medical means for dealing with this problem, as well as equipping us with the intelligence to seek out these natural solutions. God makes everyday provision for us precisely through the intelligibilities he has placed in nature and the intelligence he has given us.

To have a sufficient sense of the scope of God's sovereignty, and to trust accordingly in divine providence, requires that we do not unintelligently leap over the intelligible patterns in nature ordained by God in his wisdom. When science or medicine can help cure medical or psychological afflictions, we should not avoid these helps and instead grasp at religious practices as though they contained magical powers. Of course, prayer is always appropriate, whether natural or supernatural interventions are called for: God works through both nature and grace. Perhaps here it is helpful to remember the spiritual maxim that the Holy Spirit is also the spirit of common sense. In other words, it is not in keeping with the Spirit of God to ignore common sense in order to arrive at spiritual wisdom. The God of Creation and the God of Redemption is one and the same.

The tendency to spiritualize a psychological or medical problem prematurely is something I encounter frequently among Catholics, even among priests and religious who come seeking treatment. Often, they assume that the suffering of a mood disorder is the result of a character defect, moral fault, or spiritual failure. "I should be able to handle the stress of my life ... I'm depressed because I'm weak," and so on. This assumption is understandable; as such people tend to devote much of their time and attention to spiritual matters, they have a real feel for the spiritual drama of life. Oftentimes people who are prone to depression are remarkably sensitive to the deep things of reality. The believer who understands that all evil and suffering in the world arise ultimately from Original Sin, while misapplying that correct recognition to himself in too unmediated a way, might gravitate toward explanations that invoke a *personal* spiritual, moral, or character failure to explain depression. While this tendency may be understandable, it is most often not correct.

It is true that sin inevitably leads one into misery and a life of emotional unhappiness. It is a logical fallacy, however, to assume that the reverse is always true: that depression, as a state of profound emotional unhappiness, is always caused by personal sin or moral failure. As discussed in the previous section, while all sickness and suffering has its ultimate origin in the first human sin, we cannot make a simple and direct connection between one's personal sins and a particular instance of depression. Christian faith disavows any necessary or direct connection between a given instance of sickness or suffering and personal sin. St. John's Gospel recounts how, on seeing the man born blind, the disciples ask Jesus whether it was this man's sin or the sin of his parents that caused him to be born this way. Our Lord's answer surprises them: it was neither this man's nor his parents' sin (John 9:3). Behind this question is a faulty assumption—namely, that illness must be due to this man's (or his parents') moral failure.

It is noteworthy that Jesus does not give a full explanation as to why God has allowed this man to suffer this particular affliction. Our Lord simply indicates that a larger purpose is at work and that somehow the man's blindness provides an occasion to manifest God's glory. In this case, the glorification and larger purpose are immediately seen in the fact that Jesus heals the man of his blindness then and there. Our Lord did not, however, heal every blind person on earth. Others continue to suffer, for reasons that remain beyond our comprehension—that is, until the Last Judgment, when God will unveil how in each instance he has, by the power of the Cross, brought greater good out of each event of suffering in the long history of the world.

Depression and the Spiritual Life

Likewise, when we consider the suffering caused by mental ill-ness, including depression, we should not make the same mistake the disciples made. We should not assume that a person's afflic-tion is due to his personal sins or faults. God *will* bring a greater good from this—he would not permit this suffering on any other condition—but just what that greater good might be is some-thing that we may not come to understand before the consum-mation of history at the Second Coming of Christ. There is no immediate and simple answer to the question asked by those who suffer: Why me, why now? Where is God in this? The answer—if there is an answer that can be articulated in human terms—is somehow bound up with the great mystery of the God who suffers with and for us out of love. God's most eloquent answer is Christ on the Cross, which is an unfathomable mystery.

This is all to reiterate that depression should not be confused with personal sin. We now turn our attention to one of the sins that might, incorrectly, be conflated with depression.

Depression Versus Acedia (or Sloth)

The Fathers of the Church, especially the Desert Fathers, and subsequent Catholic spiritual writers, discuss a spiritual state called *acedia* in Latin, often translated as "sloth," one of the seven deadly sins. This is sorrow over the spiritual good that is God himself. (The related term *lukewarmness*, often used by modern spiritual writers, can be understood as a mild form of sloth, which, if left unchecked, leads to that serious spiritual disorder.) Some contemporary psychological writers, such as Andrew Solomon,[28] have noticed parallels between descriptions of acedia in early Christian writings and modern descriptions of clinical depres-sion. From this, it is sometimes assumed by modern psychologists that what was called acedia was nothing other than what we call

[28] Andrew Solomon, *The Noonday Demon: An Atlas of Depression* (New York: Scribner, 2002).

depression, and that Christian writers were turning a psychological or clinical category into a moral or spiritual one. In fact, while there may be significant overlap between depression and acedia, and while we concede that one state may lead to the other, the two states can and should be distinguished.

Acedia is a moral disorder involving flight from God. It is a disorder *to which the will freely consents*; there is an element of choice involved. Acedia is listed among the seven "deadly thoughts" in Evagrius Ponticus, which later developed into the seven deadly sins in the writings of Pope St. Gregory the Great. St. Gregory defined it as sorrow felt for the goodness of God and toward things relating to God — sorrow experienced in reaction to God's love and goodness. The Fathers, typically writing within an eremitic or monastic context, referred to this state as the "noonday demon" that may come upon the solitary monk. Rather than engaging in work, *lectio divina* (spiritual reading), prayer, or other useful activity, the monk who had fallen into acedia could be seen idly watching the sun in the sky, waiting for his one daily meal.

Like depression, acedia can involve a complex mixture of thought and emotion.

The Church Fathers, like the modern cognitive therapists such as Beck, recognized that thoughts often lead to emotions (passions) and that emotions, in turn, reinforce patterns of thinking. Both depression and acedia seem cognitively similar in that the thoughts are self-focused. However, in the depressed person, the thoughts pervade all of life, while in the acedic person, they have to do only with the things of God. As for the impact on the emotions, in a state of acedia or sloth, both irascible (anger) and concupiscible (desire) appetites are affected. Acedia could therefore have contradictory manifestations; it could involve both laziness and overactivity, both paralysis and frenzy. Evagrius noted that it often involved restlessness and an excessive need for change stemming from boredom. Depression, on the other hand, suppresses activity, as was described in Chapter 1.

In contrast to depression, the person who has fallen into sloth will typically pay too much attention to his own health, while depression usually leads to a disregard for one's health and well-ness. The acedic person is still looking forward to the next meal, while the depressed person typically loses his appetite. The desire for escape from manual work in acedia is freely chosen; depression, on the other hand, often involves an impaired ability to work, in spite of one's best efforts. The slothful person often engages in excessive activism under the guise of charity. To make up for the fact that he is not engaging in the duty of the moment (whether it be a certain kind of prayer or prescribed work), the acedic person often shows indiscreet zeal for a few ascetical practices. In depression, such activism or zeal is absent. One's lack of motivation in depression is typically global: the sense of discouragement applies to *all* of life and not just to the things of God.

For example, the depressed person may attempt a few minutes of spiritual reading. Although he wants to follow the words on the page, try as he might, he cannot bring his mind to focus on words or follow their meaning. By way of contrast, the acedic individual will simply forego spiritual reading in the first place — not because he cannot do it, but simply because he does not want to, prefer-ring other activities. The depressed person is often overtaken by morbid thoughts and feelings in regard to himself, including self-hatred and loathing. By contrast, the acedic person is typically soft on himself, reserving his feelings of indifference for God and neighbor.

While it certainly affects one's spiritual life, the psychologi-cal state of depression is not rooted typically in a moral fault, as argued in the previous section. Depression affects not just one's mood, but also one's pattern of thinking and one's bodily func-tioning. Looking only at the emotional or cognitive state may not be sufficient to differentiate depression and acedia. It can also be helpful to look at the somatic (physical/bodily) manifestations prominent in depression, mentioned in Chapter 1: appetite changes (typically weight loss) in depression, in contrast to the excessive preoccupation with food seen in acedia; low physical energy in depression, in contrast to the normal or excessive level of energy seen in acedia; the inability to concentrate experienced in depression, in contrast to the boredom or listlessness of acedia.

Clean dichotomies are often easier to draw in theory than in practice. Actual physical and mental states are complex, and typically involve a mixture of biological, psychological, social, and spiritual factors. Acedia may imperceptibly morph into mild depression. A disordered spiritual or moral state may contribute to development of a major depressive episode in an already vulnerable or predisposed individual—although, of course, depression can develop for any number of other reasons that are not attributable to a moral or spiritual fault. And causality can run the other way: depression may predispose to acedia, spiritual lukewarmness, or other moral faults. So the two states may be found together at the same time. In such cases, it is important to seek appropriate remedies for both states: medical/psychological and spiritual/moral.

Depression Versus the "Dark Night" of the Soul

Many Catholics and other Christians who are familiar with the Church's tradition of prayer and mysticism have heard of the spiritual state known as the "dark night," described by the Carmelite mystic St. John of the Cross. Actually, John of the Cross divides the "dark night" into two stages, the dark night of the *senses* and the dark night of the *spirit*, and assigns them to different stages of progress in the spiritual life. Speaking somewhat loosely and without awareness of these more technical meanings of the term, Christians will sometimes refer to any spiritual trial—dryness in prayer, doubts or difficulties with faith, or strong temptations—as "dark nights of the soul." I have evaluated some devout Christian patients who interpret their depressive symptoms as a "dark night." Believing that they are enduring a spiritual trial rather than a medical or mental illness, they are often reluctant to seek treatment with medications or psychotherapy. When they fail to find relief from their suffering from spiritual direction or prayer, they can be tempted to despair or may feel as though God has abandoned them.

What St. John of the Cross describes when writing about the dark nights of the senses and of the spirit is not, in fact, the same thing as clinical depression. It is necessary to distinguish between these two states.[29] Distinguishing them properly will help in identifying the right treatment modality, so that a person will not continue to suffer needlessly if he is depressed.

Let's begin with a brief sketch of the two dark nights as St. John describes them. The dark night of the senses is characterized by dryness in prayer, an inability to apply imagination to the mysteries of Christ, a lack of emotional satisfaction from the spiritual life, and a lack of felt enthusiasm in prayer. Nonetheless, the person in this state retains a deep commitment to seeking union with God and following Christ and does not consider abandoning the spiritual life. This feature helps to distinguish the dark night of the senses from other spiritual or moral problems, such as acedia or lukewarmness. The dark night of the senses is a *positive and normal* development indicating progress in the spiritual life. The previous spiritual or affective consolations that God granted are withdrawn, in order to advance one's faith, hope, and love by purifying one's sensory attachment to pleasure and self-will. This

---

[29] I am indebted in this section to an excellent theological and psychological study by Kevin Culligan, "The Dark Night and Depression," *Carmelite Prayer: A Tradition for the 21st Century,* ed. Keith J. Egan (New York: Paulist Press, 2003), 119-139.

helps the soul to become more selfless and attuned to God and to practice loving abandonment to him.

The dark night of the spirit occurs in more advanced stages of the spiritual life and is characterized by profound interior pain and a sense of emptiness. In this state, God allows the person to perceive his own interior disorder and depravity, the infinite gap between the sinful creature and the all-holy God. The person in this state has no awareness of God other than pure faith, and even his faith seems to him to be inadequate. As a result, the person may wonder if God can accept and forgive him. St. John of the Cross maintains that the cause of this pain is, as the theologian Kevin Culligan describes it, "the light of God's self-communication to the person, the contemplative knowledge that allows persons to see both God and themselves as they actually are, not as they had formerly imagined God or themselves to be." Culligan continues, "[T]he loss of these images [of self and God] is for the person an experience of death, with all the consequent feelings of anger, sadness, guilt, and grief."[30]

St. John teaches that both dark nights are the result of God's increasing self-communication to the person, which purifies the soul first of sensory and then of spiritual attachments. Such a state may feel like darkness to the person, but objectively it is an intensification of divine light in the soul. The individual is actually moving closer to God, not farther away. Like a person who emerges from a cave into the bright sun, the initial experience is blinding and disorienting.

The description of the two dark nights implies at least one intermediate stage. To further clarify these movements in the spiritual life and how they might relate to depression, it can be helpful to view the dark nights within the larger context of what Christian spiritual writers call the three "ways," or stages, of the

[30] Ibid., 125.

spiritual life: the purgative way, the illuminative way, and the unitive way.[31] The first stage, the purgative way, follows upon the initial conversion (sacramentally accomplished in Baptism) that launches the life of Christian discipleship. Every baptized Christian embarks upon a spiritual life whose goal, on *this* side of death, is nothing less than infused contemplation of the mysteries of the faith. To enjoy such fullness of intimate union with the Trinity requires a purging, a burning away, of unreasonable attachments to the goods of this world, so that one might be free enough to enjoy the infinite good that is God himself. If one allows this healing work, the Lord, in his goodness and mercy, purifies the soul of selfishness and sinful attachments, helping the person to grow in the virtues of faith, hope, and love.

A decisive moment comes with the first dark night, that of the senses, which leads on to the second stage of the spiritual life, the illuminative way. The illuminative way is a time when the soul feels consoled and uplifted by God. In this stage, one often has an enthusiasm to pray, to do spiritual reading, to receive the sacraments, and to serve others; the soul experiences a certain ease in following God's will, desiring holy things, and turning away from sin and worldly attachments.

From this period of illumination, the soul is led, by way of the dark night of the spirit, into a third phase, the unitive way. The unitive way is the consummate stage of Christian life on earth. Spiritual growth continues at this point, but it occurs within a stable life of perfect unity with the Trinitarian life of love. Infused contemplation of the mysteries of the faith gives rise to a love without deficiency—perfect unitive life with God. This is a life

---

[31] For a general introduction to the three stages of the spiritual life, see Benedict Groeschel, *Spiritual Passages: the Psychology of Spiritual Development* (New York: Crossroads, 1984). See also Reginald Garrigou-Lagrange, *The Three Conversions of the Spiritual Life* (Rockford, Illinois: TAN, 2002).

of holiness, of sanctity. Every Christian is called to attain this perfection of love, even before death.

Entry into this unitive way is made possible by successfully undergoing the dark night of the spirit. In this transition, the soul may experience a sense of desolation, but a "desolation" that is actually uniting the soul to God. It is imperative for properly understanding the dark nights to attend to the period of consolation—the illuminative way—in between the two dark nights. The point for our purposes is that one is not led directly from the beginning stages of the spiritual life into the dark night of the spirit. Before being led into this type of purification, the soul enjoys deep and abiding consolation in God and the things of God.

In the dark night of the spirit, it is true that the soul senses the loss of God's presence, and this causes great pain. Between the dark night of the senses and that of the spirit, however, there is spiritual consolation. (More will be said about this in the following section.) This period of spiritual consolation is key for differentiating depression from the dark night of the spirit. A depressed person is not likely experiencing the abiding consolation of the illuminative way. In this way, the basic pattern of progress in the spiritual life can help us distinguish depression from the dark nights. Both dark nights belong to the dynamism of grace, by which God brings about perfect union of the soul with himself. Love burns through the whole process, and that marks even the darkness of the senses and the darkness of the spirit that occur as God draws the Christian to the fullness of life.

Although a sense of loss is common to both depression and the dark nights, it is manifested differently. Depression involves the loss of ordinary abilities to function mentally and physically, and it can also be triggered by interpersonal loss, loss of a job, and so forth. The interior dryness of the dark night of the senses involves a loss of pleasure in the things of God and in some created things.

However, it does not involve disturbed mood, loss of energy (with cognitive or motor slowing), or diminished sexual appetite — all of which are seen commonly in depression. Those in the dark night of the senses have trouble applying their mental faculties to the practice of prayer and meditation, but do not typically have difficulty concentrating or making decisions in other areas of life.[32]

With the dark night of the spirit, as described above, there is an acute awareness of one's own unworthiness before God, of one's personal defects and moral imperfections, and of the great abyss between oneself and God. However, a person in this state does not experience morbid thoughts of excessive guilt, self-loathing, feelings of utter worthlessness, or suicidal thoughts — all of which are commonly experienced during a depressive episode. Furthermore, neither of the two darks nights involves changes in appetite, sleep disturbances, weight changes, or other physical symptoms (e.g., gastrointestinal problems, chronic pain) that sometimes accompany depression.

In his helpful article on the subject of distinguishing depression from the dark nights, Kevin Culligan writes from his own experience as a spiritual director:

> I can usually tell whether persons are depressed or in the dark night by attending closely to my own interior reactions as these persons describe their inner experience. As a disorder of mood or affect, depression communicates across personal relationships. Depressed persons typically look depressed, sound depressed, and make you depressed. After listening to depressed persons describe their suffering, I myself begin to feel helpless and hopeless, as though the dejected mood of persons with depression is contagious. I

---

[32] Culligan, "The Dark Night and Depression," *Carmelite Prayer*, 130.

also frequently feel deep pity for the "profound rejection and hatred of the self" that characterize persons who are truly depressed. By contrast, I seldom feel down when I listen to persons describe the dryness of the dark nights of sense and spirit. Instead, I frequently feel compassion for what persons suffer as they are spiritually purified, together with admiration for their commitment to do all that God asks. In fact, at these times I feel my own self being energized. It seems that the strengthening of spirit that God brings to persons through darkness is also communicated to me.[33]

What we have noted so far has to do with the dark nights of the soul occurring in the transitions between the purgative and illuminative and between the illuminative and unitive ways. But we must recognize another kind of dark night, one that is not transitional to higher stages of the spiritual life; instead, it belongs to the highest stage of spiritual life. In the perfect unitive life, one of the modes of union with God would include union with Jesus in the darkness of the Cross. This is where one must locate the dark night experienced by our Lady in her mystical, co-redemptive sorrow at the foot of the Cross—a sorrow born of an incomparably profound participation in the sorrow of Jesus. Since it is an expression of Christ's divine love, this sorrow forges a deeper union between the Mother of God and her divine Son.

An excellent contemporary example of such a dark night experienced by a saint (as opposed to the dark nights necessary to attain to sainthood) is that of Blessed Mother Teresa of Calcutta. Let us examine how this differs from depression. It came as a surprise to most people to learn after her death that Mother Teresa was in profound spiritual darkness for nearly forty years. Why were so many people shocked? Because she was so joyful. She was full

[33] Ibid., 135.

of vitality and had incredible energy and charisma to draw others into her prayer and work for the poorest of the poor. Her personal writings make clear that she spent years in a kind of profound dark night; but she was far from depressed. Anyone who met her could testify that she exuded a joy that was contagious—a joy that communicated the presence of God to those around her. We could say that the sorrow she experienced in the felt lack of God's presence in her soul is that mystical, uniquely Christian sorrow that is born from the Cross. It is a participation in Christ's own sorrow, where joy and sorrow are not opposed because both are expressive of the divine love revealed in the Cross.

As with any of the spiritual or psychological conditions discussed in this book, in actual cases, there is not always a bright and clear dividing line between healthy and ill, between one disorder and another, or between purely psychological and purely spiritual states. Because of the substantial unity of the human person, our mental and spiritual lives are intertwined, and our concrete experiences do not always fit neatly into the categories found in textbooks of psychology or theology. A person could be experiencing both a dark night in his spiritual life and an episode of depression at the same time. In such cases, we should attend to both the spiritual struggle and the medical or psychological condition.

To summarize, automatically assuming that symptoms of depression are merely a sign of spiritual weakness, or a spiritual trial sent from God that one must endure without assistance, is erroneous from the perspective of Christian faith and can delay the process of seeking help and recovering from depression. In my experience, a person's spiritual life is often improved through the process of seeking treatment. Seeking medical or psychological help can be an occasion to grow in the virtue of humility, to deepen one's self-knowledge (a central feature of good psychotherapy), and to improve one's life of prayer as the depressive symptoms improve.

All that said, with recognition of the urgent need for the person suffering from depression to get professional medical help, it must yet be remembered that when the innocent person suffers, there is a sharing in the darkness Jesus enters into on the Cross. There is a sort of dark night in the almost-limitless psychic suffering of depression that can be understood only in terms of Jesus' descent into the night of the entire world's suffering. The depressed person's sufferings have not been in vain.

Spiritual Desolation and the Discernment of Spirits

St. Ignatius of Loyola identifies two fundamental movements in the spiritual life, which he calls consolation and desolation. Understanding these can be helpful to navigate through depression. Consolation is a movement that uplifts and instills a sense of joy and peace, giving vitality and energy to one's life. Desolation, on the other hand, is a movement that is disquieting, sad, heavy, discouraging, and anxious, and that diminishes one's energy for living. According to a contemporary scholar on St. Ignatius, the founder of the Jesuits and author of the *Spiritual Exercises* presupposed a distinction between spiritual and non-spiritual consolation and desolation, observing that not all consolation or desolation has a strictly spiritual origin.[34] Even deep desolation can have a non-spiritual cause. But St. Ignatius admits that non-spiritual desolation (for example, depression) can contribute to spiritual desolation, and vice versa. As we have seen, neat and clean distinctions in actual cases are not always possible.

St. Ignatius also identifies two "spirits," one bad and the other good, that are at work in causing spiritual consolation or desolation. The action of the bad spirit is to weaken or discourage

---

[34] Timothy Gallagher, *The Discernment of Spirits: An Ignatian Guide to Everyday Living* (New York: Crossroads, 2005). The explanation of St. Ignatius's teaching in this section summarizes pages 11-46.

movement toward God. St. Ignatius teaches that the bad spirit does this by a "biting" that unsettles, by sadness, obstacles, and "false reasons" that disquiet the soul. The good spirit encourages and strengthens movement toward God through courage and strength, consolation and tears, inspirations, and a strengthening "quiet" of heart. The whole enterprise of spiritual discernment is to identify and understand the movement of the bad spirit in order to resist and reject it, and of the good spirit in order to welcome and accept it.

Spiritually speaking, there are only two fundamental directions to travel: toward God or away from God. Depending on a person's movement in the spiritual life, the good spirit and the bad spirit will act differently (and always diametrically opposed to each other). If a person is walking away from God, in a state of mortal sin, for example, then the goal of the bad spirit will be to console that person with false reasons so that he or she will continue down the road of perdition. On the other hand, the good spirit will be, for such a person, a "biting spirit" that nips at the person's moral conscience to help bring about a conversion—a return to the path toward God. In this way, we can see the good spirit at work in Peter's sorrow and tears after his denial. This sorrow was profoundly good and produced the desired fruit of repentance. It was also temporary.

In this context St. Ignatius invites the person to welcome the prick of conscience and to notice the sadness and misery that sin is producing so that the person will leave that bad place and turn toward the Lord. This type of desolation is purifying, and in the Ignatian scheme, it occurs during the "First Week" of the *Spiritual Exercises*.

However, when a person turns toward the Lord, the movement of the two spirits changes. Now the bad spirit begins to bite, trying to discourage the person with sadness, self-hatred, and false reasons to leave the path toward God, whereas the good spirit seeks to bring peace, joy, and encouragement to strengthen that person in his walk on the right path. At this stage, which corresponds to the "Second Week" of the *Spiritual Exercises*, the person should be enjoying periods of spiritual consolation. When the person was previously in sin, spiritual desolation was to be accepted as a goad to turn to God. But when the person turns and starts moving toward God, then the Lord sends consolation. Therefore, at this stage, spiritual desolation does not come from God but from the bad spirit, which is trying to disrupt or derail the consolation coming from the good spirit. The bad spirit is to be identified, understood for what it is, and resisted.

Spiritual desolation in the Second Week, like depression, is therefore not something to embrace but to reject. It is not a desolation desired by God because its aim is to discourage the person from the path that leads to God. The Lord permits this trial so that the person, by abandoning himself to God's love and cooperating with the all-sufficient grace he provides in the trial, can struggle and overcome the desolation. Although we strive always to take up our cross and follow Jesus, it is important for Christians to keep in mind that, although every suffering can and should be united to the Cross of Jesus, not every cross that comes our way is deliberately willed by the Lord.

St. Ignatius would advise that a trial or period of suffering should be subject to careful discernment. The evil one, whom St. Ignatius calls "the enemy of our human nature," would like nothing more than to pile "crosses" of his own making onto the person seeking God, with the aim of discouraging and drawing that person away from God. The only cross we should be carrying is our share in the one Cross of Jesus, which is always life-giving and always brings about a deeper union with Christ. Mother Teresa's profound and intense cross produced joy, not depression, in her. We cannot automatically assume that desolation, even spiritual desolation, is always directly willed by Jesus. Depending on our spiritual state, it could be coming from the bad spirit and therefore should be resisted.

To know whether the darkness I am feeling is authored by God directly to bring me closer to him in the union of love or whether the darkness comes from elsewhere and is merely permitted by God (although, again, even this permission is for union with him), I should carefully discern this with the assistance of a competent spiritual director.

Perhaps a person's share in the Cross of Christ is to embrace the arduous work of seeking treatment for his or her depression. Healing depression is a great good. God is good, and he desires to heal anything in us that would prevent us from receiving his love or would prevent us from loving him and others. The entire spiritual life at every stage — purgative, illuminative, and unitive — is about love.

To get a better feel for discerning the provenance of consolation and desolation, let's take, for example, the situation of two people in an adulterous relationship. They are on a path that leads them away from God. While in the sinful relationship, they may experience non-spiritual consolation in emotional and physical pleasure. At the same time, they may experience the desolation of keeping it hidden, of lying to their respective spouses, and of the hypocrisy and emptiness of such a life. Their consciences may be bothered, causing them distress, anxiety, guilt, and perhaps sorrow. The bad spirit may be tempting them to rationalize the sin with false reasons to continue. The good spirit will be pricking their consciences.

Let us suppose that they decide to end the adulterous relationship and turn toward the Lord in repentance. They may experience much desolation of grief and sorrow for the loss of the relationship. They may worry about the suffering the other person is going through. But their moral consciences would be at peace. At the same time, they may experience spiritual desolation, perhaps wondering whether God will forgive them. They may be tempted to return to the adultery, to be discouraged and filled with self-hatred for what they have done, or to doubt the Lord's mercy and goodness.

Notice this type of spiritual desolation has the aim of weakening their repentance and walk toward the Lord. St. Ignatius would say that this desolation of discouragement, self-hatred, and despair is all from the bad spirit to weaken their walk toward the Lord. The good spirit, on the other hand, is seeking to encourage them, reminding them of the Lord's great love and forgiveness, of how pleased and grateful he is for this choice and how he will bring about something beautiful in their lives if they continue down this path. To summarize: when in mortal sin, the soul should heed the desolation from the good spirit; when emerging from mortal sin and walking toward the Lord, the soul should resist the desolation from the bad spirit.

When the soul attains to greater perfection through those initial purifications and consolations, the Lord then leads it to the Third Week. The meditations of this week are devoted to the Lord's Passion. Here St. Ignatius invites the person to embark on something perhaps surprising: to ask for the grace to feel and experience what the Lord felt and experienced in his Passion, to pray for a kind of "emotional resonance" with, and participation in, Christ's suffering. He writes, "In the Passion it is proper to ask for sorrow with Christ in sorrow, anguish with Christ in anguish, tears and deep grief because of the great affliction Christ endures for me."[35]

As was mentioned earlier regarding the teachings of St. John of the Cross, Jesus does not lead a soul into a mystical participation in his sorrow without first bringing the soul through his consolation. In Ignatian terms, one cannot go to the Third Week

[35] St. Ignatius of Loyola, *Spiritual Exercises* (New York: Harper, 2000), no. 203.

(participation in Christ's sufferings) without first passing through the Second Week (spiritual consolations).

The great twentieth-century theologian Hans Urs von Balthasar observed three basic "rules" at work in the Christian's participation in the Cross.[36] He offers them in the context of discussing anxiety, but these guidelines apply to sorrow as well. First, Jesus' Cross and Resurrection ultimately offer freedom from sorrow because, in the end, the power of sin and death is conquered. Second, when a person participates in Christ's suffering, he is acutely aware of the distinction between Christ and himself. As with St. John of the Cross's dark night of the spirit, this is a clear reminder to the soul that there is only one God, and I am not he. Third, the soul is not directly led into this mystical suffering without passing through a stage of spiritual consolation.

As we have just seen, depression must be distinguished from acedia, the dark nights, and spiritual desolation. Although depression should not be confused with other spiritual states, it does have an effect on one's spiritual and moral life. It is to this theme that we now turn.

Depression's Effects on the Spiritual and Moral Life

When a person is in the thick of a depressive episode, it becomes increasingly difficult to pray, to maintain an awareness of the presence of God, to act with charity toward others, and to trust in God. As we discussed in Chapter 1, depression affects the whole person at every level—perceiving, thinking, feeling, willing, and acting. The depressed individual may be tempted to give up on the practice of prayer, frustrated at his inability to concentrate or focus his thoughts on things of God, or to maintain any sort of interior conversation with Christ. The lack of

[36] Hans Urs von Balthasar, *The Christian and Anxiety*, trans. Dennis Martin and Michael J. Miller (San Francisco: Ignatius, 2000), 96-97, 105-106, 114.

motivation and the inability to experience pleasure in any activities—including liturgical, vocal, or mental prayer—may lead a person to feel that such practices are not worthwhile or to feel that God has abandoned him.

When one is depressed, it is important to remember that God's presence in the soul is an objective fact, which is not dependent upon our subjective state or on our interior experiences. If a baptized person is in a state of grace, having confessed any grave sins and received absolution, then the Holy Spirit is present in his soul. This person remains objectively united to Christ as a member of his Mystical Body, no matter what he feels. No form of interior suffering or pain—no matter how acute and distressing—can erase this objective fact. God does not abandon us; it is only we, by our willful and deliberate sins, who abandon him.

Both the ancient pre-Christian and later Christian philosophers viewed the emotional life in close connection to the moral life. Christian doctrine teaches that experiencing an emotion such as sorrow, fear, or anger is not, in and of itself, sinful. While our emotions are part of the "raw material" of our moral life—since they incline us toward or away from interior or exterior actions—emotions themselves are morally neutral. Fear tends to make us shrink back or flee; desire tends to make us move toward the desired object, and so on. But these are tendencies, and we can always choose to act contrary to them. The morally relevant question is not, *What am I feeling?* but rather, *What am I going to do with this feeling?* How we respond to the emotions can be an occasion for strengthening either a pattern of good moral action (virtue) or a pattern of evil moral action (vice).

Therefore, merely experiencing depression (or any other physical or emotional state) is not committing sin. If the depressed person chooses to resist his depressive inclinations and, say, go to work anyway to provide for his family or seek help from a competent physician, that is actually a very meritorious and virtuous action. Struggling through a depressive episode can be the occasion for exercising even heroic virtue just by trying to get through the day. On the other hand, giving in to the depressive thoughts and feelings by committing an evil act—abusing drugs, viewing pornography, harming oneself or others—can lead to vice and, most likely, to a worsening of the depression.

As was mentioned previously, how we act also has an effect on how we feel; our choices over time shape our characteristic emotional responses. Repeated virtuous action can work to change how the acting person feels over time. This approach of developing the virtues to work against problematic or disturbing emotions is precisely the approach of thinkers such as Aristotle and St. Thomas Aquinas. Moreover, it is important to mention here that various factors—including pathological emotional states—can mitigate one's culpability in moral action. This is not to say that bad actions can be called good because of circumstances. It is to say that, depending on the circumstances, a person may not be as culpable for a wrong action as he would be if the circumstances were better; indeed, he may, in fact, not be culpable at all. One of the tragedies of depression is that it hobbles free human agency; thus, it may render actions less culpable.

Chapters 7 and 8 offer additional advice about how to maintain and develop one's spiritual life during periods of depression. There we discuss the ways in which prayer, reception of the sacraments, and ascetical practices can assist a person in recovering from depression. This illness is a trial, a cross, which God allows for reasons that are usually beyond our understanding for now. The Christian faith teaches that this suffering can have redemptive value, if it is united to the suffering of our Lord on the Cross. He has not, and he will not, abandon the person who suffers. In fact, through suffering, a person can become ever more deeply united to Christ and can thereby grow in holiness.

Chapter 3

Depression and Related Disorders

There are many reasons to seek psychiatric help when one is experiencing depressive symptoms. As we saw in Chapter 1, many medical illnesses can present with symptoms that overlap with characteristic features of depression. There is often a complex interplay between general medical conditions and depressive disorders, and both physical and mental health should be assessed in order to ensure the most effective treatment and the best outcome. Depressive symptoms, moreover, are frequently not found in pure form; they coincide with anxiety disorders and are often seen in the context of drug- and alcohol-abuse problems. There are certainly pure "textbook" cases of major depressive disorder, with no other symptoms or behavioral problems present; however, the majority of cases are more complicated.

Furthermore, there are other mental illnesses that can present with depressive symptoms, but are not in fact major depressive disorder. The most crucial psychiatric condition to rule out in evaluating depression is another mood disorder called bipolar disorder. We turn in this chapter first to the key consideration of distinguishing bipolar (what used to be called manic-depressive illness) from unipolar depression (i.e., major depressive disorder).

Bipolar Disorder (Manic-Depression)

My aim here is simply to highlight the importance of ruling out bipolar illness, a complex and often devastating illness, prior to initiating treatment for depression. Bipolar is characterized by depressive episodes, which can look identical to "unipolar" or major depression, but also manic episodes (or the less severe "hypomania," in which the manic symptoms are not as pronounced or disabling).

The term *bipolar* might suggest that at any given time, a person is either at one end of the mood spectrum or the other, either manic or depressed. While this is often the case, symptoms of mania and depression can also occur simultaneously, giving rise to so-called "mixed" manic and depressive states. For this reason, I think the older name for the disease, manic-depressive illness, is more accurate. The manic or depressive episodes tend to recur if a person is not adequately treated on an ongoing basis with mood-stablizing medications. The symptoms and episodes can come and go, and individuals with this illness may experience periods of normal mood and functioning between episodes.

Manic-depression is a disease that interrupts a young person's life without warning—usually beginning in the late teens or early twenties. It is typically chronic and unremitting. It descends like a tornado and can leave destruction in its wake. The disease involves biological factors, such as dysregulation of the brain regions responsible for mood and mental energy, which interact with psychological and social factors such as adverse events and life stressors. There is a very strong genetic component to bipolar disorder, even stronger than that found in schizophrenia or depression.

The hallmark of bipolar, which distinguishes it from depression, is mania. Mania is a chaotic state in which the person experiences racing thoughts, grandiose delusions, rapid pressured speech that is difficult to interrupt, extraordinary physical and mental energy, extreme agitation, and loss of sound judgment. When in a manic state, an individual can go for days on only a few hours of sleep, yet not feel fatigued. The manic person is typically euphoric and full of chaotic energy. Sometimes, rather than having an elevated or euphoric mood, the manic person may experience heightened irritability or become excessively quick-tempered. Individuals in a manic state sometimes get into trouble with the law or spend all their money on foolish projects, so impaired is their capacity for rational thought. Manic states typically last a week or more and are often followed by a plummet into severe depression. Suicide is common in bipolar depression, as well as in mixed states. Tragically, half of all bipolar patients attempt suicide; as many as one in six end up completing suicide.

When manic symptoms are full-blown, the picture is dramatic and obvious: family members or friends can quickly see that the individual is thinking or behaving in very uncharacteristic and obviously abnormal ways. Hospitalization is often warranted during the first full-blown manic episode in order to keep the patient safe and to initiate mood-stabilizing medication treatment. The assessment of mood disorders, and distinguishing between bipolar disorder and depression, can be more difficult in cases where the manic symptoms are less pronounced. What psychiatrists classify as "type II" bipolar disorder is characterized by more mild "hypomanic" symptoms, which are not severe enough to impair the person's normal functioning. While the symptoms of mania in these cases are more subtle and difficult to detect, it is still of crucial importance to make the correct diagnosis, as the treatment will differ between major depression and the depressive phase of bipolar. In fact, treating a bipolar patient with conventional antidepressants, in addition to generally being ineffective, can actually trigger manic or mixed symptoms and thereby make the person worse.

I treated a patient in his fifties who had suffered from severe, intractable depressive episodes for thirty years. He had been hospitalized more than twenty times, including several hospitalizations in the year prior to starting treatment with me. He had made multiple suicide attempts and was suicidal when he first came to see me. This patient had tried many antidepressant medications over the years with little or no relief of his suffering. More recently, he had had a series of electroconvulsive therapy (ECT, discussed in Part II) treatments, with no benefit. As a side effect of the ECT, he was beginning to experience short-term memory difficulties and had therefore decided to discontinue that treatment. One can only imagine his sense of discouragement and desperation. He came to see me at the recommendation of a friend, deciding to give psychiatric treatment one last try. He had been contemplating suicide for several months and had decided that he would kill himself unless he was able to find relief from his depression soon. During his initial session, this gentleman informed me that he was going to kill himself if we could not come up with something that would treat his depression.

I reviewed his medication history and discovered that he had been given adequate trials and good doses of standard antidepressant medications from every known medication class and type. Given the fact that he had failed ECT and never benefited from psychotherapy or hospitalizations, there seemed to be few options to offer him that he had not already tried. A review of his thick stack of prior medical records revealed a consistent diagnosis of major depressive disorder from multiple psychiatrists — both in hospitals and in outpatient clinics. However, there had been occasional and brief periods, especially while he was being treated with some of the antidepressants, where he had experienced subtle cognitive symptoms — racing thoughts, a sense of interior restlessness — that may have suggested mild mania. This was nowhere near a textbook case of bipolar, where the symptoms and behaviors are dramatic and readily observable. But I hypothesized that perhaps he had failed antidepressant treatments because he had been misdiagnosed. The signs were subtle and not definitive, but he may have been an individual with bipolar who spent 95 percent of the time in the depressive phase, with only occasional mild mixed or hypomanic symptoms. I suggested treating with a standard mood stabilizing medication for bipolar and discontinuing his antidepressant.

He returned to the clinic two weeks later, still alive and fortunately much improved. He reported that this was the best he had felt in ten years. He had decided that week not to go through with his suicide plan. Over the next few weeks, his depressive symptoms continued to improve. He has maintained good mood stability on the medication now for several years and credits this medication with saving his life. This case serves to illustrate the importance of getting the correct diagnosis and of distinguishing between one type of mood disorder and another.

Generally, primary care physicians have less experience evaluating and treating bipolar disorder than they have with depression. So it is better to seek consultation with a psychiatrist first, if one is available, than an internist or a family-medicine physician. Of course, in some rural areas, there can be a shortage of psychiatrists or other specialists, in which case a primary care physician is the only available option—and certainly a better option than avoiding medical care altogether.

Substance Abuse

Having briefly described an important illness to rule out before diagnosing depression, we now turn to consider briefly the two most common types of disorders associated with depression: substance abuse and anxiety disorders. A full account of drug and alcohol addictions lies well beyond the scope of this book and may be the subject of a future volume. At what point heavy alcohol use becomes "problem drinking" and exactly how one defines an "alcoholic" are subjects of debate within the medical and mental-health professions. Problem drinking can take many forms, and excessive alcohol intake can cause a range of problems—from medical disorders, such as seizures and liver cirrhosis, to work-related or relationship problems. Likewise, the myriad problems associated with drug use—both the use of "street" drugs, or the abuse of prescription medications—are many and varied, and widely recognized. Spiritually oriented treatments, such as Alcoholics Anonymous' Twelve-Step program and others like it, which encourage a "conversion" of one's life and behavior, are often the most effective ways to deal with alcoholism and other addictions.

For the purpose of this book, it is important to note that drug use and alcohol abuse occur at higher frequency in individuals who are depressed. In some cases, the drugs or alcohol cause or contribute to the depression. In other cases, the abuse of alcohol or drugs is an attempt to "self-medicate" the depressive symptoms. The substance is used to numb the symptoms temporarily or at least to allow the person to "check out" momentarily and try to escape suffering. Over time, the self-medicating through drug or alcohol abuse makes the problem of depression worse. In many cases, the interplay between the mood disorder and the drug or alcohol abuse is complex: the depression may be due to drug intoxication, to drug or alcohol withdrawal (when this is not done safely in a medically supervised detoxification program), or to the chronic effects of the drug in the body. The psychological or social consequences of drug and alcohol abuse can also contribute to depression, or make the depression more difficult to treat.

St. Thomas Aquinas demonstrated a remarkable insight into human nature when he wrote that no man can live without joy, and this is why anyone deprived of spiritual joy will seek joy in carnal pleasures. This turn to carnal pleasures often takes the form of sexual misbehavior, drugs, or alcohol abuse. It is precisely the inability to feel joy, what psychiatrists call *anhedonia*, that makes depression such a terrible illness. But the attempt to find true and lasting joy—spiritual joy—in a counterfeit coin such as sexual misbehavior, drugs, or alcohol abuse only compounds the suffering. The ability to experience spiritual joy must be restored, so that joy can once again be found in what is really true, good, and beautiful.

In many cases, it takes skilled psychiatric assessment by someone with clinical experience in treating chemical dependency and addictions to figure out how the depression and the substance-abuse problems are related. In most cases, both the mood disorder and the substance abuse need to be addressed. Comprehensive treatment for both may involve biological, psychological, social, and spiritual interventions. An individual or his family should not attempt to address problems of this magnitude on their own. With tough love, if necessary, family members and friends should encourage the person with the drug or alcohol problem to acknowledge that he needs assistance and help him to find a program in which he can receive a full assessment and comprehensive treatment. It is best to find a program with psychiatrists on staff who treat "dual diagnosis" patients (i.e., patients with both an addiction and a co-occurring psychiatric problem such as depression or anxiety).

Depending on the nature and severity of the problems, an inpatient rehabilitation program may be warranted. In other cases, intensive outpatient treatment or a "partial hospitalization program," in which the person is at the program most of the day but is home at night and on weekends, may be sufficient. In cases where recovery has progressed sufficiently and a period of sobriety has been established, outpatient treatment with a psychiatrist or psychotherapist may be sufficient. Twelve-Step groups often play an important role in a person's recovery. Since treatment recommendations can vary depending upon the nature and severity of the problem, a psychiatric consultation, or an initial interview at a hospital-based chemical-dependency program is the best place to start.

Anxiety Disorders

In the current diagnostic and disease classification system used by psychiatrists (the DSM-IV), mood disorders such as depression, dysthymia, and bipolar disorder are categorized separately from anxiety disorders. The latter category includes such things as phobias (fears of particular objects or situations), obsessive-compulsive disorder (OCD), post-traumatic stress disorder (PTSD), panic attacks, and generalized anxiety disorder (GAD). However, sharply distinguishing the categories of mood from anxiety disorders can be somewhat misleading, since depression and anxiety often go hand in hand. In most cases of depression, there is a clinically significant component of distressing anxiety as well. This is sometimes diagnosed as a separate anxiety disorder, like OCD, but often the depressive disorder is qualified as having "anxious features."

Brain research indicates that depression and anxiety are closely related to one another biologically. Genetic findings suggest that depression and anxiety share some of the same predisposing genes. For example, certain changes in the serotonin transporter gene can predispose to both depression and anxiety. Rather than having two distinct disorders, an individual suffering from depressive symptoms and excessive anxiety may have a single disorder that manifests itself with both types of symptoms. The periods of depression and anxiety may alternate or may occur simultaneously. In some situations, the same environmental or situational factors can lead to both types of reactions: a severe trauma such as rape, for example, can lead to symptoms of post-traumatic stress as well as depression. Anxiety and depression often share the same biological vulnerabilities and the same psychological or social factors.

Because of these possible underlying biological commonalities, the medication treatments for depression and anxiety often

Depression and Related Disorders

overlap. As will be discussed in Part II, antidepressant medications that act on the brain chemicals serotonin and norepinephrine can be very beneficial in both depression and anxiety disorders. When depression and anxiety are present together, sometimes a single medication is sufficient to treat both types of symptoms.

A skilled psychiatric evaluation can help to tease out and clarify the many features of a complex clinical picture. A comprehensive and detailed evaluation—examining medical conditions, co-occurring psychiatric disorders, and behavioral problems such as addictions and other related issues—is necessary for formulating the most effective strategies to treat all of these problems. When we attend to depression, we often need to address not only the depressive symptoms, but also the other related conditions, behaviors, addictions, and so on. As with depression, the spiritual perspective is important in the treatment of anxiety disorders and addictions.

Chapter 4

Depression and the Tragedy of Suicide

I was sitting in my wife's hospital room, where she had just delivered our second child when my phone rang: one of my former patients had taken her own life. This was a woman in her seventies who had suffered from intractable depression for many years. She had not responded well to psychotherapy, nor had she benefited from several trials of different antidepressants. I had seen her briefly in the clinic a few weeks prior to her death. She came to see another attending physician for the initial dose adjustment of a surgically implanted device called a vagal nerve stimulator (VNS), a cutting-edge treatment for refractory depression. This colleague who had seen her for the VNS adjustment was now on the other end of the phone line, informing me that she had cut her own wrists and bled to death. I looked over at my newborn son, a fragile life full of promise, only recently come into the world, and wondered what he would have to suffer in his lifetime.

This patient was not the first person I had known to commit suicide. A close high school friend, who had been diagnosed with bipolar disorder when I was in medical school, had taken his own life during my second year of residency training. We had spoken on the phone just a few weeks prior to his death. In my grief, I believed that with my medical and psychiatric training, I should have been able to see the warning signs. Despite his three prior attempts on his life, I did not see this one coming. He had been a graduate of the Air Force Academy and a varsity collegiate distance runner before receiving a medical discharge from the military due to his mental illness. Since then, he had struggled to find meaningful work and had suffered recurrent bouts of serious depression. The last time we spoke, however, he seemed to be in fairly good spirits and mentioned very little regarding his internal struggles. A few weeks later, at twenty-nine years of age, he shot himself. This fourth suicide attempt would be his final one.

Suicide is a difficult topic about which most people are reluctant to speak. If it is mentioned at all, a person's death by suicide is typically talked about only in hushed tones and with discomfort. I have now attended two funerals of young men who died by suicide. In such a setting, people are confused regarding the appropriate way to discuss the person's death. If the circumstances surrounding the death are at all ambiguous, as, for example, in a medication overdose, we try hard to find alternative explanations—an accident, a medical problem, anything other than suicide—to explain the person's demise.

This awkward discomfort stems from our innate intuition that taking one's own life is an unnatural, possibly immoral, act. Indeed, as will be discussed further below, suicide runs contrary to the natural moral law inscribed in the heart of every human being. We Christians know by faith that suicide strikes at the heart of God's gift of life to us. To attempt to control the timing and circumstances of one's own death in this way amounts to a vain endeavor to become what we are not: the sole author of the story of our lives. This highest authority can belong only to God.

What drives a person to such despair that he engages in self-inflicted violence? What must a person be suffering, such that he would even consider suicide as an option, a "way out" of his anguish, or a solution to his problems?

The mental state of depression, as described in the preceding chapters, is all too commonly associated with death by suicide.

Depression and the Tragedy of Suicide

The rate of completed suicide in major depression is four in one hundred, far greater than the rate in the general U.S. population, which is eleven per hundred thousand. In this sense, it is accurate to say that untreated serious depression is a potentially fatal illness. In this chapter, we will discuss why depression puts a person at risk for suicide and how to lower this risk and perhaps prevent this tragic outcome. In this context, we will also examine the role of spiritual practices in suicide prevention. The chapter concludes with some reflections on the extraordinarily painful process of grieving after the suicide of a loved one.

Mood Disorders and Suicide Risk

The Anglican clergyman and poet John Donne suffered from bouts of depression. Often during these episodes, he was driven to suicidal thoughts. He wrote, "Whensoever any affliction assails me, methinks I have the keys of my prison in mine own hand, and no remedy presents itself so soon to my heart as mine own sword." As Donne experienced firsthand, when a person is in the depths of a depressive episode—with one's body sluggish, one's mind rigid and constricted, and one's emotional reserves completely drained—death may appear to be the only way in which the suffering will cease. Many suicidal individuals truly believe in their moments of anguish that suicide is the only means to end their torment. This view of suicide as a "solution" to suffering is of course a lie, a trick of the diseased mind, but one that is easier to believe when in the throes of serious depression.

In the United States, someone commits suicide every seventeen minutes, accounting for an astonishing thirty-three thousand deaths per year. It is estimated that a majority of these people were suffering from some form of depression at the time of death, either the depressive phase of bipolar disorder, major depression, or alcohol- and drug-induced depressive states. According to some research, 95 percent of those who commit suicide have a diagnosed mental disorder of some kind. In addition to mood disorders such as depression and bipolar, schizophrenia is associated with 10 percent of suicides, and dementia or delirium with 5 percent of suicides. Suicide is the third leading cause of death overall among young people in the United States aged fifteen to twenty-five. Suicide rates among young people have risen over the past several years. An astonishing one in ten college students and one in five high school students seriously considered suicide during the past year.

Women attempt suicide three times more often than men, but men complete suicide twice as often as women. This is because men tend to use more violent and deadly means, such as guns, hanging, or jumping from heights, whereas women tend to use methods less often fatal, such as cutting their wrists or overdosing on medication. Over half of suicides are catalyzed by alcohol, which is not surprising when one considers that alcohol intoxication makes one more impulsive and impairs one's reasoning and judgment. In a drunken state, an individual who has been thinking about suicide is much more liable to act impulsively on these thoughts.

Statistics alone cannot tell the whole complex and tragic story of suicide. In the end, whenever a person takes his own life, we are left with an intractable enigma that cannot ever be completely unraveled in this life. We do know that people who attempt suicide are typically ambivalent; that is, part of them wants to die and another part of them wants to live. They are internally divided, as is evident by the fact that many people change their mind midway through the attempt. This can perhaps provide a modicum of consolation to those who survive the departed: the divided mind of the suicidal person may have had a few moments before death to turn to God in repentance for the self-destructive act. We will return to the moral question about suicide later in this chapter.

Depression and the Tragedy of Suicide

The number-one suicide spot in the world was, until recently, the Golden Gate Bridge in San Francisco. Someone jumped from this bridge approximately once every two weeks. An astonishing sixteen hundred people died there before the city finally voted to erect a suicide barrier. Such barriers have been proven to save lives, since suicide not only requires internal motivation but also easy access to means. Only a handful of people who have jumped from the Golden Gate Bridge have survived. This rare but fortunate outcome requires hitting the water at just the right angle, and overcoming the resultant serious injuries. A reporter interviewed those few who had survived the jump. It takes about four seconds after jumping from the bridge to hit the water, and the reporter put this question to the survivors: "What was going through your mind as you were in the air for those four seconds?" Every one of them responded that they regretted having taken the leap. As one man put it, "I realized then that all of the problems in my life that I thought were unsolvable were in fact solvable—except for having just jumped." This is the ambivalent "divided mind" of the suicidal person. To mitigate the risk of suicide, we try to appeal to the healthy "part" of a person's mind. To be sure, not all suicides can be prevented, but perhaps some can.

Suicide Prevention

• *Safety plans.* People rarely joke about suicide. Talking about committing suicide should not be considered "normal" for anyone, including for teenagers. Studies have shown that teens who mention suicide, however offhandedly, are indeed at higher risk for suicidal behavior. Family or friends should therefore take seriously any talk of suicide. The individual who thinks, writes, or makes comments about committing suicide is someone requiring clinical attention from a skilled psychiatrist or psychologist. If you have recently considered suicide but have not confided this to · anyone, whether out of shame or because you do not believe you would actually act upon the thoughts, I strongly advise that you seek clinical attention. All suicidal thoughts should be discussed openly and in detail with a physician or therapist. The discussion should include whether or not you have formulated a plan of how the suicide might be carried out and whether you have access to means such as firearms.

There are several factors that increase a person's risk for suicide. Unmarried or widowed persons and those with a family history of suicide are at higher risk. Men or women living a homosexual lifestyle are at significantly increased risk for suicide. Drug and alcohol abuse also substantially increase one's risk, as does a history of physical or sexual abuse. Any form of social isolation is detrimental. By contrast, those with closer ties to family and friends are less likely to attempt suicide. Marriage lowers one's risk, for example. It is exceedingly rare for a child prior to puberty to attempt suicide, but teenagers and those in their early twenties are at higher risk than people in other age groups. Being wealthy, famous, or highly intelligent does not protect a person from suicide. In fact, some studies suggest that higher social status actually confers greater risk. Every year, bright and well-off college freshmen at Ivy League universities take their own lives.

Although we can study and quantify some of these risk factors, ultimately, suicide is a very difficult event to predict. Many patients whom clinicians consider to be at high risk end up surviving long-term, while other patients end up committing suicide unexpectedly. Nevertheless, some measures can be taken to keep safer those in danger and to reduce the chances that they will take their own lives. Many who think about suicide act upon these thoughts only in a state of acute distress, anxiety, or substance intoxication. Such states tend to be transient: if measures are taken to prevent harm during this period, then the acute risk of suicide can pass. Some people mistakenly assume that a person who survives a serious suicide attempt will sooner or later try again and eventually complete suicide. "If they are going to do it, you can't stop them—they'll find a way," is how the argument goes. Research has shown this to be incorrect in most cases. Most people who survive a suicide attempt subsequently go on to do well long-term. A majority do not repeat the suicide attempt, and if they do, subsequent attempts often do not prove fatal. Most factors that incline a person to suicidal behavior—depression, relationship difficulties, or financial problems—are eventually treatable or reversible.

What can be done to help people safely through periods of suicidal thinking? The nature and type of protective measures taken depend upon the person's particular circumstances and individual level of risk, so we will not go into too much detail here. A safety plan is best worked out in conjunction with a doctor or therapist who has experience treating depression and suicidal patients. Often a brief phone conversation with the therapist or a suicide help line can assist the person in the moment of distress. The person's access to easy means, such as firearms, should be restricted during this period, and his or her medications should be administered by a family member and kept away from the patient, who might attempt an overdose.

What should a person do who discovers journals or other writings that make reference to suicide? What if another person confides in you that he is considering suicide? The first step is to speak with the individual who expressed thoughts of suicide and strongly encourage him to talk immediately with a doctor or therapist about his suicidal thinking. If he refuses, a call to 911 will allow the police to bring the person to the emergency room for evaluation. While this might seem like an extreme measure, it can end up being life-saving. A priest who hears a penitent in the confessional make reference to suicide or say things in confession to the effect that "life is no longer worth living" is in a more delicate situation due to the strict seal of the confessional. He should ask the penitent to continue speaking to him immediately after the confession and, at that point, discuss the suicidal thinking in more depth. A priest who hears about suicidal thoughts outside of confession or in the context of spiritual direction can recommend that the person talk with a doctor or therapist immediately about the suicidal thoughts. If the person is in danger of acting on the suicidal thoughts, the priest should strongly encourage him to be brought to the ER for evaluation.

Sometimes in these circumstances, hospitalization, even involuntary hospitalization, is necessary to ensure the person's safety. It bears repeating that such a measure can be life-saving. Family members or friends who are aware that a person may be at risk for suicide should bring the person immediately to the emergency room for evaluation. If the potentially suicidal person is unwilling to go to the ER, then family or friends should not hesitate to initiate the process of involuntary hospitalization by calling the police. Be aware that bringing a person to the ER for evaluation, or calling 911 so that the police can bring the person to the ER, does not necessarily mean that the person will be hospitalized. But it will ensure that the decision of whether to hospitalize will be made by an experienced clinician.

• *Spiritual practices.* A significant body of research demonstrates that suicide is an area within psychiatry where Christian faith has proven beneficial and even life-saving. Research findings consistently show that religious faith and spiritual practices lower the risk of suicide. Spiritual practices such as prayer, participation in the sacraments, spiritual direction, and growth in the virtues are discussed in Chapters 7 and 8. Here, I will limit the discussion to a brief review of the ways in which religious commitment and the spiritual life can be protective against suicide.

Research data strongly suggests that the more religiously committed and devout a person is, all other things being equal, the lower the risk for suicide. Large epidemiological studies, going back to the seminal work of sociologist Emil Durkheim in the nineteenth century, consistently demonstrate this finding. In addition, Durkheim's data suggests that among Christians, suicide rates are lower in Catholic countries than in Protestant ones. Some social scientists have hypothesized that this may be due to Catholicism's greater emphasis on community—as in, for example, the doctrine of the Communion of Saints or communal liturgical practices—in contrast to the greater emphasis placed on individuality in Protestant theology and practice. Non-religious factors may also be at work here: many Catholic countries tend to have better, warmer climates than many Protestant ones, perhaps reducing the risk for seasonal affective disorder (consider the difference between the balmy French Riviera and a blustery fjord in Norway).

In any case, Christian faith in general—whether Catholic or Protestant—and some other forms of religious belief have been shown to be protective against suicide in many subsequent scientific investigations. The reasons for religion's protective role are threefold. On the most basic level, religious communities support believers through social networks and ties of mutual solidarity. Church participation, friendships, and small groups, which commonly develop in and around parishes or religious communities, are an effective antidote to the sort of social isolation that worsens suicide risk. Durkheim demonstrated that suicide rates in various countries are inversely proportional to the degree of social cohesiveness and community solidarity. The social fragmentation we increasingly witness in our culture might be one factor contributing to the rising rates of suicide among young people in recent years.

At a moral level, religious belief is protective against suicide because our moral teachings often deter those who would otherwise consider this option. One of my patients, a young man who suffers from anxiety and depression, told me point-blank: "I don't believe in God, so I don't see anything wrong with suicide." He frankly admitted that he had given his mother permission—his own blessing, as it were—to commit suicide, if she decided to, due to her own depression. This patient saw suicide as a viable option if he could not find a way out of his financial difficulties. Contrast this with one of my Catholic patients, another young man who struggles with depression, who admitted, "I would probably have killed myself already, but I'm terrified of going to hell." I am happy to report that this healthy fear of judgment got him through his suicidal period, and he is now doing much better.

The third, and most important, protective factor conferred by Christian faith is the indispensable theological virtue of hope, bestowed in Baptism and subsequently developed in the life of faith. Christianity offers hope in the midst of difficulties and pain. Through our faith, in hope, we can find redemptive value even in and through suffering. The psychiatrist Aaron Beck, a pioneer in cognitive therapy, did a long-term prospective study of eight hundred suicidal patients to determine which risk factors were most closely linked to suicide. He studied individuals who had been hospitalized after a suicide attempt or for suicidal thinking. Beck managed to follow these patients for the next ten years to see who survived and who eventually completed suicide. In trying to find the key differences between the survivors and those who died by suicide, Beck examined the patients' diagnoses, the number and type of mental and medical symptoms, the degree of physical pain a person was in, social and economic factors, and so on.

The results surprised some behavioral scientists. The one factor most predictive of suicide was *not* how sick the person was, or how many symptoms he exhibited, or how much pain he was in. The most dangerous factor was a person's sense of *hopelessness*. The patients who believed their situation was utterly without hope were the most likely candidates for completing suicide. There is no prescription or medical procedure for instilling hope. This is the domain of the revelation of God's loving goodness and baptismal efficacy. We can have a natural sort of hope when things clearly appear hopeful. But when our situation appears or feels hopeless, the only hope that can sustain us is supernatural—the theological virtue of hope, which can be infused only by God's grace.

One of my patients, who had suffered sexual and physical abuse at the hands of both of her parents, once told me, "If it were not for my relationship with Jesus, I would have killed myself a long time ago." I have no doubt that this statement was true. She is still here today because of her faith and her hope in the God who loves her. As an adult, she was received into the Catholic Church. In spite of her tremendous suffering, she has found hope—hope in God, who became man to suffer and die with us and who rose from the dead for us. We will return to the virtue of hope in the final chapter.

The Church's Teaching on Suicide

The Church has a clear—and yet nuanced and sensitive—teaching regarding suicide, founded upon Sacred Scripture and developed in Tradition. The basic principles are articulated in the following paragraphs of the *Catechism of the Catholic Church*:[37]

> Everyone is responsible for his life before God who has given it to him. It is God who remains the sovereign Master of life. We are obliged to accept life gratefully and preserve it for his honor and the salvation of our souls. We are stewards, not owners, of the life God has entrusted to us. It is not ours to dispose of.

[37] *Catechism of the Catholic Church*, nos. 2280-2283.

Suicide contradicts the natural inclination of the human being to preserve and perpetuate his life. It is gravely contrary to the just love of self. It likewise offends love of neighbor because it unjustly breaks the ties of solidarity with family, nation, and other human societies to which we continue to have obligations. Suicide is contrary to love for the living God.

If suicide is committed with the intention of setting an example, especially to the young, it also takes on the gravity of scandal. Voluntary co-operation in suicide is contrary to the moral law.

Grave psychological disturbances, anguish, or grave fear of hardship, suffering, or torture can diminish the responsibility of the one committing suicide.

We should not despair of the eternal salvation of persons who have taken their own lives. By ways known to him alone, God can provide the opportunity for salutary repentance. The Church prays for persons who have taken their own lives.

This teaching bears careful reading and reflection. In considering it in relation to suicides that I have dealt with, I have come to appreciate more deeply the wisdom contained in these sentences. Let us try to unpack them a bit in order to understand more deeply the problem of suicide from the perspectives provided by faith and reason.

A sense of God as the creator and author of life is necessary for understanding and appreciating these doctrines and moral teachings. The *Catechism* begins this section with an affirmation of our responsibility before God for our own life, which is a gift from God. This responsibility is grounded in our human freedom, another gift we have been given as rational, spiritual creatures.

Depression and the Tragedy of Suicide

Our happiness and salvation hinge on the good use of our freedom. In order to be saved and to become holy, we must respond to and cooperate with sanctifying grace. We freely act as stewards, not as full owners or dispensers, of the life God has entrusted to us. To attempt to dispose with this life on our own terms is to act wrongly and irresponsibly, as though God did not create or redeem us.

By faith in God's revelation, we know that we are persons created in his image and likeness. Even apart from the supernatural gift of faith, our human reason can perceive that God is the source of life and that we have a natural inclination to preserve and perpetuate our own life. This universal human inclination is inscribed in our biological constitution: the fundamental will to survival underlies many features of human psychology and behavior. One feature that indicates how serious and unhealthy severe depression can be is the fact that it so often inclines a person toward suicide—an objectively disordered, unnatural, and irrational act. Aside from other considerations, this feature of depression should be sufficient for the depressed person to seek immediate medical, psychological, and spiritual assistance.

The *Catechism* explains that suicide is contrary to love in three ways. First, it is contrary to *love of God*, for the reasons just described. Second, according to the natural moral law, it is contrary to a proper *love of self*, also for reasons just described. Appropriate love of self includes the desire and intent to preserve one's own life, even in the midst of suffering or hardship. Third, suicide is contrary to *love of neighbor*. Even if we are suffering, we continue to have obligations toward our family, nation, and society. Anyone who has tried to comfort loved ones in the wake of a suicide can see clearly the unimaginable suffering that suicide causes for those left behind. Grieving after a suicide, as discussed in the last section of this chapter, is tremendously painful and almost unbearable.

I recall a patient in his twenties who was hospitalized for depression and a personality disorder. This unfortunate young man already had spent several years in mental hospitals. Every time the doctors attempted to discharge him, he returned for readmission, unable to function on his own in the outside world. His psychiatric pathology was in large part induced when he was only eight years old. This child witnessed his mother commit suicide by shooting herself in the head. The psychological trauma was almost indescribable. This event tore at the very fabric of his psyche, and the damage may have been irreparable. On subsequent admissions to the hospital, his anger, self-hatred, and pathological need for attention and care were manifested by continually swallowing objects (whatever he could get his hands on—a toothbrush, a pen, and other such things), which had to be removed surgically. In my experience, suicide is not something that family members and close friends eventually "get over" in the same way that people can grieve after other forms of death and loss.

The *Catechism* next warns that voluntary cooperation in suicide is also a grave sin. Furthermore, if the person committing suicide intends to set an example, especially for the young, the act takes on the additional gravity of scandal, that is, influencing other impressionable individuals to commit the same sin. This teaching challenges the mistaken view that what I do to myself does not hurt anyone else. Even if the person does not intend to be scandalous, his act of suicide often sets an example that others imitate. Research studies show that suicide is often socially "contagious." Vulnerable individuals are moved to act on suicidal thoughts when they see others—particularly famous individuals—doing the same. Most celebrity or high-profile suicides reported in the media trigger "copycat" suicides in which others even employ the same method. These socially influenced suicides produce a measurable increase in the total deaths by suicide. Many of these cases are people who might not have otherwise taken their own lives, but for the bad example set by others and broadcast by the mass media.

The *Catechism* clarifies that suicide, if done with full knowledge and full consent of the will, is gravely immoral. Must we, then, despair of the salvation of those who take their own lives? Not necessarily. A careful reading of this section shows that the issue is more nuanced. The *Catechism's* teaching in this regard can provide comfort and succor for those who have lost a loved one to suicide.

The Church, drawing upon findings of modern medicine and psychology, acknowledges that grave psychological disturbances—such as states of serious depression, anguish, or grave fear of hardship or suffering—can diminish one's responsibility or culpability for suicide. As mentioned above, research on suicide indicates that most people who take their own lives are suffering some degree of mental impairment, most often induced by depressive states. In severe depression, when psychotic features can often be present, the person's rationality and freedom may be seriously impaired or totally incapacitated, which again diminishes or nullifies one's ability to make rational or free choices. Objectively, the act remains wrong and immoral, but the person's subjective guilt or culpability may be diminished, or even eliminated, in such mental states.

For these reasons, the Church teaches that *we should not despair of the eternal salvation of persons who have taken their own lives.* How can they be saved? "By ways known to him alone, God can provide the opportunity for salutary repentance," says the *Catechism.* It goes on, "The Church prays for persons who have taken their own lives." And so should we.

After a Suicide

I know of no ready-made formula or straightforward method to help family or friends grieve after a loved one commits suicide.

In my clinical experience, some people who are grieving become overly concerned with whether they are going through this in a healthy or normal way. Patients often ask me about this, wanting me to assess whether they are grieving "normally." Certainly it is important to distinguish non-pathological grief or bereavement from clinical depression, which we discussed in Chapter 1. But if a person is not clinically depressed, a medical or therapeutic approach to bereavement may not prove the most helpful. Surrounding yourself with loving and supportive family members and friends, allowing time to do its work, and pouring out your heart in prayer consistently and patiently is the only real advice I can offer. Grief often comes and goes in waves; it can overtake you at unexpected times. Let the waves of grief come when they will. The emotional pain of loss hurts deeply, and there is simply no way to sidestep the hurt (nor should we attempt to).

The bereavement self-help books are full of advice, much of it rather glib. This is probably even more the case in regard to grieving after a suicide. While there is some truth contained in the various schemas for the "grieving process" that might be of interest to psychologists, little of it actually proves helpful for the grieving person. A person need not spend time fretting over which of Kübler-Ross's well-known five stages of grieving he or she happens to be enduring at the moment. I have found few books that provide real relief or assistance to those suffering through the process. Two notable exceptions might be Peter Kreeft's thoughtful *Love Is Stronger than Death* and C. S. Lewis's fine work *A Grief Observed*, a sober and unsentimental personal account of his own anguish and spiritual struggles following upon the death of his wife.

Rather than dispensing advice here, like so many other well-intentioned but ineffectual self-help books, I prefer to conclude this chapter with a personal account of one mother's experiences, which I include here with her permission. Perhaps this account can be of more benefit than discussing an abstract "process" or "method" of bereavement.

Her phone call woke me at three in the morning. Somewhat dazed, I was surprised to recognize the voice on the line, a reporter who had recently interviewed me. Christine was planning to write a story about a project I had started at UC Irvine called the Psychiatry and Spirituality Forum. A few weeks prior to this phone call, she had attended one of the forum events, a lecture I had given on the topic of spirituality and suicide prevention. As I would soon discover, her interest in this topic would become more than just professional or academic.

"My son Gabriel just committed suicide," she informed me. Her voice sounded distant, stony, as of one still in a state of shock. Gabriel was twenty-three years old. "I did not know who else to call," she explained. I arrived at her house a half-hour later and tried to do what little I could to assist her, her husband, and their surviving son. In my line of work, I see people daily who are suffering tremendously, but I have rarely witnessed the sort of human pain that these three were enduring that night.

Christine later wrote about her experience with suicide in an article for the magazine *Christianity Today*.[38] In this moving essay, she attempted to convey some of her guilt and grief in the months that followed Gabriel's death:

> Early on, the suicide felt like a cruel cosmic joke. It was as if God, or the Devil, or some Job-like combination thereof, was mocking and toying with us. Had my husband and I not been devoted, if imperfect, parents? And what kind of awful irony was it that our boy with the sunny disposition, the one whose story embodied the pro-life message, would take his own life? Would his legacy be reduced to symbols

[38] Christine A. Scheller, "In the Valley of the Shadow of Suicide," *Christianity Today* (April 2009).

of social stigma instead, in birth and in death? Had I not the previous day submitted a story about the Psychiatry and Spirituality Forum at the University of California, Irvine to a news outlet, my interest having been piqued by parental concern? I had even blogged about a Forum lecture on suicide prevention. Surely I should have recognized the warning signs.

Such experiences of self-blame and guilt are invariably present after a suicide. "Why did I not see the warning signs and intervene?" or "What could I have done to prevent this?" These are questions that every family member or friend asks herself. Christine went on in the article to describe firsthand the chronic ruminations that cycle through the minds of those who are left behind, and left wondering:

> We survivors replay final conversations with the deceased in our minds—like the one Gabriel had with a friend days before he died in which he made passing reference to the means he would employ. Or the one I had with him before he walked out the door that evening: "Gabe, honey," I had said, "what's going on? Your eyes look dead." He had simply shrugged, and I let him go.

These ruminations neither heal the pain of loss nor banish the guilt. Christine's writings did not attempt to mask or gloss over her difficulties. As she described, most suicide-survivor literature proved inadequate in helping her to grieve; it was typically "full of clichés for banishing guilt, such as, 'If love could have saved your family member, they'd still be alive.' It's a Band-Aid approach that helps in the short run but offers little lasting relief." She found more adequate and lasting help in her faith, although this was a faith that passed through the purifying and testing fire of suffering. Her writings do not attempt to mask her struggles in maintaining faith and hope in the midst of this ordeal. She eventually came to recognize that it was in the end precisely her faith that provided healing and comfort, where the suicide-survivor self-help books had fallen short. She describes it in this way:

> When I think of all that Gabriel suffered in this life, I do not understand. I find it difficult to trust God or engage him with the intimacy I once enjoyed. And yet every day, I inhale moments of grace. I am immeasurably grateful for the privilege of being Gabriel's mother. By faith, I now see my serendipitous meeting with Aaron Kheriaty not as a cosmic joke, but as evidence of God's immanence. As Gabriel was walking out the door of this life, I called out after him, "I love you." Love is as strong as death, wrote Solomon. The love of God is stronger.

Such an outlook requires heroic faith. Ours is not a religion that provides easy answers or quick fixes to tragic and inexplicable events such as suicide. Magical incantations that cast out suffering are not part of the Christian life. Rather, at the center, we find Christ on the Cross, the Incarnate God-Man who suffers real pain and real death. In this we find hope — not a sweet salve or a miracle drug, but a hope that can help when other means inevitably fail.

A few days after Gabriel's death, Christine asked me if I would say some words at his funeral. She wanted me to mention something about his depression, which impressed me as courageous on her part. Although I had no idea what words I could offer on such an occasion, I could not decline this request. The night before the funeral, still at a loss as to how I should proceed with this delicate topic, I prayed to the Holy Spirit for assistance and somehow managed to jot down some remarks. I conclude this chapter with an excerpt from my brief comments at the funeral:

For reasons that are quite beyond our comprehension, God allowed Gabriel to suffer from a terrible illness. Words fail us here because the typical word used to designate this mental illness is *depression*, a pale word for such a terrible affliction. But as terrible as this affliction is, it is an illness that mostly remains hidden from the rest of us. The person suffers not on the outside, where we can see the effects of the illness, but on the inside, which is hidden from our view.

And depression affects not just a person's moods and emotions; it also constricts a person's thinking—often to the point where the person feels entirely trapped and cannot see any way out of his mental suffering. Depression can destroy a person's capacity to reason clearly; it can severely impair his sound judgment, such that a person suffering in this way is liable to do things, which, when not depressed, he would never consider. Gabriel's death issued from an unsound mind that was afflicted by a devastating disorder.

All of you who knew Gabriel know beyond doubt that he would never deliberately do anything to cause you anguish or grief. But like other illnesses that are less hidden, Gabriel's illness is one that too often proves fatal. I want to be careful here. For if any of you, or any people you know, also suffer from depression or related illnesses, I want you to know that your situation is not hopeless. Help is available. You have options, and there are treatments that can often alleviate this terrible form of suffering. I implore you, if you are afflicted in this way, to please seek help from a competent psychiatrist. You have nothing to be ashamed of.

Gabriel suffered from this illness through no fault of his own. Neither he nor anyone else here is to blame. Why our Lord allows such suffering we do not know. And yet we know that God does not allow us to suffer alone. For he is a God who descends to our level, who comes to meet us in our suffering, our illness, and our affliction. This was the message that God delivered to Mary through his own angel Gabriel—the message that God would come among us as one of us and endure our human pain with us to the end.

On the Cross and in his agony, our Lord suffered not just our physical afflictions, but our mental anguish as well. Out of the depths we cry to him. And he reaches down into our depths to raise us up with him. God knows the depth of our suffering; he knows our fragile heart. And Christ's own heart—a heart of flesh, a heart both human and divine—is merciful beyond measure. It is in this mercy that we place our hope. It is into these hands, stretched out on the Cross in a gesture of love, that we entrust Gabriel.

May his angel greet him; may all the angels welcome him to that place where his grief will be extinguished, where he will suffer no more. We pray that he may rest in peace, in God's peace, which surpasses all understanding.

Part II

Overcoming Depression

Chapter 5

Medication and Other Biological Treatments

"Then Zeus's daughter Helen thought of something else.
Into the mixing-bowl from which they drank their wine
She slipped a drug, heart's-ease, dissolving anger,
Magic to make us all forget our pains . . ."

Homer, *The Odyssey*

In this Homeric passage, a modern reader might recognize some-thing remarkably contemporary. The drug surreptitiously intro-duced by Zeus's daughter Helen may strike us as nothing more than a very rapid-acting, extraordinarily effective antidepressant medication. For the Greeks of Homer's time, such a fantastical concoction could have originated only in the magic plied by chil-dren of the gods. Helen of Troy's "heart's-ease" is clearly superior in efficacy to current antidepressant medications; nothing that we prescribe acts with such swiftness or such dramatic results. Yet living as we do in the "age of Prozac," we take for granted our abil-ity to alter mood states through manipulation of brain chemistry.

Today's antidepressant medications are considered by some to be cause for celebration; by others, they are a cause for concern. People often ask whether I think antidepressant medications are over-prescribed. My answer is both yes and no. Some individuals who do not need them are prescribed antidepressants; others who need them do not seek treatment or refuse to take them. In this chapter, I try to provide a balanced account of the benefits and risks of using medications to elevate our moods. After discussing antidepressant medications, I will touch on other ways of addressing depression—through diet, exercise, and complementary or alternative approaches. The chapter will conclude with a brief glance at some medical procedures that are being developed for the treatment of severe depression.

Antidepressant Medications

Ever since the Hippocratic physicians of ancient Greece posited that an excess of "black bile" (melan-choler) in the body was responsible for depression, medical science has recognized a strong biological underpinning to this disorder and therefore has pursued physical remedies. Thanks to medical advances, we no longer resort to bloodletting or laxatives (as was popular from ancient times through the Renaissance) to purge excess bodily fluids in an effort to treat depression. Rather than attempt to decrease levels of "black bile," today we typically aim to alter brain chemistry. Medications that have proven helpful in depression elevate brain chemicals, specifically the monoamine neurotransmitters, which include norepinephrine, serotonin, and dopamine. The monoamines are among the brain chemicals responsible for signaling between one neuron (brain cell) and another.

The success of antidepressant medications has often led to the oversimplified explanation that depression itself is nothing but a "chemical imbalance in the brain." Efforts to promote this idea are well intended enough. Often the aim of such reductionistic biological explanations is to destigmatize the diagnosis of depression, a laudable and worthy goal. If depression is nothing but a chemical imbalance, it is fundamentally no different from other medical illnesses such as diabetes.

As should be clear from Part I, however, the illness of depression is more complicated than the simplistic "chemical imbalance"

Medication and Other Biological Treatments

explanation suggests. Depression certainly involves abnormalities in brain chemistry, but generally neurochemistry and the soul are inseparably connected. Certainly, changes in our brain can affect what we think and how we feel. But the arrow moves in the other direction as well: what we think and how we feel influence our brains profoundly. This is certainly the case with depression. For example, psychotherapy for depression has been shown to make changes in the brain similar to those made by antidepressants. So, while depression involves chemical changes in the brain, it cannot be simplistically reduced to these terms. What is happening in the brain is only part, although an important part, of the story. Likewise, in considering treatments, medications should be considered a part of the answer—often an indispensable and even life-saving part—but not the whole answer.

A full explanation of commonly used antidepressant medications lies outside the scope of this book. The details of specific medication benefits and risks are best discussed with your physician after a thorough evaluation. Here, I will touch on only a few general principles. First, we need to dispel the myth that antidepressant medications are addictive or habit-forming. They are not. On the other hand, some of the medications used short-term for immediate relief of anxiety, such as benzodiazepines like Valium or Ativan, do have abuse potential and should be used carefully under the supervision of a skilled doctor.

Among the newer antidepressants, the two main classes are the SSRIs (selective serotonin reuptake inhibitors) and the SNRIs (serotonin/norepinephrine reuptake inhibitors). These medications are generally well tolerated and safe, even in overdose. Common side effects include minor gastrointestinal complaints such as nausea, or mild headaches for the first few days. The most common side effect is decreased sexual desire, although this also is a common symptom of depression itself and may improve as the depression is treated. To avoid sexual side effects, the medications buproprion (Wellbutrin) or mirtazapine (Remeron) can be used, although each of these has its own unique potential side effects. Buproprion is also indicated to assist with smoking cessation, so this can be a good antidepressant for individuals who are also trying to quit smoking.

Some people are under the false impression that newer always means better when it comes to medications. While the newer antidepressants often have fewer side effects and are safer in overdose, the older antidepressants—the tricyclics and MAOIs (monoamine oxidase inhibitors)—have sometimes been shown to be more effective for severe or refractory depression. The tricyclic antidepressants can cause dry mouth or sedation and must be used carefully if one has heart problems. The MAOIs are generally well tolerated, but they require a diet that has some restrictions, such as avoiding food with the amino acid tyramine (including aged cheeses, fermented beverages, and other not-so-commonly consumed foods), and have potential drug-drug interactions with other medications.

Again, a full account of these medications would cause us to get bogged down in medical details. Furthermore, advancements are being made all the time in medicine, so by the time you read this book, there may be new antidepressant medications available. Rather than trying to figure out by reading this book or researching on the Internet whether medication might be appropriate or which medication to take, a consultation with a competent psychiatrist is the best source of information. Medication advances occur at a rapid pace, and the lists of adverse effects found in the package inserts tend to be very long, scaring away most readers. Your physician can explain which side effects occur with some degree of frequency and advise you regarding minimizing potential side effects.

Unfortunately, there is no medication treatment for depression that works immediately. All of the antidepressant medications

Medication and Other Biological Treatments

take about four to six weeks to take full effect. Sometimes benefits will be noticed sooner, perhaps two or three weeks into treatment. But typically a person needs to be on an antidepressant medication at an adequate dose for at least a month to know whether the medication is effective. I see many patients who tell me they tried and "failed" one or more antidepressant medications, only to find out that they were not on any of them long enough to see whether they would have worked. If I see an immediate effect from an antidepressant in the first few days or weeks, this often suggests that the benefit is due more to a placebo effect than to the actual medication. A frequent problem that I see in clinical practice is that a medication will be started at a low dose by a family doctor or internist, giving the patient only partial relief of symptoms. Often, a higher dose is necessary to receive the full benefit from the medication. As long as the medication is well tolerated, increasing the dose within the approved dosing range is typically more advisable than adding a second medication to augment the first.

The first symptoms to improve with a medication are often the difficulties with energy, concentration, and motivation. The last symptoms to improve are often the low mood and feelings of hopelessness. A person might notice that his energy and motivation have improved in the first couple of weeks on a medication, whereas it may take a few more weeks before his mood follows suit. For this reason, the first month or two on an antidepressant can be a vulnerable period. Suicide risk should be carefully monitored and assessed, and the person taking the medication should be clearly informed and periodically reminded that the mood may take longer to remit than other symptoms. A person who is depressed and thinking about suicide may not have the energy, concentration, or motivation to formulate and carry out a suicide plan. However, if these symptoms improve prior to the depressed mood or the sense of hopelessness, the person may then have the energy and cognitive ability to act upon a suicidal plan.

Although the data is mixed and inconclusive, some research suggests that this initial suicide risk may be especially present for adolescent patients who are starting on an antidepressant. The other factor that can increase the risk for suicide after starting an antidepressant was mentioned in Chapter 3: in an undiagnosed bipolar (manic-depressive) patient, an antidepressant may switch the patient from a depressive into a manic or mixed state, which can put the individual at risk for acting impulsively on suicidal thoughts. For these reasons, careful monitoring by the treating psychiatrist is important when initiating treatment with antidepressant medication. Patients and families should also keep in mind that untreated depression puts a person at risk for suicide. While some case reports suggest that the first month may be a vulnerable period, recent research studies also show that treatment with antidepressant medications *overall* reduces the incidence of suicidal behaviors. Antidepressant medications can save lives.

How well do antidepressant medications work? Research supports the "rule of thirds": in about one-third of patients, an antidepressant will lead to complete remission of symptoms; in one-third of patients, a medication will have a clinically significant benefit but without treating all of the symptoms; and in one-third of patients, it will have little or no measurable benefit. While these results may not sound stellar, the "rule of thirds" also applies to other commonly used medication treatments such as antihypertensive medications used for high blood pressure. What happens if a patient falls within the one-third of patients who do not respond to the first antidepressant medication? Research suggests that if a second antidepressant medication is tried, either another medication from the same class or a medication from a different class of antidepressants, the "rule of thirds" repeats itself: one-third remission, one-third response, one-third no benefit. With persistence and time, a medication treatment can be found that can provide at least some benefit for the majority of patients with depression. For those "refractory" cases of depression that do not seem to respond at all to multiple medication trials, other treatment options are available. These are discussed later.

The science of why some depressed patients respond to a particular medication while others do not is still unclear. The general classification of "depression" or "major depressive disorder" may in fact encompass more than one disorder—what we call depression may be a related collection of illnesses with somewhat different underlying biological causes or contributing factors. As our knowledge of neurobiology continues to improve, the ways in which we classify depressive disorders might become more precise and may in the future include different subtypes of depression that respond differently to treatments. Furthermore, we know that individuals vary widely in the ways in which they absorb and metabolize different medications. There are also individual differences at the level of brain biology where the medications have their therapeutic effects.

The science of psychopharmacology is making advances in the understanding of these individual variations. Some lab tests can show, for example, how a person's genetic profile may affect the way he or she metabolizes some antidepressants. EEGs and other tests of brain functioning are beginning to be used in some settings to predict response to medications. Such tests currently have some, although limited, clinical usefulness. As this science progresses, psychiatrists hope to be able to tailor initial treatments to the unique biological traits of the individual. Medication metabolism and response is quite complicated, however, since it is affected not just by genetics, but also by environmental factors such as diet, cigarette smoking, and other medications. Thus, medication management remains an "art" for which clinical experience, careful evaluation and observation, and good doctor-patient communication are indispensable. Patients who do not feel satisfied with medication treatments may benefit from a second opinion or consultation with another skilled psychiatric physician.

"Cosmetic Drugs"

Recent scientific advances have made antidepressant medications more tolerable, safer, and easier than ever to prescribe. Our technological ability to alter moods through pharmacology is well known, in part due to the "direct to consumer" television advertisements for antidepressant medications. In our day, many prescription medications have become household names, including some antidepressants. The word *Prozac* is every bit as familiar to the man on the street as *Viagra*. An online search yields an astonishing sixty-two recent books with *Prozac* in the title. (*Viagra* had only thirty-five.)

With the proliferation of aggressive pharmaceutical marketing, the question arises whether antidepressants are sometimes given to individuals who do not really need them. Here a few brief comments will have to suffice. In addition to treating mental diseases, it has been suggested that we should also use these medications in people who are not mentally ill. Beyond elevating moods in the depressed, newer antidepressants appear at times to alter personality traits in healthy individuals. Some commentators have dubbed this "cosmetic pharmacology," analogous to "cosmetic surgery." The idea behind so-called cosmetic drugs is that these medications are useful to treat individuals who are not suffering actual disorders. If we have the power to tinker with brain chemistry to improve the condition of unhealthy individuals, why not do the same in healthy individuals to "enhance" performance or mental functioning? Moving beyond the medical goals of treatment to utopian visions of "enhancement" would involve not just making the sick well, but making the well feel "better than well." As a physician grounded in the Hippocratic tradition of healing, and wary of utopian *Brave New World* scenarios, I am skeptical of these proposals.

Personality traits are generally understood by psychiatry to be unique dispositions and tendencies that endure through the vicissitudes and changes of one's thoughts and moods. We have long known that certain substances can modify personality traits. For example, alcohol temporarily makes some people more extroverted or more impulsive. However, until recently, the medications we had at our disposal effected these changes only temporarily. A person may appear to have a different "personality" when intoxicated, but he inevitably returns to his old self after the hangover clears. By contrast, cosmetic drugs offer the possibility of permanent personality changes. It now appears that biotechnology is, or may soon be, capable of altering these fundamental features of human nature.

Questions about human nature are at the heart of much philosophical and theological reflection: What is the essence of the human person, and in what does his happiness and flourishing consist? Is genuine "self-improvement" possible, and if so, how? Can virtue be learned only by years of hard moral training, or can it now be acquired by faster and easier technological means, such as medication? Perhaps what in former days required ascetic effort and struggle will someday be available by popping a pill. Our willingness to use or to avoid cosmetic drugs will depend upon our convictions about our ultimate end or goal: Is man nothing but an organism that is well or poorly adapted to his environment? Or is he also, as understood in the Christian tradition, a beloved creature made in the image and likeness of God, a wayfarer and a pilgrim, a being who is never entirely at home in this world and whose perfect contentment cannot ultimately be found in this mortal life?

According to Catholic teaching, the human person must be understood as a total unity of body and soul—an "ensouled body" or an "embodied soul"—that is made in God's own image and likeness. Soul and body are profoundly united and separated only at death. And that separation cannot last forever; God will bring about the resurrection of each of our bodies at the consummation of history. Man is neither a pure spirit, like the angels, nor a merely material biological organism, like other animals; he is a wayfaring creature in between. He is "sacramental," the visibility of the invisible world of spirit, the world of knowing and loving. Man bridges the material and spiritual dimensions of the world. If we see spirit and body in this way as an inseparable whole, we can discern the value in a healthy individual's physical endowment. This view of the human person leads to a more humble, more respectful approach to what is "given" in the human individual, including one's unique biological makeup with its capacities and limitations. At the same time, this view also offers a more exalted view of the human animal, revealing the great dignity of the human person, since both the human soul and the human body point beyond themselves to God in whose image we are made. Christianity also reveals that every human person has been redeemed by Christ's Sacrifice on the Cross and is called to enjoy eternal life with God, both in soul and body.

In this context of receiving our life from a good God who means to make us eternally happy, inborn traits of temperament or acquired traits of character should be seen neither as totally unalterable and untouchable nor as completely plastic and open to manipulation. The body is neither the whole of the self, nor a foreign tool to be altered at will. A person's natural biological makeup should call for appreciation and respect, not for overbearing control arising from Promethean pride. Even natural weaknesses are not always bad. Struggling with such weaknesses can result in the development of virtue in a person. Cultivating this attitude of reverence for our unique God-given endowment will help physicians and patients resist the temptation to reach for a pat, literally encapsulated, solution to every problem encountered on our pilgrim way. It will help us to maintain that *healing*, not "enhancement," is the proper end of medicine. It will help us avoid pursuing utopian social projects, beginning with the commodifying manipulation of the human body.

With a view to the eternal life for which we hope, St. Teresa of Avila described this earthly life as "a bad night in a bad inn." This is not pessimism, but a realistic assessment of our human predicament. No medication can make us completely at home in the world; no technical fix can rid us of all discontentment, nor should we want it to. Each of us senses in our depths that—for all its undeniable beauty and goodness—this world is not our final home.

Returning to our main theme, it must be said that depression is a real and serious illness, and its relief is a great blessing. For those afflicted with depression, antidepressant medications have provided tremendous relief from suffering. While unnecessary prescriptions of antidepressants may be a current or future problem, we need not throw out the baby with the bathwater. The misuse of something does not negate its proper use. Are antidepressants on the whole overprescribed? I would suggest that perhaps the wrong people are sometimes getting them. A recent major national study showed that only half of those suffering from depression during the previous year received healthcare treatment (of any kind) for it. Of the half who received treatment, only half of those (that is, a quarter of those who suffer from depression) received *adequate* treatment.[39] This is troubling, since inadequate treatment of major depressive disorder can lead to relapse and recurrence. Indeed, the majority of individuals in this study who

[39] R. C. Kessler, P. Berglund, O. Demler, et al., "The epidemiology of major depressive disorder: results from the National Comorbidity Survey Replication (NCS-R)," *Journal of the American Medical Association* 289 (2003): 2095-3105.

had depression reported significant functional impairment from their illness.

Diet and Dietary Supplements

Browse any bookstore, and you will find diet books by the dozens. Try to combine their recommendations, and you will find contradictions left and right. The obesity epidemic in America, and our desire for better living through eating just the right foods, seem to feed an insatiable appetite for diet books and cookbooks to complement the latest dietary fad. With this flood of new books—many written by physicians—promising weight loss, more energy, longer life, and disease prevention, it is easy to get confused, throw our hands in the air, and go for a slice of pizza. Is there any scientific consensus regarding the connection between nutrition and mental health?

The best research suggests that we can confidently recommend what has been called a Mediterranean diet. For the sake of keeping things simple, we can describe this diet as basically heavy in: (1) brightly colored vegetables, (2) fish, (3) olive oil or vegetable oil. It is moderate to light on: (1) meat, (2) complex carbohydrates (rice, pasta, bread). It avoids: (1) simple carbohydrates (sugars) (2) and processed foods.

Dietary supplements often promise more than they deliver, but there may be some supplements worth using for depression. The omega-3 fatty acids, found in fatty fish, such as unprocessed salmon or tuna, as well as in some vegetables, have been studied extensively in relation to depression and other mood disorders. Overall, research shows that a diet high in foods with omega-3s, or supplemented with fish oil or omega-3 supplements, can help prevent depression and help stabilize one's mood in bipolar disorder. Epidemiological research suggests that countries where the diet is higher in omega-3s, such as Japan, where fish intake is high, have lower rates of bipolar disorder compared with other countries.

Medication and Other Biological Treatments

Omega-3 supplements alone are not robustly therapeutic or curative for moderate to severe depression; they cannot substitute for medications, psychotherapy, or other treatment measures. They can, however, help these treatments to be more effective and can help lower the risk of developing depression if taken consistently. Many studies suggest that the dose of omega-3s needs to be fairly high to be effective. (See your physician for specific dosing recommendations.) One potential difficulty is that many individuals find that they have trouble tolerating the supplements at doses sufficiently high to achieve the therapeutic effect.

Based upon a growing amount of research in this area, I routinely suggest fish-oil or omega-3 supplements to patients with a history of a mood disorder. The American diet, moreover, tends to be low in B vitamins and vitamin D; the latter may be important in the treatment of seasonal affective disorder. A multivitamin, or B and D supplements, are indicated if lab tests show abnormally low levels. For all patients, a multivitamin and mineral supplement is a good health measure in general, although there is typically no need to go overboard with expensive supplements.

Herbal supplements should be understood as being more akin to medications than to vitamins or dietary supplements. Many herbal remedies have pharmaceutical properties—acting on the brain or the body in ways similar to medications. While some herbal supplements may have potential benefits, as with medications, they also come with inherent risks and potential side effects. The perception that they are automatically safer or more "natural," simply because they are naturally occurring, is false. Risks and benefits should be weighed, and research data examined carefully, to determine the efficacy and safety of these compounds.[40]

For example, some evidence suggests that St.-John's-wort, the most commonly used herbal supplement for depression or anxiety,

[40] The website www.naturalstandard.com is a good evidence-based resource on complementary and alternative medicine.

works in a fashion similar to the SSRI medications. Evidence suggests that it can be effective for mild or moderate depression, but experimental results for severe depression are more limited. In addition to having its own potential side effects, St. John's wort can interact with other medications, causing potentially serious adverse reactions. For this reason, patients should always mention any herbal or dietary supplements to their doctor when asked about medications they are taking. Many patients are reluctant to do so, out of fear that their mainstream physician may disapprove of alternative medicine; however, this information is important for the doctor to know in order to ensure safety and to help find the most effective treatment.

One of the potential problems associated with dietary or herbal supplements is the lack of quality control. Medication quality, even for generic medication brands, is closely monitored by the U.S. Food and Drug Administration (FDA). So, with medications, you can be reasonably certain that what is on the label is actually what is in the bottle. Studies of supplements, however, show that the amount, quality, and purity of the compounds in question can vary widely from one product to another. If you are going to use supplements, it may be necessary to do some market research to ensure quality. As one example among many, with fish-oil (omega-3) supplements, it is important to find one that has been tested and found free of heavy-metal contamination, as lead and mercury have been reported in some fish-oil supplements.

Physical Exercise

Research consistently demonstrates that regular aerobic exercise is beneficial for mild to moderate depression, particularly for elderly individuals. Evidence suggests that it is less effective for severe or melancholic depression, not to mention the fact that it is very difficult for a person in that state to find the motivation to sustain a regular exercise routine. For cases of mild to moderate depression, several studies suggest that exercise may work as well as antidepressant medications, having similar physiological effects to antidepressants. For example, exercise lowers levels of the stress hormones cortisol and norepinephrine, reduces platelet aggregation, and promotes the release of endorphins—the body's chemicals responsible for the so-called "runner's high." Most studies suggest that exercise must be sufficiently rigorous to be effective. Recommended regimens of aerobic exercise are twenty-five to thirty minutes five times per week or forty-five minutes three times per week. Both routines are equivalent in terms of their benefits for depression.

Aerobic exercise can take many forms, such as jogging, swimming, biking, or using a treadmill, a StairMaster, or a stationary bike. Stop-and-go exercise, such as tennis or weightlifting, during which there are pauses between moments of exertion, are probably less effective. A basic rule of thumb is that your heart rate should remain consistently elevated (75 to 80 percent of maximum heart rate, which you can measure after a sprint). Milder exercise, such as walking, is probably better than nothing. Exercise has the advantage of having no side effects, other than the risks of exercise-related injuries, and can be done at low cost. One need not join an elite gym or hire a high-end personal trainer.

The difficulty with exercising while depressed is obvious. The very symptoms of depression—low energy, lack of motivation, inability to find pleasure in activities—typically make the very idea of exercise sound unappealing at best and downright repugnant at worst. But exercise will turn out to be most beneficial for your physical and mental health precisely when it is most difficult to motivate yourself to exercise, if you can bring yourself to do so. Most people find a regular schedule and routine necessary to sustain an exercise regimen. For most people, exercising with a friend or as part of a class at a gym is more effective than exercising alone and can help sustain motivation. The psychological benefits of social interactions while exercising add to the physical benefits of the exercise itself.

While the effects of exercise on depression are often not completely curative, they are significant in terms of at least partial relief of symptoms and improvement in functioning. For those who have mild depression and would like to avoid taking antidepressants, an aerobic exercise regimen can be an effective place to start. For those who are taking antidepressants, adding exercise can make the medications work better and shorten the time needed for recovery from depression. For these reasons, I recommend regular exercise to all my depressed patients.

Sleep Hygiene and Social Interaction

We have seen that sleep is often disturbed in depression. In someone who has recovered from a depressive episode, sleep-pattern disruptions may be one of the first symptoms that depression is re-emerging. An inability to sleep and early-morning awakening are typical symptoms of depression. A characteristic feature of so-called atypical depression is excessive sleeping. In these circumstances, too much sleep or lack of activity while alert may contribute to sustaining the depressive episode or making it more difficult to treat. In bipolar disorder, too little sleep can trigger a manic episode, and too much sleep can contribute to depression.

Therefore, for both prevention and treatment of depression, it is important to maintain good "sleep hygiene." This term refers to healthy sleep patterns and behaviors: going to bed and waking up at roughly the same time every day (give or take an hour), not allowing yourself to lie in bed (awake or asleep) excessively during the day, avoiding caffeine and alcohol in the evening before bed, and seeking treatment for insomnia when it becomes a problem. In addition to good sleep-hygiene habits, treatments for insomnia can include behavioral therapy, cognitive therapy, or medications. If the insomnia is caused by an underlying mood or anxiety disorder, then the best treatment is to address the under-lying disorder, rather than just treating the sleep symptoms.

In his magisterial seventeenth-century compendium, *The Anatomy of Melancholy*, probably the longest book on depression ever written, Robert Burton wisely advises the following for all forms of depression: "Give not way to solitariness and idleness. Be not solitary, be not idle."[41] Contemporary research on mood disorders confirms this sage advice. Research examining mood stabilization in bipolar or depression points to the role played by daily routines—meals, work, interacting with other people, and so on. What has been dubbed "interpersonal and social rhythms therapy" is a fancy way of saying that routine is good for mood disorders. Our moods do best with the proper balance of rest and leisure, work and study, meals and time with family and friends. These studies recommend not only getting up and going to bed at consistent hours, but also establishing consistency and balance in our times for eating, being with others, activity, rest, and so on.

The symptoms of depression tend to push people toward social isolation. Depressed individuals feel they have neither the energy nor the ability to engage meaningfully with other people. Just as the depressed individual may have to struggle more—sometimes heroically—to get out of bed in the morning or to get a bit of exercise, so also the depressed person who is prone to social isola-tion should fight against this tendency. It is good for one's mood to be with others (the right kinds of people, at least), even if it does not feel so good in the moment. Waiting too long in the morning before encountering another person is not good for one's mental health. If friends or family are not around during the day, or if professional work tends to isolate you, try to find ways to avoid eating alone, and try to seek out cultural or social events with others rather than watching TV by yourself every evening.

[41] Robert Burton, *The Anatomy of Melancholy* (New York: New York Review Books, 2001), 970.

"Neuromodulation" Treatments

I will conclude this chapter by discussing four treatments that collectively fall under the category of "neuromodulation," a fancy way of describing any procedure or technique that affects the conduction of electricity in the nerves of the brain or body directly. As mentioned earlier, antidepressant medications work on "neurotransmitters"—the chemicals that go from one nerve cell to another and allow neurons to communicate with one another. But when a nerve cell fires, it does so by conducting electricity down the cell. So, in a sense, the currency of the brain is electricity, with chemicals playing the role of communicating between cells and thereby indirectly affecting electrical conduction. While medications affect brain chemistry, neuromodulation techniques affect nerve cells directly and alter their electrical conduction more immediately.

Because these techniques are sometimes invasive, typically costly, and must be administered at a hospital or doctor's office, they are usually reserved for those cases of severe depression that do not respond to medication treatment or medication treatment combined with psychotherapy. There are four neuromodulation procedures that have been approved by the FDA for the treatment of refractory depression: electroconvulsive therapy (ECT), vagus nerve stimulation (VNS), transcranial magnetic stimulation (TMS), and deep brain stimulation (DBS). While ECT is widely available, at least in larger urban settings, the other three techniques are newer and less available. Also, because of the higher costs associated with these treatments, approval for insurance reimbursement can sometimes be challenging.

• *Electroconvulsive therapy (ECT)*. Among these four techniques, ECT has been around the longest and is also the most effective. Public perception of ECT is often negative, colored by Hollywood portrayals such as that of Jack Nicholson flopping around on a table while sadistic doctors zap his brain in the movie *One Flew Over the Cuckoo's Nest*. In days past, with cruder methods and lack of adequate anesthesia, this technique was much less pleasant, although it was often life-saving. Today, someone observing the administration of ECT would see a benign procedure that takes only a few minutes: the patient lies anesthetized and asleep with barely a muscle twitch. The technique itself is non-invasive, other than having an IV inserted to administer the anesthetic and muscle relaxants; it does not involve surgery.

ECT delivers an electrical current to the brain that is sufficient to produce a seizure. While this may sound strange, it turns out to be therapeutic for depression. I like to think of it as hitting the "reset" button on the brain, similar to what a defibrillator does to the heart. When things "boot up" again, as after defibrillation the heart beats normally if all goes well, so also after ECT the brain functions more adequately. It is a gross oversimplification, but the truth is that after many years of research and lots of hypotheses, scientists are still not entirely sure exactly how ECT works. Research has definitively demonstrated, however, that it does work and is remarkably safe. The main side effect is short-term memory loss, usually for a few hours before and after the procedure. Long-term repeated ECT treatment may begin gradually to cause more marked impairments in memory. Unlike many medications, ECT is safe and effective during pregnancy, and may be a good option for moderately or severely depressed pregnant women who want to avoid medications that could potentially harm their babies.

In most cases, a treatment with six to twelve sessions is sufficient to resolve moderate to severe depression. Less-frequent maintenance treatments are sometimes used to prevent recurrent depression. ECT can also be effective for bipolar mania and psychosis. Overall, ECT tends to work faster than medications, with some individuals noticing significant benefit even after the first treatment. Attempts are currently being made to develop other techniques, such as magnetic seizure therapy or focal electrically administered seizure therapy that would have the benefits of ECT without the potential cognitive or memory side effects. These techniques, however, are not yet well developed or researched sufficiently to have clinical application.

• *Vagus nerve stimulation (VNS)*. VNS was initially developed to treat epilepsy, but later was found to be effective for depression as well. In 2005 it became the first FDA-approved implantable device for treatment of chronic or recurrent depression that did not respond to medication treatments. The vagus nerve helps the body communicate with the brain, and vice versa, and is involved in regulating autonomic processes in the body, such as heart rate and digestion. The VNS device, which is similar in size to a pacemaker and shaped like a large coin, is implanted surgically beneath the skin in the chest and attached to the portion of the left vagus nerve that sends signals from the body to the brain. The device sends a tiny electrical signal to the vagus nerve at fixed intervals. The "dose" of the signal is adjusted by a psychiatrist with a non-invasive handheld device that can communicate at close range with the VNS device. Side effects are fairly minimal, usually just a cough or a slight change in one's voice (due to the fact that the vagus nerve is close to the nerve that controls the larynx). These side effects often improve by adjusting the electrical impulse dose.

Unfortunately, VNS, which can take up to three months to take effect, does not work nearly as quickly as ECT. If patients have a partial response to medications, it is recommended that they stay on the medications while being treated with VNS. Only about half of those treated have significant benefit, and only about one-third of those treated have complete remission of symptoms. This may not sound very impressive, but it is important to recall that the device is tested and used only in the most severe and refractory cases of depression—individuals who have tried and failed to respond to several medications or other treatments. Benefitting half of the patients in that category is no small achievement. Prior to getting this treatment approved, a person needs to have tried and failed at least four medications or ECT, or both. Because insurance approval is difficult, VNS is perhaps not used as frequently as it could be for depression.

• *Transcranial magnetic stimulation (TMS)*. In 2008 TMS became the most recently FDA-approved neuromodulation technique for the treatment of depression. Guidelines require that a person fail to respond to at least one adequate trial of an antidepressant medication before receiving TMS. The technology works on the basis of the electromagnetic laws of physics: a strong electrical charge going through a copper coil produces a magnetic field, which in turn produces at a distance another electrical current in a second coil of wires. Rather than producing the second electrical current in a wire, however, a TMS device can modulate (through the skull, but non-invasively) electrical currents in the nerves of the brain. The magnetic field produced by the device is similar in strength to the magnetic field produced by an MRI machine. The technique is limited by the short distance that the magnetic field acts on, so only the outer surface (or cortex) of the brain, and not the deeper structures, can be affected.

Because it is non-invasive—it does not require surgical implantation of a device, nor does it require anesthesia—TMS has the advantage of being administered on an outpatient basis. A standard course of treatment would be five sessions per week for four to eight weeks in a row. The device is on for about a half-hour for each treatment. The most common side effect is a headache or discomfort during the procedure, which stops when the device is turned off. Patients generally tolerate the procedure well, and discontinuation rates are low. The response is typically not as robust as that seen with ECT, yet TMS is less expensive, safer, and easier to administer.

• *Deep brain stimulation (DBS)*. DBS was originally developed for the treatment of Parkinson's disease, and later found to be effective also for the treatment of depression. It involves a neurosurgical procedure whereby tiny electrodes are implanted in specific areas within the brain. These electrodes deliver small electrical charges that affect the adjacent brain structures. In contrast to other forms of neurosurgery, DBS electrodes are adjustable and reversible—they can be turned off. As in VBS, a small pacemaker-size battery for the electrode is implanted under the skin in the chest wall. The FDA recently approved DBS under its "humanitarian device exemption program"; that is, it can be used experimentally in restricted clinical situations for intractable, severe, and disabling obsessive-compulsive disorder. Studies have shown that when used for OCD patients, DBS also displays antidepressant effects. In the near future, it may be studied, and perhaps approved, for use in severe, disabling, and refractory depression. Obviously, this is an invasive and potentially risky neurosurgical procedure. However, it must be kept in mind that severe depression itself carries inherent serious health risks, including risk of death by suicide.

Chapter 6

Psychotherapy: Its Benefits and Limitations

*"Which of us is not so utterly alone that it is the cool
clinical touch of a stranger that best serves to cure his aloneness?"*
Walker Percy

☞

One of my goals in this chapter is to demystify the process of psychotherapy. An excellent definition of *psychotherapy* is given by
psychiatrist Jerome Frank: "Treatment typically involves a personal relationship between healer and sufferer. Certain types of
therapy rely primarily on the healer's ability to mobilize healing forces in the sufferer by psychological means. These forms of
treatment may be generically termed psychotherapy."[42] The key
ingredient for all good therapy, regardless of what methods are
used, is the quality of the therapeutic relationship. Like Socrates,
the skilled therapist is analogous to a midwife: he does not impose
an external cure, but helps to marshal the patient's own internal
resources for healing and growth. The good therapist will help
the patient understand his motivations and see connections that
perhaps the patient did not previously recognize. Good therapy
can improve a patient's thinking, feeling, and behavior; it can
help him overcome vices and grow in virtues. The process relies

[42] Jerome Frank and Julia Frank, *Persuasion and Healing: A Com-
parative Study of Psychotherapy*, 3rd ed. (Baltimore: Johns Hopkins
University Press, 1991), 1.

heavily on the patient's own character strengths, however attenuated these may be due to various disorders.

How exactly the "talking cure" works continues to be the subject of ongoing research and debate. That it does indeed work for many people, and that it can be a remarkably powerful means of psychological healing when done skillfully, are well researched and widely accepted facts. But just as there are inherent risks as well as benefits for medications, so also with psychotherapy. It can be done well or poorly, and when it is not done well, it can do harm rather than good. I cannot exhaustively treat all methods and modalities of psychotherapy in this chapter. Rather, I intend here merely to introduce a few of the methods and potential benefits of psychotherapy relevant to depression.

While it may appear a bit mysterious at first glance, it should come as no surprise to the Christian that healing can come through words. After all, the world was created through and for the Divine Son, the *Word* of the Father, and he as the Incarnate Word redeems and heals us. And as St. Paul writes, "Faith comes through hearing" (Rom. 10:17). Many of the early Church Fathers, foremost among them St. Augustine, recognized the power of words to effect healing in the soul of the listener. A saintly pastor and expert rhetorician, he understood his own preaching in terms of "the cure of souls."[43] Likewise, the power of deep, intensive listening to convey psychological benefits has long been appreciated by Christian thinkers and incorporated into pastoral practices of spiritual direction and the sacrament of Confession.

The reader may object that there is nothing very unusual or particularly difficult about listening to a person's problems. Why pay a professional psychotherapist when you can get the same services from a good friend, or even from a sympathetic bartender for the price of a beer? First, good psychotherapy clearly involves

---

[43] Paul R. Kolbet, *Augustine and the Cure of Souls* (Notre Dame, Indiana: University of Notre Dame Press, 2010).

more than merely attentive listening. Yet even in regard to just listening we can ask: When was the last time someone (a friend or a bartender) gave you a continuous hour of his or her time and did *nothing but* listen with complete attention—actually hearing everything you said and probing deeper for more insight? For most people most of the time, listening tends to be rather superficial, a part-time job. A good listener hears the other person, but may still be thinking of what he is going to say next, or perhaps puzzling over how to respond appropriately with answers to the person's problems. The listening that occurs in psychotherapy ought to be deeper and more intensive. It actually helps that the psychotherapist is someone you need not see or deal with outside of the treatment setting. This type of relationship creates a unique and safe "holding" environment, where sincerity and disclosure of difficult issues are made easier.

The term *psychotherapist* needs some clarification since several types of mental-health professionals provide psychotherapy. *Psychiatrists* are physicians, MDs, who after college have undergone four years of medical school and another four years of residency training in psychiatry. If his training was rigorous and balanced, a psychiatrist will be skilled both in prescribing medications and in other biological treatments described in the previous chapter, and in providing good psychotherapy. Many psychiatrists today, however, choose to limit their professional practice to providing diagnoses and treating with medications, referring to other mental-health practitioners for psychotherapy when it is indicated. *Psychologists* are those who have obtained a doctorate in psychology after college, and generally are of two types: research psychologists (the degree is a PhD) or clinical psychologists (the degree is a PsyD). Other licensed *therapists* will have a master's degree (MA) in mental-health counseling or social work (LCSW: Licensed Clinical Social Worker, or MFT: Marriage and Family Therapist). It is important to know whether your practitioner is licensed, either to practice medicine in the case of psychiatry, or to practice clinical psychology or counseling, in the case of other therapists.

Legally, anyone can advertise himself or herself as a "therapist." The term alone is not a professional designation that is regulated by any accrediting body. It is a good idea to find out, first, the type of therapist, the training the therapist has received, and whether the therapist is licensed by the relevant board to practice. *Psychoanalysts* are psychotherapists who have been trained and certified according to the methods of psychoanalysis, a type of therapy developed by Sigmund Freud and his followers. This form of therapy is by and large passé, and there are far fewer fully trained psychoanalysts than there used to be. A good psychoanalyst, however, is often skilled at long-term depth, or psychodynamically oriented, psychotherapy (described later).

Regarding the different psychotherapy modalities covered in this chapter, it is important to note that most therapists tend to be "eclectic" in their approach: they avoid restricting their practice exclusively to one therapeutic approach or technique. There certainly are therapists, such as cognitive-behavioral therapists, who tend to utilize one or two approaches exclusively. But most skilled therapists try to tailor their approach to the particular needs of the patient, adapting the techniques and methods as the symptoms and circumstances dictate.

Many Christians who suffer from depression naturally have a preference for finding a therapist who shares their religious convictions. Some patients have had counterproductive or distressing experiences with therapists who contradicted or blatantly disparaged their religious beliefs, or who discounted their moral convictions. Patients should be aware that advice proffered by the therapist will be colored by the therapist's own worldview, and may be distorted by the therapist's own biases. Since the quality of the therapeutic relationship, which includes above all the element of trust and confidence, is central to the success of the psychotherapy, and since a person in a vulnerable state is liable to be harmed by following bad therapeutic advice, it is important to find a therapist who is trustworthy. The right fit is the foundation for effective psychotherapy.

Yet, as mentioned previously, shared religious and moral convictions alone do not guarantee a trustworthy therapist. He or she must also be well trained, competent, compassionate, and skilled in the difficult and demanding craft of psychotherapy. When therapy is warranted and a competent Christian therapist is not available, a skilled therapist who respects and honors the patient's religious and moral convictions is, in my opinion, preferable to no therapist at all. It is worth citing here St. Teresa of Avila's opinion regarding spiritual direction: if she had to choose between a holy spiritual director and a knowledgeable spiritual director, she said that she would opt for the knowledgeable one.

In introducing a few of the common methods of psychotherapy, it is useful to recall the view of the human person—both philosophical and theological—mentioned in the Introduction. On the philosophical level, human persons are rational (able to grasp the truth), volitional and free (able to desire and will to live according to the truth), and relational (able to enter into relationships of love with other human persons and with God). In this chapter, I will discuss therapeutic strategies that aim at the rational aspect of the person (cognitive therapy) and the volitional aspect (behavioral therapy). We will then look at interpersonal, marital, and family therapy, which all focus on the relational aspect. Finally, we will look briefly at depth, or psychodynamic, therapy, which attempts to get to the conscious and unconscious roots of thinking, willing, and feeling. Cognitive therapy focuses on our thinking, behavioral therapy on our willing and choosing, interpersonal therapy on our relationships, and depth psychotherapy on all of these areas, with particular attention given to our affective and emotional life. The reader who has some knowledge of philosophy and theology will likely see many connections between psychotherapy and these two liberal arts that attend to human thinking, willing, feeling, and relationships. Psychotherapy is not essentially an empirical or "hard" science like biochemistry, although it is informed by the hard sciences. Rather, it is, in the words of Paul Vitz, "an applied philosophy of life."[44]

Cognitive Strategies—Changing Habitual Thought Patterns (Intellectual)

The therapeutic strategy of changing our emotions and behaviors by way of changing our thoughts is a tradition in the West stretching back to the ancient Greek philosopher Socrates. The theme continues through the writings of the Desert Fathers, such as St. John Cassian, and the Christian philosopher St. Boethius. It is carried on in modern medicine in the writings of the American physician Benjamin Rush, who is considered the "father of American psychiatry" (and who was also one of the signers of the Declaration of Independence and founders of the American Psychiatric Association). The psychiatrists Alfred Adler and Aaron Beck are perhaps the best representatives of this approach in the twentieth century. It was Beck who coined the term *cognitive therapy* and wrote a very influential book on cognitive therapy for depression.

Beck recognized that our emotional state could affect our thinking. When we are depressed, our thoughts tend to focus on the negative and the morbid, ruminating on themes of hopelessness. But he also argued—and this was a key insight that tapped into a long philosophical tradition—that our thinking can affect our emotional state. In other words, the arrow moved in the other direction as well. This insight is the foundation for cognitive

[44] Paul Vitz, "Psychology in Recovery," *First Things* 151 (March 2005): 17-21.

therapy. Negative patterns of thinking color our emotions, thus contributing to or sustaining a depressed mood. Rather than aiming therapeutic measures at the mood or emotional state directly, Beck devised therapeutic techniques to help challenge and alter unrealistic patterns of negative thinking. In other words, changing our habitual patterns of thought will alter our moods, and the effects will be more lasting. The thought patterns, or "schemas," upon which he focused attention are often automatic; that is, they are habitual patterns of thinking that run like a tape player in the back of our minds. These patterns of thinking are so ingrained that we are often only dimly aware of their ongoing presence and influence.

For example, a person with a tendency toward depression may have an automatic negative thought, "I'm bound to fail my exam today." This thought, in turn, may grow out of a deeper underlying assumption, "If I try something challenging, I'm sure to fail." At an even deeper cognitive level, this assumption may be rooted in a deeply held "core belief" that is broad and largely unexamined, such as, "I'll never succeed at anything." Depressed individuals tend to have selective perception and attention. They automatically focus only on negative aspects of situations, persons, or circumstances. Beck described what he called the cognitive triad for depression: negative thoughts about oneself, about the world or one's circumstances, and about the future. Many people who have experienced depression and recovered can describe this triad, and recall how pervasive and habitual such distorted thinking was during a depressive episode.

Cognitive therapy attempts to identify and to challenge these negative "hot thoughts" and eventually uncover and challenge the underlying assumptions and core beliefs that drive such negative or unrealistic thinking. This work involves much more than just "positive thinking" or repeating mantras to make us feel better. This shallow form of self-help was satirized in the old *Saturday*

Night Live skit featuring a psychological guru named Stuart Smalley, who constantly repeated trite affirmations such as "I'm good enough, I'm smart enough, and doggone it, people like me." It was comical because it was obviously ridiculous and absurd. Good cognitive therapy is not about telling ourselves things we like to hear, which will not work anyway, since no matter how often we repeat them, we will not really believe them without solid evidence in their favor.

Instead, the cognitive therapist and the patient begin with the assumption that a person's negative thoughts (e.g., "I'm going to fail the exam") may in fact be true; but then again they may not be true. The process is not so much about developing "positive" thinking as such, but about developing more realistic and rational thinking. If the negative thoughts are false, the patient should not allow such thoughts to continue to run his life and dictate his moods. Cognitive therapy involves changing bad habits — in this case, a habit of thinking that affirms a particular idea that is untrue or exaggerated. As is the case with quitting smoking or interrupting a habit such as chewing fingernails, in order to break this bad habit of irrational thinking, cognitive therapy requires more than simply smiling and saying nice things to oneself while looking into a mirror.

The cognitive therapist starts by helping the patient recognize these thought patterns and become aware of just how often such thoughts arise and under which circumstances. Then, through a series of written exercises, the therapist helps the patient to examine such thoughts, assumptions, and core beliefs in light of actual evidence. Is the thought accurate, or does it need to be altered or modified in light of reality? If so, how can the patient learn to gradually replace these automatic patterns of irrational or unrealistic thoughts with more balanced and accurate thinking? In the process of this work, characteristic "cognitive distortions" are identified that tend to run through many aspects of the patient's inner life. For example, the person may have a tendency to catastrophize, always expecting the worst even when the situation or evidence does not warrant this expectation.

The cognitive therapist assists the patient with identifying these patterns of thinking through specific homework assignments of writing daily "thought records." Systematic logical reasoning and experimental testing are brought to bear on these thoughts to identify those that are distorted, unrealistic, or untrue. Cognitive-therapy exercises help a person to work systematically to correct these automatic negative thoughts about the self, the world, and the future. The mood or emotional aspects of depression tend to improve as the distorted thinking that was sustaining them is corrected.

Cognitive therapy aims to keep the patient focused on the "here and now" and does not tend to look at the past or delve deeply into prior experiences. Assumptions and core beliefs are taken as a given; the question of how the person's life story or past experiences shaped these assumptions and core beliefs is not typically examined in cognitive therapy. The idea is that these patterns of thought can be altered in the present, regardless of how they developed in the past. Cognitive therapy bypasses the work of finding out *why* the patient thinks or feels the way he does, and instead proceeds with practical means to alter these thoughts in order to improve current emotional states.

Cognitive therapy has been one of the more extensively studied therapies for depression. Research suggests that it has beneficial effects comparable to those of medications, at least for mild to moderate depression (severe depression responds less well to therapy and better to medication). Cognitive therapy is associated with fewer adverse effects than medications, and patients tend to stick with cognitive-therapy treatment longer than medication treatment. Some studies also suggest that the beneficial effects of cognitive therapy last longer after therapy is discontinued than the beneficial effects of medication after medication is discontinued. This may be related to the fact that cognitive therapy teaches patients techniques and skills that they can continue to practice on their own, even without the aid of the therapist. They develop new habits of thinking that are more accurate. As a habit, it begins to function spontaneously, becoming "second nature," with its own positive momentum. Research shows that the combination of medications and cognitive therapy tends to work better for depression than either approach alone.

The reader may be familiar with the claim that cognitive therapy, and perhaps interpersonal therapy, is the only type of therapy that research has proven to be beneficial for depression. This claim should be taken with a grain of salt. Some kinds of therapy lend themselves more readily to research than other types. Their techniques are replicable and can be put in the form of a manual for therapists, thereby standardizing the procedure for research purposes. They also tend to be time-limited and short-term, making them more cost effective to research. For these reasons, far more research has been conducted in recent years on cognitive therapy than on psychodynamic or other forms of therapy. This does not mean that the other therapies are ineffective, or even that they are less effective. It simply means that their outcomes have not been researched as extensively because they are more difficult to research.

Behavioral Strategies — Changing Habitual Acts (Volitional)

Just as cognitive therapy changes moods by way of thoughts, so behavioral therapy changes moods by way of altering habitual patterns of behavior. If cognitive therapy begins with the intellect, behavioral therapy begins with the will. Behavioral techniques have found more application in the treatment of anxiety disorders, such as phobias, than in the treatment of mood disorders, such as depression. However, behavioral therapy can often be combined with cognitive therapy in what is termed (surprise!) *cognitive-behavioral therapy*, or CBT. Like cognitive therapy, behavioral therapy tends to stick to the here and now, without delving deeply into the patient's past. It does not ask how or why behavioral patterns developed in the first place. Instead, it takes these patterns as the starting point and attempts to alter them in ways that promote the individual's freedom and flourishing.

Behavioral therapy is especially helpful in assisting individuals to gradually overcome habitual patterns of avoidance, which tend to cause problems or contribute to stress. A depressed patient, for example, may have a tendency habitually to avoid situations involving confrontation. A skilled behavioral therapist can assist such a person, first, in recognizing this pattern, then in understanding more clearly how it contributes to stress and subsequently to depression. For example, one might avoid such situations and thereby not address interpersonal problems adequately, which in turn causes undue stress, contributing to a depressed mood. This behavior may be so repetitive that it becomes a habit, more or less automatic, of which the person is often only dimly aware. Once the pattern is recognized and appreciated by the patient, techniques can be utilized that teach the person to tolerate the anxiety associated with the situation that he is avoiding and gradually train himself to approach and confront the situation. This can be done all at once in a jump-in-and-swim behavioral technique known as "flooding" or, more commonly, in a process of gradual exposure.

Behavioral therapy is also a very important and frequently effective approach for addressing related behavioral disorders such as alcohol or drug abuse, eating disorders, or suicidal ideation, which often co-occur with depression. In the next chapter, in the section on so-called "positive psychology," I will briefly discuss the role of virtue development — patterns of good and healthy thinking and behavior—for general mental health and for recovery from depression. The positive psychology project revives the ancient and medieval approach of virtue development. Growth in character strengths and virtues such as courage, patience, magnanimity, and generosity works against the feeling of helplessness so often found in a depressive episode.

Interpersonal, Marital, and Family Therapy (Relational)

Interpersonal therapy focuses on the fact that human persons are intrinsically relational. These therapies recognize, at least implicitly, that man is a "social animal," that we can flourish only in relationships of love and trust. Interpersonal therapy (IPT) is a form of individual therapy that has been extensively researched and found to be effective for the treatment of depression. IPT begins with an understanding of depression as closely linked with loss, especially the loss of, or damage to, important relationships.

Like the previous two approaches, IPT focuses less on digging into the patient's past and more on current relationships. It recognizes that early attachment patterns, especially early relationships to one's parents, can result in insecure attachment styles that negatively affect current relationships. A patient may have developed, for example, an insecure "avoidant" attachment style, by which he tends to keep other people emotionally at a distance, often out of unconscious fears of vulnerability grounded in prior experiences of being emotionally hurt in close relationships. This avoidant style can lead to current difficulties forming close or intimate relationships, alienating family members, friends, or a spouse, and resulting in loneliness. Other insecure attachment styles addressed by IPT or depth psychotherapy include anxious or ambivalent attachment styles, which involve excessive fear of loss and a consequent emotional "smothering" of others in relationships, hypersensitivity to criticism, or similar traits that lead to problematic relationship patterns.

Psychotherapy: Its Benefits and Limitations

These unhealthy patterns of relating to others often put an individual at higher risk for depression. IPT focuses on correcting unhealthy current relationship patterns, working through grief after interpersonal loss, and resolving or mitigating conflicts or other problems in the patient's current relationships.

Marital therapy and family therapy are similar to interpersonal therapy in the sense that both focus on resolving difficulties in current relationships. These approaches differ from IPT mainly in the fact that the therapist works not just with the individual patient in sessions, but with the spouse (marital therapy) or with the spouse and children (family therapy). This approach allows the therapist to observe directly each family member's interactions with the others, rather than relying only on the person's own (possibly biased) reports regarding their relationships. In a sense, the "patient" in marital or family therapy—the subject of treatment—is not the individual, but the *marital relationship* itself or the *family system* itself.

If the social stress leading to a depressive episode is rooted primarily in a problematic marriage or in family difficulties, then these approaches can be effective ways to address depression. They also can be used in combination with medications and in combination with individual therapy. In the latter circumstance, it is typically advisable that the individual therapist and the marital/family therapist not be the same person. Separating these roles can help avoid the delicate issues of patient confidentiality, and help the therapist to remain more objective and avoid bias in the marital or family context.

Psychodynamic, or "Depth," Psychotherapy (Emotional)

If cognitive therapy aims at the intellect, and behavioral therapy at the will, then the collection of approaches that go under the name of *psychodynamic*, or depth, therapy attempts to probe deeper into that aspect of the person which Sacred Scripture calls the heart. The heart, according to biblical anthropology, is not just the emotional or affective part of the soul; it is the seat or root, the interior depths, from which spring all the person's thoughts, memories, desires, behaviors, passions, and emotions. Obviously, if a patient allows the therapist to probe into these recesses of the soul, then the therapist should be a person who is highly ethical, trustworthy, skilled and competent, empathetic, and compassionate. This kind of therapeutic work goes beyond examining the patient's current thoughts and feelings, and delves deeper into the person's life story, often revisiting emotionally painful memories or experiences. This kind of therapeutic work — and it is indeed work — can sometimes be emotionally exhausting. The patient may temporarily feel worse before beginning to feel better. A decision to engage in the long, laborious, and difficult work of depth psychotherapy requires discernment and prudence.

The methods of psychodynamic therapy are many, and the theories underlying them are varied. A brief list would begin with Freud's psychoanalytic theory and techniques, later modified by other analysts such as Melanie Klein, who developed object-relations theory, the self-psychology of Heinz Kohut, and later the attachment theory of John Bowlby. Over time, the practice of psychodynamic therapy has moved away from psychoanalysis, in which a person lies on the couch for an hour a day at a frequency of four or five days per week for a period of months or years, and free-associates while the therapist makes only rare comments. Today, depth psychotherapy is typically more time-limited — perhaps once or twice per week — although it still may last for a period of months or years. Space does not allow us to assess these theories or practices in detail. Instead, I will try, using a simple analogy, to identify a few key features of these therapies as they pertain to depression.

Suppose you have an old wound on your arm that gets infected. As the infection gradually grows, it develops into an abscess. Time alone is often not sufficient to heal such a wound, and simply ignoring it will not make it better. The infection can spread, and the abscess can grow and expand. If it is ignored for too long, the infection may spread away from the localized site of the wound and begin affecting the rest of the body, even vital organs. The person may choose to ignore the infection and hope that it will go away or resolve on its own without medical intervention. But, eventually, he may see that this will not work and may reluctantly approach a physician for a cure. The patient may have grown used to the dull pain of the abscess and may have learned to guard the arm so that the unhealed abscess is not touched, as this can cause much more intense pain.

What does the good physician do? First, he must examine the person; he must probe and palpate to find the source of the infection. This examination can hurt, and the patient may wince or jump when the doctor finds the abscess. If the person wants to be cured, if the body is to heal the infection, the patient will have to allow the physician to get out his scalpel and lance the abscess. This will, of course, hurt. The results can be distasteful as the pus is drained. But this is the only way the wound can begin to heal. A permanent scar may remain, but the area is no longer painful and the rest of the body is no longer adversely affected by the spreading infection. In the short term, when scalpel cuts into skin, the problem feels much worse. In the long term, however, the patient eventually feels much better. Ultimately, there is no other path to healing this kind of problem. Avoiding the problem will not make it disappear.

Let us apply this physical analogy to our psychological life. Psychodynamic therapy often involves probing for old, unhealed wounds. A skilled therapist can recognize, as he or she takes a detailed psychological and social history, where the painful or unhealed psychological wounds or emotional conflicts are located. The process of "lancing the wound" may involve recalling and talking through problems or experiences that the person has avoided or guarded with characteristic psychological "defenses," often for many years. The work of therapy and the emotional catharsis involved can in the short term be quite difficult, and the therapist needs to be skilled in providing a safe "holding" environment in which this can occur. The person who undergoes such treatment, like the patient who goes under the knife of a surgeon, is in a vulnerable state. Many people try to avoid this level of vulnerability at all costs. But if such treatment happens at the hands of a skilled and compassionate therapist, then deep and lasting healing can occur.

Compelling new research, summarized in the work of Bob Enright and Richard Fitzgibbons, has found that many of these unhealed emotional wounds or conflicts that drive depression can be most effectively addressed by facilitating the process of forgiveness.[45] I have already mentioned that depression has sometimes been characterized as anger turned inward. While this is not the case for all depressive episodes, it is a key factor in many cases. In contrast to the Freudian view of this anger or aggression as an innate or inborn drive, the concept of forgiveness sees anger as a response to an injustice or real harm. Such harm may be physical, psychological, emotional, or moral. Seen from this perspective, the emotion of anger is the natural human reaction to an injustice and can move a person to correct the injustice.

According to psychoanalytic theory, anger/aggression is a primary drive that must "go" somewhere; that is, it must have some release. But excessive expression of anger—letting it "vent"—has not been found to be very effective in healing anger problems or depression. Expression of anger tends to beget more anger, thus intensifying depression. Furthermore, excessive anger

[45] Bob Enright and Richard Fitzgibbons, *Helping Clients Forgive: An Empirical Guide for Resolving Anger and Restoring Hope* (Washington, DC: American Psychological Association Press, 2000).

expression tends to harm a person's relationships. A more effective way to resolve such anger is through the process of forgiveness. Research studies on forgiveness have shown improvement in depressive symptoms, diminished anxiety, increased hope, improved self-confidence, and a decreased preoccupation with offenders. Clinical experience with forgiveness work has shown less-impulsive behaviors, improved ability to manage anger, and less displacement or overreaction with anger.

Forgiveness therapy is not "value neutral," as many forms of therapy dubiously claim to be. In reality, any psychotherapy, because it is fundamentally an applied philosophy, always presupposes a certain view of the world and of the human person and thus presupposes certain values. Forgiveness therapy asks the patient and the therapist to identify wrongs or injustices—specific acts or omissions by which the patient or someone he or she loves was emotionally hurt or threatened—and to help the patient recognize that other behaviors and attitudes, such as mercy, can be right and good. It starts with identifying unresolved anger, bitterness, or resentment, which is the natural reaction to having been threatened or hurt. Such ongoing anger is typically accompanied by sadness and grief, and can be a core feature, or underlying cause, in many cases of depression.

In addition to feelings of anger, bitterness, or resentment, associated thoughts can include such things as awareness of the injustice, a plan to respond in kind (revenge), or a fantasy that the other person will suffer in ways that he deserves. People who have been hurt are often angry without a clear awareness of the cause. The emotion is conscious, but its origin is unconscious. Awareness of the problem causing the anger is the first step toward freeing a person from anger. Avoidance, or merely the passage of time, will not necessarily make the emotion dissipate. It is simply not true that time automatically heals all wounds. Anger that is not resolved is often displaced onto other people or objects; it "spills over" in inappropriate contexts. Why do some angry people punch a wall? They are not angry at the wall, but at a person, displacing this anger onto an inanimate object. Unresolved anger can lead to acquired patterns of irritation, annoyance, and acrimony toward others who are not the cause of the anger. Consider the father who comes home from work and yells at his kids, when he is really angry at his boss.

Acknowledging anger and finding its origin can be difficult. People often unconsciously mobilize strong defenses against acknowledged anger. They do not want to admit anger toward a person they are supposed to love; for example, a parent. But the goal of therapy in uncovering the anger is not to make the patient more angry, but to allow him, through forgiveness, to be freed from the anger. This can begin to happen only by facing the truth, not by ignoring or denying it.

Forgiveness therapy can be characterized by four phases. First, in the uncovering phase, the patient realizes he is suffering emotionally because of another's injustice, noting the protracted anger that gets directed toward himself and which perhaps gave rise to self-destructive behaviors, thoughts of taking revenge along with conflicted feelings as the unjust person is someone he is supposed to love, etc. An awareness of this emotional pain can be a motivator for change through forgiveness. Second, in the decision phase, the therapist educates the patient to clarify what forgiveness is and what it is not. The decision to forgive at this stage is cognitive—at the level of thinking and not yet at the level of feeling or behavior. The decision to forgive is only the beginning. What follows is the hard work of extending the forgiveness into one's emotions and behavior. Next, in the work phase, the patient begins to see that the offending person is more than the offense he has committed. The focus shifts from the self (uncovering phase) to the offending person, which is a different focus from many other modes of therapy. Cognitive and behavioral exercises are encouraged to help the patient understand the offender. This does not mean excusing his actions, because forgiveness can occur only by acknowledging the truth, including the evil committed. Acknowledging the truth, nevertheless, also means recognizing the wider context of the evil action. As in CBT, emotional transformations toward the offender may follow from cognitive decisions to forgive. Finally, in the deepening phase, insights and changes may lead to further explorations: Have I ever needed another's forgiveness in the past? What was it like for me when I was forgiven? Is there any meaning or purpose to my experience of suffering; can anything good come out of it? Exploring such questions may lead to a cycling again through the first three phases in a deeper way.

Forgiveness therapy often takes considerable time and effort. The work of forgiveness has an inescapably moral dimension, and often a deeply spiritual and religious dimension. As Christians we have been taught to pray by our Lord himself, "Forgive us our trespasses, as we forgive those who trespass against us" (Matt. 6:12). It is important to remember that the person who forgives has been treated unjustly by the other person, and this injustice is not excused or explained away in the process of forgiveness. The wrongdoing is still affirmed as wrong. Justice can coexist with forgiveness; for example, the wronged person may simultaneously seek payment for damages and work on forgiving the offender. Forgiveness as a moral virtue goes beyond what strict justice may require. It is not owed as a matter of justice, and therefore, the decision to forgive must be freely made; it can only be a free gift, an act of charity, of love. Patients should not be unduly pressured by the therapist or by other family members to forgive. As a free act of mercy, it is centered in the forgiver's genuine desire for good toward the one who unjustly hurt him. When a person is merciful, he gives another person good things that the other does not deserve and refrains from a punishing stance that may be deserved. In this way, the person acts like God himself, who cried out as he was being crucified, "Father, forgive them. They know not what they do" (Luke 23:34). The freedom of the gift is what makes forgiveness therapy so liberating and healing: patients discover that forgiveness makes them stronger than the wrong that was done to them. It paradoxically gives them a power over the evil that has been inflicted.

To summarize, Enright and Fitzgibbons define forgiveness as follows:

> People, upon rationally determining that they have been unfairly treated, forgive when they willfully abandon resentment and related responses (to which they have a right), and endeavor to respond to the wrongdoer based on the moral principle of beneficence, which may include compassion, unconditional worth, generosity, and moral love (to which the wrongdoer, by nature of the hurtful act or acts, has no right).[46]

A Catholic reader can readily see how this heroic act of virtue is fundamental to our moral lives as followers of Christ. It has powerful healing effects psychologically and spiritually. It may form a core part of the healing of many cases of depression in which unresolved anger or hatred is a contributing factor.

Forgiveness is more than just a "coping strategy" or a "skill." It is a virtue. It says something about one's character, a quality connected with one's very identity. Thus, forgiveness therapy involves not just a healing technique or method, but also a process of transforming a patient's character and identity.

The Permanent Limits of Medicine and Psychotherapy

As helpful as it is, psychotherapy has limitations that will never be overcome by scientific advances. These limitations are

---

[46] Enright and Fitzgibbons, *Helping Clients Forgive*, 24.

permanent because science and human techniques cannot provide solutions to all human problems.

First, in regard to medical or psychological evaluations of the
person, the following considerations should be kept in mind. A
psychiatrist or psychologist does not have the luxury of omni-
science; if he is skilled, learned, and experienced, he may develop
remarkable powers of observation and keen diagnostic acumen.
Even so, he has no infallible or magical access into the recesses
of the human soul. A skilled therapist will have the humility to
remember the limits of any one perspective, and the futility of
a "total" or "comprehensive" medical or psychological theory
about his patients. As the psychiatrist and philosopher Karl Jaspers writes:

> The object of psychiatry is man ... When we know him,
> we know something about him, rather than himself. Any
> total knowledge of man will prove to be a delusion brought
> about by raising one point of view to the status of an only
> one, one method to the status of a universal method.

In short, Jaspers says, "Like every person, every patient is
unfathomable."[47]

Pope Pius XII, in an address on the topic of applied psychology, said something very similar:

> The best psychologists are aware of the fact that the most
> clever use of existing methods does not succeed in pen-
> etrating the area of the psyche which constitutes, one
> might say, the center of the personality and which always
> remains a mystery. At this point, the psychologist cannot
> but acknowledge with modesty the limitations of his pos-
> sibilities and respect the individuality of the man on whom

[47] Karl Jaspers, *Selected Essays,* trans. E. B. Ashton (Washington,
DC: Regnery Gateway, 1963), 213.

he must pass judgment; he should strive to perceive the divine plan in every man and help develop it insofar as it is possible. Human personality with its specific characteristics is in fact the most noble and wondrous work of creation.[48]

The indispensable attitude here for any evaluating physician, psychologist, or therapist should be one of *reverence*. I am not necessarily talking about a mystical or religious awe, although that may be present as well, but about the scientist's original sense of wonder at his object of study. If the therapist possesses this virtue of humble reverence, he will be wary of simplistic attempts to reduce patients to their symptoms or traits; he will be wary of incomplete "nothing but" explanations, which are the offspring of an impoverished and impoverishing pseudo-science.

This leads to some ethical consequences for the therapist, of which the patient should be aware. Out of respect for the patient's freedom and human dignity, the evaluating psychiatrist or psychologist should in no way intrude upon, or even subtly coerce his way into, the depths of the person's mind. It is true that psychological or medical evaluations and psychotherapy require that a patient become vulnerable, revealing intimate parts of his or her interior life. But this must always be done voluntarily, with full freedom and consent of the patient, facilitated in an atmosphere of respect and discretion. Pius XII puts it this way:

> Psychology also shows that there exists a region of the intimate psyche—particularly tendencies and dispositions—concealed to such an extent that the individual will never know of them or even suspect their existence. And in the same way as it is illicit to take what belongs

---

[48] Pius XII, Address of His Holiness to the Rome Congress of the International Association of Applied Psychology, April 10, 1958.

to others or to make an attempt against a person's corpo-
ral integrity without his consent, neither is one allowed to
enter his interior domain without his permission, whatever
may be the techniques or methods used.

The best physician will approach the mystery of his patient both
from below, with a fully human biology, and from above, with a
psychology informed by a sound philosophy of the human person.
All the while the physician realizes that these two approaches aim
toward, without ever attaining, the invisible horizon where spirit
and matter, body and soul, meet. Here, the physician treads on
sacred ground. He gazes into a personal and unfathomable mystery, whose depths he can never fully plumb. The person he sees
was known by God before the foundation of the world.

The language of therapy—of psychiatry and clinical psychology—has often replaced the language of morality and religion in
the modern world. The writer Philip Rieff dubbed this "the triumph of the therapeutic."[49] But a therapeutic approach to human
problems, helpful as it sometimes is, is limited. Therapy or medicine cannot cure our deepest disorders. These disorders are, first,
the problem of sin, and second, the problem of death. For these
two problems, psychiatry has very little to offer, and it would be
unfair to expect this science or these techniques to provide such
answers.

The following story indicates the limited perspective that a
merely human psychology (without the aid of divine revelation)
will have on ultimate mysteries such as death. In a recent conversation, a fellow psychiatrist and I were discussing with a group of
medical students the case of a narcissistic teenager. This colleague,
a seasoned and skilled psychiatrist for whom I have great respect,

---

[49] *The Triumph of the Therapeutic: Uses of Faith After Freud* (New
York: Harper & Row, 1966).

was arguing that some denial of reality was healthy—going so far as to endorse the fostering of some delusions. He was referring specifically to fostering the denial of death as a healthy defense. I took issue with this. To be lied to, or to lie to ourselves, contradicts our nature as rational creatures who should orient our life according to the truth.

According to my colleague, a lie is sometimes better—or at least, healthier—than the truth. He thought that spending much (if any) time thinking about death was unhealthy. I conceded that it is certainly possible to have morbid preoccupations with death that are pathological. But an outright denial of death as a healthy defense struck me as fundamentally wrong. I was reminded of the traditional Catholic practice of meditating frequently on "the four last things" (death, judgment, heaven, and hell). This practice is a staple in the Catholic spiritual tradition and also, in my opinion, psychologically healthy.

Without doubt, the denial of death is common, and probably more so today than in the past because of the widespread denial of God and because of the technologically enabled bureaucratic administration of life and death in the modern nation-state. In times past, contact with death and dying persons was a part of people's ordinary reality, rather than being a sanitized process that occurs only in hospitals and nursing homes. The denial of death can even operate at the civic level. For example, the City of San Francisco has banned cemeteries within the city limits, as though its citizens did not need space for burial. But just because a behavior is widespread, that does not mean it is good or healthy.

My colleague believed that the denial of death is necessary because "the truth," as he sees it, is too unpalatable. We are, he explained to the medical students, merely material beings floating on a speck of dust in an enormous universe. We occupy a minuscule space for a brief period of cosmic time, and our greatest achievements mean nothing in the end. What my colleague was putting forward was not medical science but his own philosophical presuppositions about the world. I had to admit that a world without God, where a human person is simply a bundle of molecules, would make the thought of death intolerable. But, fortunately, such is not the world we inhabit.

He turned to me for confirmation, and I responded that he and I held vastly different worldviews. Regarding our being a very small part of a vast material cosmos: as Chesterton put it, we should never let mere size dwarf the spirit. Only from his erroneous materialist premise did it follow that we are "dust in the wind," that life was fundamentally meaningless and death therefore intolerable. This was a premise that I could not accept. We know by reason and by faith that God exists and that human beings have an immortal soul, created by God for eternity, which will outlast all the matter in this universe. Therefore, our human acts, the work we perform in our mortal bodies, can be meaningful and carry an eternal weight.

So we have no necessary reason for the denial of death, and such denial for a Christian cannot be characterized as a healthy defense. We Catholics frequently ask for assistance from our Lady at the hour of our death; we repeat the word *death* itself over fifty times during the Rosary. This is not a word that we avoid, nor is death a reality that we need to deny. God himself has destroyed the power of death through his Cross and Resurrection.

The denial of death—or any other denial of reality—is indeed psychologically unhealthy; it is a type of delusional thinking, and we should not encourage it in our patients. I am convinced that all good psychotherapy rests on the premise that the truth is better than a lie, even when the truth is difficult or painful. While good psychotherapy can help cure our denial, it cannot solve the problem of death's finality—nor should we expect it to. For these answers we turn to the science of reason (philosophy) and the science of faith (theology).

The Catholic Guide to Depression

There is an equally prevalent denial of sin today. As with the denial of death, the denial of sin is not helpful from the perspective of mental health and human flourishing. T. S. Eliot examined this denial of sin in his play *The Cocktail Party*. In the story, the protagonist, a young woman named Celia Copleston, is having an affair with a married man. When she suddenly realizes the emptiness of this relationship, her life is shaken profoundly. Like many people today, in her distress, she turns to a physician for advice. There is something not quite right, she tells him:

> I should really like to think there's something
>> wrong with me—
> Because, if there isn't, there's something wrong
> Or at least, very different from what it seemed
>> to be,
> With the world itself—and that's so much more
>> frightening!
> That would be terrible. So I'd rather believe
> There is something wrong with me, that could
>> be put right.

She tries to name her disorder. Finally, after floundering, she comes up with the only diagnosis to explain her symptoms:

> *Celia*: It sounds ridiculous—but the only word for it
>> That I can find, is a sense of sin.
> *Doctor*: You suffer from a sense of sin, Miss Copleston?
>> That is most unusual.
> *Celia*: It seemed to me abnormal ...
>> My bringing up was pretty conventional—
>> I had always been taught to disbelieve in sin.
>> Oh, I don't mean that it was never mentioned!
>> But anything wrong from our point of view,
>> Was either bad form, or was psychological.

Psychotherapy: Its Benefits and Limitations

> ... And yet I can't find any other word for it.
> It must be some kind of hallucination;
> Yet, at the same time, I'm frightened by the fear
> That it might be more real than anything I
>   believed in.
>
> *Doctor:* What is more real than anything you believed in?
> *Celia:* It's not the feeling of anything I've ever done,
>   Which I might get away from, or of anything in me
>   I could get rid of—but of emptiness, of failure
>   Towards someone, or something, outside of myself;
>   And I feel I must ... atone—is that the word?
>   Can you treat a patient for such a state of mind?

The answer, of course, is no. Freud himself recognized these limits when he said, "It would be absurd for me to say to a patient, 'I forgive you your sins.'" The psychotherapist has no power to do this. Someone once asked Mother Teresa what the biggest problem with the modern world was. Her answer: the loss of a sense of sin. Our contemporaries are like Celia before her conversion. While they may have a vague sense that all is not well, they do not have the religious vocabulary to diagnose the disorder accurately.

Sin is the worst—the deadliest—sort of pathology, since it attacks the life of the soul itself. And death is the human problem for which we will never discover a medical or psychological solution. Life in this world will always be terminal. A clinician may be able to assist someone with complicated grief. But he or she cannot solve the mystery of death or the problem of sin. The solution to these problems lies beyond the competence of the clinician. Only Christ has this key. St. Paul, who considered himself the "chief of sinners," nonetheless chides death almost gleefully: "O death, where is thy victory; O death, where is thy sting?" (1 Cor. 15:55). Such a statement makes little sense outside of the Christian faith.

The Problem of Guilt

Excessive feelings of guilt or guilty ruminations are a central feature of depression, one of its cardinal symptoms. Yet the emotion of guilt, or the knowledge that one has done something wrong, is not in itself abnormal or pathological. Quite the contrary, an inability to feel guilt when one has committed an evil act is the central feature of a profoundly pathological personality known as sociopathy (or antisocial personality disorder). The analogy to a diseased body is apt for understanding this condition: sociopathy is a spiritual disease of the worst sort. Citing psychiatrist Albert Görres, who argued that the capacity to recognize guilt belongs essentially to the spiritual makeup of man, Joseph Ratzinger (Pope Benedict XVI) explains:

> [Guilt] is as necessary for man as the physical pain that signifies disturbances in the normal bodily functioning. Whoever is no longer capable of perceiving guilt is spiritually ill, "a living corpse" ... No longer seeing one's guilt, the falling silent of conscience in so many areas is an even more dangerous sickness of the soul than the guilt that one still recognizes as such. He that no longer notices that killing is a sin has fallen farther than the one who still recognizes the shamefulness of his actions, because the former is further removed from the truth and conversion.[50]

Conscience is an organ that requires proper development. In trying to distinguish normal guilt from pathological guilt, the following comparison may be helpful. Consider an analogy between the problem of psychological guilt and the problem of physical pain. Under normal circumstances, pain is a sign that something is wrong in the body. The best cure for the pain is to correct the

---

[50] Benedict XVI [Joseph Cardinal Ratzinger], *On Conscience* (San Francisco: Ignatius Press, 2007), 18-19.

underlying cause of the pain. However, in some physical disorders, patients may develop a pain syndrome in which they feel pain despite having no underlying organic pathology or injury to cause the pain. In this situation, the pain itself is pathological and causes problems with normal functioning.

But if, on the other hand, a person felt no physical pain even when the body was harmed, that would be a huge problem of a different sort. In fact, there exists a rare neurological condition in which individuals are incapable of feeling physical pain. You might think that does not sound too bad, but the problem is that such individuals are never aware of when their hand is touching a hot stove, or when they stub their toe, and so on. These unfortunate individuals very quickly develop serious injuries and infections, which eventually prove to be fatal. Physical pain is a normal and healthy mechanism to maintain the body's integrity. Likewise, guilt is a normal and healthy mechanism to maintain the soul's integrity.

Guilt is analogous to physical pain in the following respect. Under normal circumstances, a person feels guilty when he has done something wrong, and the feeling or awareness of guilt can be an impetus for the person to seek forgiveness from God, to rectify the wrong when possible, and to make amends to the person who was wronged by his action. As Pope Pius XII said in an address on psychotherapy and religion, the sense of guilt is "the consciousness of having violated a higher law, by which, nevertheless, one recognizes himself as being bound, a consciousness which can find expression in suffering and psychic disorder."[51] To call this sort of guilt pathological in itself and to try to cure it by means of psychotherapy (or by means of medications to dull the

---

[51] Pius XII, "On Psychotherapy and Religion," An Address of His Holiness to the Fifth International Congress on Psychotherapy and Clinical Psychology given on April 13, 1953, no. 34.

guilty feeling) would be misguided. Such an approach could do a grave disservice to the guilty person. Pius XII goes on to say:

> Psychotherapy here approaches a phenomenon which is not within its own exclusive field of competence, for this phenomenon is also, if not principally, of a religious nature. No one will deny that there can exist—and not infrequently—an irrational and even morbid sense of guilt. But a person may also be aware of a real fault which has not been wiped away.[52]

Such efforts to distinguish normal from pathological guilt are essential in the sound treatment of psychiatric disorders or the work of spiritual direction. Such efforts by physicians go back at least as far as the Renaissance physician and clergyman Timothie Bright, who devoted several chapters in his 1586 work *A Treatise on Melancholie* to differentiating those who suffered from dejection due to a guilty conscience from those who suffered from pathological guilt associated with melancholia.[53]

We should recognize that an irrational and morbid sense of guilt is found frequently in persons suffering from depression. Depression's effects on perception, cognition, and emotion are such that the guilty feeling is often far out of proportion to any wrong the person may have committed. In this case, the guilt is like physical pain that has taken on a life of its own, unmoored from an underlying cause. This irrational and morbid guilt (e.g., "I have committed a grave sin by running a yellow light; I am a totally worthless and unlovable person," etc.) should be carefully distinguished from normal guilt resulting from sinful behaviors or vices.

[52] Ibid, no. 35.
[53] Stanley Jackson, *Melancholia and Depression: From Hippocratic to Modern Times* (New Haven, Connecticut: Yale University Press, 1986), 328.

Psychotherapy: Its Benefits and Limitations

On the other hand, it is clear that when we perform an act that we judge to be immoral, we typically (at least, if we have a well-formed conscience) experience feelings of shame, thoughts of regret, and so on. The resultant guilt should not be mistaken for a psychological disorder, but should be dealt with by appropriate spiritual means.

Pius XII goes on in the address quoted earlier to describe the problem and its solution:

> Neither psychology nor ethics possesses an infallible criterion for cases of this kind, since the workings of conscience which beget this sense of guilt have too personal and subtle a structure. But in any case, it is certain that no purely psychological treatment will cure a genuine sense of guilt. Even if psychotherapists, perhaps even in good faith, question its existence, it still perdures. Even if the sense of guilt be eliminated by medical intervention, autosuggestion or outside persuasion, the fault remains, and psychotherapy would both deceive itself and deceive others if, in order to do away with the sense of guilt, it pretended that the fault no longer exists. The means of eliminating the fault does not belong to the purely psychological order. As every Christian knows, it consists in contrition and sacramental absolution by the priest. Here, it is the root of the evil, it is the fault itself, which is extirpated, even though remorse may continue to make itself felt. Nowadays, in certain pathological cases, it is not rare for the priest to send his penitent to a doctor. In the present case, the doctor should rather direct his patient towards God and to those who have the power to remit the fault itself in the name of God.[54]

---

[54] Pius XII, "On Psychotherapy and Religion," no. 37.

The Catholic Guide to Depression

As I have mentioned already, according to its Greek root, the word *psychiatrist* literally means "doctor of the soul." And yet, the psychiatrist has no cure for this greatest of all psychological maladies — the problem of sin, and the resultant guilt that sin causes. If he is astute, a good psychiatrist can perhaps define and describe guilt and help the patient recognize and detach from irrational or morbid guilt, but he can in no way cure the guilty conscience. All of our human attempts to do so, whether by psychological defense strategies, medical ministrations, or therapeutic techniques, ultimately prove insufficient.

But we need not despair. For our own failures suggest to us what faith has already revealed: in the last analysis, there is only one true and effective Doctor of the soul. The Fathers of the Church called our Lord the "Divine Physician." This brings us to the next chapter, on the theme of our spiritual life as it relates to depression.

Chapter 7

Spiritual Help for Depression

"Whoever suffers from mental illness always bears
God's image and likeness in himself,
as does every human being."
Pope John Paul II[55]

As was already suggested in Chapter 2, comprehensive treatment for depression should address not only the physical and psychological realms, but also the individual's spiritual life. It should attend to both nature and grace. Offering widely applicable spiritual advice to depressed individuals is challenging, since each person follows a unique path. Each reader comes to this book with his or her own life story, with unique problems and difficulties, with a personal and unrepeatable vocation.

Several years ago, a journalist asked Joseph Ratzinger, before he became Pope, "How many ways are there to God?" This is a question that many people today are asking, and those who suffer from depression often have more difficulty finding their path to God. His answer may surprise us. To the question, "How many ways are there to God?" Ratzinger responded simply, "As many as

---

[55] John Paul II, Address to participants in the international conference sponsored by the Pontifical Council for Pastoral Assistance to Health Care Workers, December 11, 1996.

there are people." He went on to explain, "For even within the same faith, each man's way is an entirely *personal* one."[56]

Cardinal Ratzinger elaborated further on his answer: "We have Christ's word: *I am the way* (John 14:6). In that respect there is ultimately one way, and everyone who is on the way to God is therefore in some sense on the way of Jesus Christ." So for everyone we can say: to find God, seek the face of Jesus Christ. That is the first step applicable to all. Jesus Christ is the *one* way that encompasses the *many* paths. Being a Christian does not just mean accepting some abstract or lofty idea, however noble; neither is it just the result of an ethical choice we make. Being a Christian means encountering a person—the person of Christ. Ratzinger concluded, "This does not mean that all ways are identical, in terms of consciousness and will, but on the contrary, the one way [of Jesus Christ] is so big that it becomes a personal way for each man."[57]

The process of healing from depression is analogous: it is a personal way for each one. Among the many unique paths there are commonalities—typical means of healing widely known to be beneficial. But a person whose depression is deeply rooted in his or her genetics may have a different process of recovery from another individual whose depression is more related to life experiences, unresolved interpersonal conflicts, or early-childhood abuse or neglect.

Acknowledging the wide variety of causes, in this chapter, we will touch on spiritual themes relevant to depression. I hope to offer some practical means that may be applicable to individuals suffering in diverse circumstances. The spiritual practices discussed and recommended here have broad applicability because

---

[56] Benedict XVI [Joseph Cardinal Ratzinger], *Salt of the Earth: The Church at the End of the Third Millennium*, trans. Adrian Walker (San Francisco: Ignatius Press, 2002), 32.

[57] Ibid.

they are deeply rooted in our Catholic tradition—and thus are universal.

Positive Psychology and Growth in Virtue

Good character will not necessarily prevent one from developing depression. Character strengths and virtues, however, can help a person to cope more effectively with life stressors and persevere through the difficult process of recovery from depression. Changing ourselves and changing our habits is not easy. According to the ancient Greek philosophers, such as Socrates, Plato, Aristotle, and the Stoics, we attain happiness by living in accordance with the virtues—by developing good habits of character. This is done by paying intelligent attention to the actual good to be found in one concrete situation after another and acting according to the virtues thus developed throughout our lifespan. The great Christian thinkers St. Augustine and St. Thomas Aquinas expanded this theme in the light of Christian revelation, showing how the classically recognized virtues come fully alive by the power of the most important virtues, ones unknown and unknowable by the ancients, the theological virtues that lead us to God directly. The virtues are to be understood as character traits and habitual dispositions that perfect our nature, that make us more human and more free, and that therefore lead us to happiness and a flourishing human life.

The Greek philosophers listed four "cardinal," or chief, virtues, which were the hinges of all the other virtues. *Prudence*, or practical wisdom, helps us to choose the good and right course of action in specific situations and complex circumstances. *Justice* is the virtue that regulates our relationships and life in society, the virtue by which we habitually give others what is due to them. *Temperance* is the virtue through which we regulate our appetites for food, drink, sex, and so on. *Fortitude*, or courage, is the virtue through which we boldly face and overcome difficulties, or patiently endure them, as the circumstances may dictate. Augustine and Aquinas endorsed these "natural" virtues and, following St. Paul's teachings, added the three "supernatural," or "theological," virtues: faith, hope, and love. These virtues are necessary because they lead us to more than what the natural virtues can provide; they lead us to the Good itself. The theological virtues enable us to attain our final destiny and fulfillment, which is union with God.

A few years ago, the former president of the American Psychological Association, a researcher named Martin Seligman, started a new movement known as "positive psychology." Seligman argued that psychologists and psychiatrists had for too long focused only on mental disease, disorder, and pathology—only on what could go wrong in the mind, not on what could go right. The psychological sciences had learned a lot in the twentieth century by studying people's weaknesses and vulnerabilities. But Seligman argued that it was time also to study, in a rigorous scientific way, those positive traits and habits that lead to happiness, health, and human flourishing.

The results of much historical research and many studies in the social sciences on this theme are summarized in his book with Christopher Peterson, *Character Strengths and Virtues*.[58] The positive-psychology researchers distilled the traits that led to mental health and flourishing down to six. According to these psychologists, the central virtues and their respective character strengths that lead to health and happiness are: (1) wisdom—including creativity, perspective, and love of learning, (2) justice—including social responsibility, loyalty, fairness, and leadership, (3) temperance—including forgiveness and mercy, humility, prudence, and self-control, (4) courage—including bravery, persistence,

---

[58] Christopher Peterson and Martin Seligman, *Character Strengths and Virtues: A Handbook and Classification* (Oxford: Oxford University Press, 2004).

integrity, and vitality, (5) humanity—including love, kindness, and social intelligence, and (6) transcendence—including humor, hope, gratitude, appreciation of beauty, and spirituality. The list will be reminiscent to Christians familiar with our own tradition of virtue ethics.

These researchers were not setting out to reinvent the Christian tradition, and their research sources included many non-Christian texts and traditions (everything from pagan philosophers to Hindu sacred texts to the Boy Scout Manual). In other words, historical research and scientific inquiry confirmed from a different perspective and using different methods what had already been discovered and described by a long Christian tradition of philosophy and theology. Growth in virtue and good habits of character are essential for our mental and spiritual health. As already mentioned, developing one's character will not make a person immune from depression—recall that many virtuous and holy individuals have suffered this affliction. However, the virtues can enhance our ability to cope with stress, loss, setbacks, and other factors that can lead to, sustain, or worsen depression.

It would take a separate book to comment on each of the virtues and vices that are relevant here. (See Appendix 1 for further reading on the subject of the virtues.) I will mention briefly, in connection with depression, just one relevant consideration.

Our love for God is bound up with love for our neighbor; one cannot exist or grow without the other. Regarding love of neighbor, consider one vice that frequently undermines this virtue: the deadly sin of envy—perhaps one of the hidden vices of our age. Envy is a form of sadness. It can contribute to depression, or in extreme cases, it might be at the root of depressive symptoms. All the various causes of sadness are too many to enumerate here, and not every cause of sadness can be remedied or removed. But some can, including this one.

Envy is defined in the *Catechism* as, "sadness at the sight of another's goods and the immoderate desire to acquire them for oneself, even unjustly." The *Catechism* elaborates upon the problems associated with this sin and provides its remedy: "Envy represents a form of sadness and therefore a refusal of charity; the baptized person should struggle against it by exercising good will. Envy often comes from pride; the baptized person should train himself to live in humility."[59] It goes on to quote St. John Chrysostom on the subject: "Would you like to see God glorified by you? Then rejoice in your brother's progress and you will immediately give glory to God. Because his servant could conquer envy by rejoicing in the merits of others, God will be praised." Those who struggle with depression—indeed, all of us—would do well to examine our conscience to see if perhaps envy may be playing a role in worsening our mental state. This vice, like the others, can be uprooted with the help of God and the means of grace that will be described in the following pages.

Unity of Life

As we grow in the virtues, our life becomes characterized by a more profound unity. We see in the saints this unity of life: they do not wear masks or have fractured personalities. A person of integrity is the same person on Monday morning at work as she was on Sunday morning at church. Much mental distress or disorder, including some cases of depression, are caused or sustained by a person's trying to live a series of contradictions.

The following is admittedly a very extreme example, but I cite it to illustrate my point: forensic psychiatrists who study sociopaths and mass murderers tell us that when these people recount their autobiographical narrative, their thought process is fragmented, inconsistent, and full of internal contradictions.

---

[59] *Catechism of the Catholic Church*, no. 2540.

This is a severe example of how evil and interior brokenness are characterized by *disunity* and *dishonesty*—with others and even with oneself. By contrast, goodness, health, and wholeness are characterized by *unity* and *integrity*.

In our age, in which a secular culture tries to push religious faith completely into the private sphere, there is a great temptation for us to live a sort of double life: on one side, an interior life, a life in relationship with God; and on the other, a separate and distinct professional, social, and family life, full of everyday earthly realities. This tendency toward disunity is not just cultural or social, a product of a particular place and time; at a deeper level, it is the result of the fracturing and fragmenting effects of sin—Original Sin and our own personal sins.

St. Josemaría Escrivá, the founder of Opus Dei, put the matter this way: "We cannot lead a double life ... There is just one life, made of flesh and spirit. And it is this life which has to become, in both soul and body, holy and filled with God. We discover the invisible God in the most visible and material things."[60] Mature Christians do not have a split personality; they do not lead a double life. We should not hang our faith at the door like a hat when we walk into the office. My wife would understandably be hurt if I took off my wedding ring when entering a bar. Just so with our faith: it is a full-time, integral part of our identity, informing everything we do. The Greek root of the verb *to heal* literally means "to make whole." The more unified our exterior and interior lives become, the healthier and happier we will be. My hope is that you come away from this book with some suggestions to set you on a path toward becoming less fragmented and more whole.

I mention in this context two common traps to avoid. The first is what you might call "mystical wishful thinking." This is a

[60] Homily, "Passionately Loving the World," no. 51, in *In Love with the Church* (London: Scepter, 1989).

sort of daydreaming that involves entertaining a series of fantasies and what-ifs: "If only my talents were put to better use ... If only I were more appreciated by my spouse or my employer ... If only I made more money ... Perhaps if I had pursued a different line of work, or had not gotten married, or had married someone else ... then I could really be happy, then I could really be holy." This sort of wishful thinking is at best a waste of time; at worst, it may be a temptation to abandon our God-given vocation. Wasting time nurturing such fantasies can lead to a chronic sense of discontentment and may contribute to sustaining a depressed state.

Researchers have found that one key factor that contributes to many cases of depression is the inability to adjust our expectations—expectations of ourselves, of others, and of the world. Mystical wishful thinking prevents us from coming to terms with our life and our circumstances as they are. It prevents us from adjusting our expectations accordingly. It can blind us to opportunities for improving our situation right where we are, right where God has placed us. It can prevent us from accepting ourselves, accepting those around us, and accepting the situation in which God in his providence and goodness has placed us.

An important spiritual task for all of us is this: to become convinced that God has placed us here in this family, or with these friends, or in our job, for a reason. There is something divine, something beautiful, hidden there—not on the other side of the fence, where we believe the grass must be greener. And it is up to us, with God's help, to discover that "divine something" right where we are, in the ordinary events and circumstances of our life.

The second trap or pitfall is our tendency to become "workaholics"—to drive ourselves into the ground with frenetic activity and consequently to burn out. This is a common contributing factor in many cases of depression. Recent research on depression shows a growing trend of work-related stress to be a major factor contributing to rising rates of depression. Ironically, this tendency toward workaholism is sometimes combined with laziness outside of work. The workaholic can often be seen "freaking out" at work and "vegging out" at play. We Americans have this peculiar tendency to oscillate between frenetic, busy activity on the one hand and flabby, wasteful inactivity on the other. The late novelist Walker Percy dubbed this disorder "angelism-bestialism"; it involves excessive time and energy consumed by high-stress work and low-value entertainment.

What may appear on the surface to be two disorders is really one: the two problems can be understood as flip sides of the same coin. Both are manifestations of what the desert fathers called *acedia*, which we have already discussed in relation to depression in Chapter 2. Acedia, you will recall, is a type of spiritual laziness that leads to a sense of discontent or demoralization. The reader might object at this point: the workaholic does not appear to be lazy. But if you look deeper, you will see that his activism and nervous energy are a substitute for an impoverished interior life. These may be a distraction from having to face the deep truth about himself or his situation. Now, as we stressed in Chapter 2, depression must not be conflated with acedia. However, we seem to be witnessing a rising confluence of these two conditions.

Disordered rest often takes the form of excessive drinking, pornography consumption, or other unhealthy and morally problematic behaviors. When we pour another shot or open that illicit website, we always tell ourselves the same thing: "I deserve this." The truth is we deserve better. Our leisure activities should be true recreation — literally, "re-creation"; that is, they should reflect Sabbath rest. This means doing activities that renew and refresh us, but that also ennoble us. Keeping holy the Sabbath and using our leisure time wisely are not only essential for our spiritual life; they also happen to be among the best and most widely applicable prescriptions for good mental health. When one is depressed, it may very well be necessary to rest more and, in consultation with a doctor, to remove oneself from the stress and strain of one's typical work for a time.

The Tranquillity of Order

We hear a lot of talk about peace — about making peace, about establishing peace, about promoting peace. Peace in the world. Peace in the home. Inner peace. There is a lot of talk. All of us want this; we long for it. But peace is often misunderstood: peace is not merely the absence of conflict, the absence of war. It is not just something negative. Peace is something positive.

Augustine formulated a classic definition of peace. Peace, he said, is the *tranquillity of order*. There is a relationship between peace and the virtue of order. Order is necessary for interior peace. If you lack peace, ask yourself if you have order in your life. Exterior disorder typically contributes to interior disorder. Likewise, disorder in our interior lives or in our relationships contributes to disorder in our external world. Our exterior activity will typically mirror our interior disposition. Both interior and exterior disorder can contribute to depression.

I will cite just one example of exterior disorder commonly found in our lives. People today get on average 20 percent less sleep than people did a hundred years ago. But we have not evolved to the point where we suddenly need less sleep than our great-grandparents. We have already discussed at length the links between sleep and mood disorders. We cannot tax our bodies in this way indefinitely, without suffering consequences for our moods. If we are to get adequate sleep, ordering our time may involve saying no to some activities or projects, even worthy projects.

Just as we should try to bring order to our environment, even more important, we need to learn to order our loves and our commitments properly. St. Thomas Aquinas wrote about the *ordinis caritas* — the "order of charity." The idea here is that our loves must be properly ordered: God first, then family and friends, followed by acquaintances, strangers, and so forth. Our use of time should reflect this order of charity. It is good to examine our conscience and review our life from time to time, looking at our daily activities and schedule. We may discover a need to re-prioritize how, and with whom, we spend most of our time. The order of charity can guide us here: do our commitments really correspond to whom and what we should be most devoted to?

Let us conclude this section with a consideration that may help us to order our life and our loves, by putting things in their proper perspective. In the conclave homily just prior to his election, Pope Benedict said that in our work, in our lives as a whole, all of us want to produce lasting fruit—fruit that abides. "But what abides?" he asks. "Money does not last. Buildings do not last, or books. After a certain time, more or less long, all this disappears. The only thing that abides eternally is the human soul—man created by God for eternity. The fruit that abides, therefore, is the one we have sown in human souls: love, knowledge; the gesture capable of touching the heart; the word that opens the soul to the joy of the Lord."[61] This is a great ordering principle for putting our daily lives and our work in the proper perspective: the only thing that abides eternally is the human soul.

A Plan of Life

Recovery from depression involves making a treatment plan, prioritizing various elements, and putting them into effect—psychotherapy, medication, exercise, changes in one's social or family life, and so on. This plan should attend to one's spiritual life as well. It may surprise some that our Lord recommends the same kind of approach in the spiritual life; we begin by taking stock of our resources and making a concrete plan:

[61] Cardinal Ratzinger's Homily in Mass Before Conclave, April 19, 2005. Available at http://www.zenit.org.

For which of you, desiring to build a tower, does not first sit down and count the cost, whether he has enough to complete it? Otherwise, when he has laid a foundation, and is not able to finish, all who see it begin to mock him, saying, "This man began to build, and was not able to finish." Or what king, going to encounter another king in war, will not sit down first and take counsel whether he is able with ten thousand to meet him who comes against him with twenty thousand? And if not, while the other is yet a great way off, he sends an embassy and asks terms of peace. So therefore, whoever of you does not renounce all that he has cannot be my disciple (Luke 14:28-33).

Of what does our spiritual plan of life consist? Among other things, it should include some of the commonly recommended norms of piety that we will discuss in the rest of this chapter: prayer, reception of the sacraments, spiritual reading, spiritual direction, and so on. We need not reinvent the wheel here. The Church's faith and tradition provide ample and time-tested means. And just as all of us have our own path to God, so our plan should be individualized; it should fit us like a glove. A spiritual director can be a great help to us in this regard, working with us to craft a plan of life that suits our circumstances. It is good to begin modestly, with a few things, doing them well and consistently. This is more important than piling one devotion on top of another and carrying them out in a half-hearted manner. The norms in our plan of life are not just a daily checklist of things to get done. Rather, they are simple daily encounters with Christ, which we attend to with love for God.

When one is struggling with depression, the plan must be kept very simple and doable, so that it does not become an occasion for undue stress or scrupulosity. And particularly when one is depressed, there is no need to berate oneself for not fulfilling a plan of prayer perfectly. God is looking for love from us, not self-punishment.

Prayer

Blaise Pascal, a seventeenth-century scientist and philosopher and a deeply committed Christian, claimed that "all men's miseries derive from not being able to sit in a quiet room alone." If this was true in his day, it is even truer for us today. Karl Jaspers claimed that "all great things happen in silence." But our contemporary mentality suggests just the opposite: that sitting alone in a quiet room is not "productive" and that silence is a waste of time. Is it not rather the case that great things happen amid fanfare, with bright lights shining and television cameras rolling? Yet, deep down we still crave silence; we sense the need for contemplation. The word *contemplation* might intimidate some of us, but it need not.

We find our way to God only in prayer. As a relationship, each individual's prayer life will be unique and personal. There are many forms of prayer — liturgical, vocal, meditative, and contemplative, or unitive, prayer. We can begin with some advice on mental prayer, especially as it bears on our mental health. A growing body of scientific research, starting with the studies of Herbert Benson at Harvard Medical School, has shown that contemplative or meditative practices have wide-ranging health benefits, including benefits for depression and anxiety. Several studies suggest that fifteen to thirty minutes of contemplative prayer or meditation twice a day has robust health benefits, including lowering blood pressure, reducing rates of heart disease, ameliorating chronic pain, and helping with insomnia.

Of course, we pray in order to enter into deeper union with God. If we pray just to lower our anxiety or improve our mood (i.e., if we use prayer as a means to another end), then we may not in fact really be praying. However, if we come to see the value of prayer in itself, for its own sake, then the mental-health benefits can accrue as a "side effect" as we develop a more consistent and habitual life of prayer. If we are seeking God in prayer, then prayer is good for us on the spiritual, psychological, and bodily levels. The mental and physical health benefits are secondary gains, which augment the primary gain of growing closer to God and becoming more the persons we are created to be.

It should not surprise us that prayer is natural and healthy, both for the body and for the soul. Because we are made in the image of God and made for union with him, we are made for prayer. When we act in accord with our nature, good things tend to result. We know that being in good relationships helps people heal psychologically. But the most important relationship of all is a right relationship with God. So it should come as no surprise that deepening our relationship with him results in better psychological health.

The practice of mental prayer, which encompasses both meditation and contemplation, although unfamiliar to many Christians today, is deeply embedded in our tradition and universally found in the lives of the saints. Christians have no need to seek out other forms of meditation (where the self, not God, often becomes the focus of attention), nor do we have to learn esoteric techniques in order to meditate. Our own tradition already contains untold riches. The practice of mental prayer need not be overly complicated. Methods can be helpful to avoid distraction or dryness, but simplicity and sincerity are the keys to effective mental prayer. "You say that you don't know how to pray?" St. Josemaría Escrivá wrote. "Put yourself in the presence of God, and once you have said, 'Lord, I don't know how to pray!', rest assured that you have begun to do so."[62] Beginning on the path of prayer is that simple.

---

[62] St. Josemaría Escrivá, *The Way* (Princeton: Scepter, 1982), no. 90.

Spiritual Help for Depression

St. John of the Cross described mental prayer as "a simple gaze upon God in silence and love," and St. Teresa of Avila defined it as "a close sharing between friends; it means taking time frequently *to be alone with him whom we know loves us.*" Mental prayer is nothing more than being in conversation with Christ. This interior dialogue can occur with or without the use of words. Seeing one of his parishioners who spent long periods in prayer in front of the Blessed Sacrament, St. John Vianney asked him what he said to the Lord during his visits. The man responded, "Nothing. I look at him, and he looks at me." Mental prayer is for everyone; it is not the sole prerogative of priests, monks, and nuns. We simply need the desire. It takes practice and dedication, to be sure, but mostly it is a gift of grace. So we must ask God for it. Prayer is not our own personal accomplishment; it is God's work in us.

If you are distracted in prayer or do not know how to begin, you can employ a simple method that has been recommended by many who are advanced in the ways of prayer, from St. Ignatius to St. Josemaría. Open the Gospels, and select one of the scenes. Read the passage slowly and engage the scene with your senses through your imagination. Place yourself as one of the people in the scene. Imagine what you see, hear, and smell. Imagine our Lord's appearance, his voice, words, and gestures. Play the scene like a film in your mind's eye. What emotions are at play in the scene? What kinds of thoughts and choices are there to consider? Ask the Holy Spirit to help you see and to draw close to Jesus. We know by faith that Jesus is present and to be encountered in the sacred text of Holy Scripture. This method can lead you on to a simple gaze upon God in silence and in love.

It is also noteworthy to observe the psychological benefits of engaging the imagination in prayer. According to brain physiologists, using the imagination engages emotional centers of the brain that are typically less activated by the process of pure logical reasoning. God is not an abstraction; he is the Word who became *flesh*. We have found remarkable success in helping people heal emotionally by helping them bring their emotions into their prayer life via the imagination. Our spiritual life involves the whole person, not just our intellect and will.

Many other methods could be suggested here, but there is a danger of getting too hung up on following a method. In prayer, freedom is the rule. I will mention just one more, a simple four-step method for mental prayer that comes from a wise retreat director. It is described by the acronym ARRR (think of a pirate to jog your memory): acknowledge, relate, receive, and respond.

First, *acknowledge* what is going on in your heart. Sometimes we think that to pray we have to "look our best," and so we might push aside the ugly, messy, and difficult things in our heart—what Mother Teresa calls our "poverty." But the subject of our prayer is simply the subject of our life, so if our life is messy and difficult, that is precisely what we bring to our prayer. Since God is God, he already knows everything about us, so there is no reason to hide anything. Those closest to God were quite honest in showing him their sorrow, fear, and even anger. As in human relationships, honesty helps to create a sincere and deep relationship with God.

Second, *relate* what you acknowledge to the Lord. Prayer is not a matter of solitary navel gazing; it is a relationship with the living God. If you are churning a personal problem over in your mind in a sort of sterile monologue, then take this same problem and turn it into a fruitful dialogue with the Lord. He does not expect us to succeed on our own, and in fact we cannot do anything good without his help. So we show him with sincerity exactly what is going on.

Third, *receive*. The Lord wants to meet us in that difficulty or the poverty of what we have acknowledged and related to him. He wants to love us there; in fact, he prefers to meet us and to love us in our poverty and humility, which can at times feel humiliating. But that is where we give him the most room to work. It is there that we are faced with our own inability and perhaps our failure. Being receptive does not mean being lazy or passive. It is an active receptivity and engagement in the relationship with God. It is the receptivity that our Lady showed when she said, *"Fiat mihi secundum verbum tuum"* — "Be it done unto me according to your word" (Luke 1:38).

Finally, *respond*. Having received grace from the Lord, we are able to respond in love both within our prayer and in acts of love toward others. The precise ways in which we respond in love to Love will be entirely personal for each one of us.

The first order of business for many depressed individuals in trying to pray is to learn to *quiet* themselves. While the depressed person may appear sluggish on the outside, interiorly he can often be full of agitation and disquiet. During my psychiatry residency, I once asked a psychotherapy supervisor what to do during a therapy session when there was a long pause or several moments of silence. He answered, quoting a distinguished psychoanalyst: "Listen to the silence."

This advice is also helpful in the spiritual life. Recall the prophet Elijah on Mount Horeb, who heard God not in the strong driving storm, or in the earthquake, or in the fire, but rather in the gentle whisper (1 Kings 19:12-13). But in our loud and hectic world today, we are not used to listening to the silence for God. Another mentor of mine in residency liked to joke that he had acquired "occupationally induced attention-deficit disorder." The frantic pace of modern life and work leads many of us into this kind of frazzled state, which leads to interior disquiet and exterior disorder. Quieting ourselves in order to pray is essential not only for our sanctity but also for our very sanity.

One simple technique is to slow our breathing down by inhaling through our nose and exhaling through our mouth. We can even imagine inhaling the Lord's love and grace and exhaling all the garbage and sorrow we feel. We can employ the ancient practice of the "Jesus Prayer," which comes from the Desert Fathers and developed in eastern Christianity, by repeating quietly or silently, "Lord Jesus Christ, have mercy on me, a sinner." These spiritual masters say that the entire Gospel is encapsulated in this one phrase. It can even be united to the same breathing technique: inhaling, "Lord Jesus Christ" and exhaling, "have mercy on me, a sinner."

An important aspect of interior silence is unplugging a bit from our technological gadgets, which have proliferated in recent years. When doctors counsel nicotine addicts or alcoholics on smoking cessation or sobriety, we often get the retort: "I don't have a problem. I could quit anytime I want to!" Right. Sure. Just as the doctor might suggest avoiding smoking for twenty-four hours, I put the same challenge to readers who have become addicted to their Blackberry or iPhone, who waste many hours on Facebook, e-mail, or other technological time drains: take a hiatus from these for one day every week. Take a Sabbath rest from your e-mail. Take a bit of time every day to set aside these distractions and focus your attention only on the presence of God.

St. Augustine famously wrote, "You have created us for yourself, O Lord, and our hearts are restless until they rest in you." Well, as it turns out quite literally, our hearts—and the rest of our bodies—are restless, anxious, hypertensive, and stressed, until they rest in God. Prayer benefits us on the natural level, calming our anxieties and modulating our erratic moods. On the supernatural level, prayer is indispensable: it is oxygen for our souls. St. Teresa of Avila said that she could not guarantee heaven to anyone who did not pray for at least ten minutes a day. Without this daily conversation of friendship, without these periods of gazing upon the One we love, we cannot maintain the presence of God during daily periods of intense and busy work. Spend a bit of time with Jesus, in front of the Blessed Sacrament when possible, in prayer every day. Prayer is indeed good medicine.

Spiritual Help for Depression

In addition to the practice of mental prayer, our Catholic tradition offers a rich patrimony of vocal prayers—from the public liturgy of the Mass, the Liturgy of the Hours, and prayers associated with eucharistic adoration, to private devotions such as the Rosary and the Divine Mercy Chaplet. Traditional vocal prayers are tremendously helpful and should not be neglected. Even those who are advanced in mental prayer do not abandon vocal prayer.

Such prayers can be especially helpful during times of mental distress—such as depression—when our minds may have a difficult time focusing. For someone in a severely depressed state, mental prayer may simply prove to be impossible. In such cases, vocal prayers can be especially beneficial; we can allow the wise and holy people from the past to give us the words to pray in our present moment of anguish. Such commonly known prayers are found in many Catholic prayer books, such as the *Handbook of Prayers*; a small selection is provided in Appendix 2.

Two common difficulties encountered in the practice of prayer are interior dryness and distraction. With dryness, a lack of affective consolations or a mental fog can make perseverance in prayer more difficult. It could stem from the spiritual desolation, whether demonically or divinely originated, as discussed in Chapter 2. With distraction, we find it difficult to focus our mind on conversation with God.

Dryness and distraction are common challenges for anyone who sets out to establish a habit of prayer, but they are more frequent and more pronounced during times in which one is struggling with depression or anxiety. During periods of dryness or distraction, vocal prayers can provide the material for our conversation and help quiet and focus our mind. For example, we can slowly meditate on the Lord's Prayer, savoring each word or phrase. The repetition of the Rosary, as another example, has a calming effect on our mind.

The words of these vocal prayers can help quiet our inner rest-lessness, making it easier to attend to the mysteries we are con-templating. The tradition of praying the *Angelus* in the morning, at noon, and in the evening, or of praying a daily Rosary (with family members, if possible), or of reciting some of the liturgi-cal hours of the Divine Office can help establish and mark the rhythm of our day. These daily norms allow us moments of more focused contact with God every day. More will be said about litur-gical prayer when we discuss the Holy Mass.

It is important that when we find ourselves distracted in prayer we do not become discouraged and demoralized. Instead, we should allow the Lord to gently turn our attention back to him, offering him our imperfections, even the mental pain and frustration of depression. If a time of prayer is a constant oscil-lation between attentiveness and distraction, and yet we try to persevere, that is excellent prayer.

Spiritual Reading

Good spiritual reading, which can be as simple as spending a few minutes a day reading from the Scriptures and from other spiritual classics, can help sustain our spiritual life and feed our prayer. Deep reading has proven therapeutic for many who suffer from depression, and there is no better written source of consola-tion and strength than the Bible, along with the books written by those whose lives were shaped by the Sacred Scriptures. Fur-thermore, the practices of spiritual reading and prayer are mutu-ally enriching. Spiritual reading will feed our prayer, and prayer will make our spiritual reading more fruitful. The daily reading of good books can be a remedy for sadness, a comfort in distress, and a helpful way to foster hope and fortitude. Good spiritual reading can help us feel less isolated; it draws our thoughts to eternal, spiritual, and divine realities. This can help to pull us out of our often myopic and narrow view of our present circumstances. The psychologist and philosopher William James survived and eventually recovered from bouts of severe depression in part through deep and serious reading.

Along with the Gospels, the Psalms can be an excellent source of spiritual reading in times of difficulty or distress. In an address given at the Vatican conference on the subject of depression, Cardinal Jose Saraiva Martins pointed out that expressions of faith in the midst of severe depression are found in the Psalms. Several psalms can be read as "expressions of a depressive state," with symptoms of sadness, lack of interest, diminished capacity for work, sleep disturbances, physical wasting, an overwhelming sense of guilt, a desire to cry, and perhaps even suicidal thoughts. Cardinal Martins cites Psalm 55 as an example: "My heart pounds within me; death's terrors fall upon me. Fear and trembling overwhelm me; shuddering sweeps over me." He also mentions the distressed tone of Psalm 102, where the psalmist laments, "I am withered, dried up like grass, too wasted to eat my food." At the same time, many psalms, including those with depressive themes, simultaneously exalt the goodness of God and the created world. They offer a response and a remedy to ease the apparent hopelessness of the depressed state. The conviction that "man is always loved and appreciated by God," that the world is not wholly hostile but fundamentally good, and that it is normal to express one's emotions—all this can be found in the reading of the Psalms. This is another reason the Liturgy of the Hours, which is built around the Psalter (the cycle of readings from the Psalms), is ardently recommended by the Church and is a required part of the rhythm of the day for clergy and religious.

Confession and Spiritual Direction

The sacrament of Confession, or Reconciliation, is saving medicine for the soul. While it is not curative of depression, it can be effective medicine for both spiritual and psychological health.

One research study in Europe showed that Catholics who confess regularly are less neurotic than Catholics who do not. Confession is not something dark and dreary; it is, as John Paul II said, the sacrament of joy. It is the sacrament that restores and strengthens our hope. It brings profound peace, psychologically and spiritually. There is no reason to be afraid of this practice, even if it has been years since we made a good confession.

Our spiritual life is one of conversion and reconversion, of beginning and beginning again. St. Philip Neri, who was called the apostle of joy and was recognized during his lifetime as a living saint, said on his sickbed at the age of eighty: "When I get well, I intend to change my life." One of St. Josemaría Escrivá's most popular sayings, which comes from Father Pio Bruno Lanteri, the founder of the Oblates of the Virgin Mary, was *"Nunc coepi"* — "Now I have begun!"

These close friends of God, who lived in deep union with him, always saw their lives on earth as a continuous conversion. They would never consider themselves as having "already arrived" in the spiritual life. There is no better way to make a new start and to deepen our conversion than by making a good confession, and going to confession regularly, even monthly or weekly. The procedure, although sometimes difficult, is simple: open up your wounds and show them to the priest. If you have forgotten how to confess, just tell the priest, and he will gently guide you through it. Let Christ, the truest Physician of the soul, cleanse your sins and help you to begin again.

Confession addresses our emotional life by concretizing the things that are keeping us from God and forgiving these sins. Confession allows us to verbalize our wrongdoing, getting it "off our chest." Verbalizing our sin before the priest, who represents both God and the Christian community, breaks us out of the isolation and despair that sin produces. Moreover, we believe that Christ is actually present in the person of the priest, giving his absolution. The penitent hears the words addressed to him by Jesus: "I absolve you from your sins ..." The penitent can be consoled in a very concrete, personal way by the mercy and love of God. Moreover, in confession, the Lord also gives grace to help the penitent avoid those sins in the future. It is important to recall that confession is protected by the strict seal of the confessional: the priest may *never* reveal what is said in confession, even under pain of death. What safer place could we find to verbalize the dark corners of our soul, to bring them out into the light to be ministered to and healed?

But why would one need to confess his sins to a priest? It seems rather humiliating, after all. Cannot a person just go straight to God? The simple answer is that our Lord arranged things this way: we are creatures of flesh and blood, and we therefore come close to God by seeing, hearing, and touching. God's invisible grace is communicated through visible instruments, such as water, oil, or the audible words of the priest. This is the basis for the sacramental principle in Catholic theology and the liturgy. Jesus knows that we are made of flesh, that our knowledge comes to us through the senses of sight, hearing, touch, smell, and taste. He made us this way. This is why he breathed the Holy Spirit onto his Apostles after the Resurrection, giving his chosen representatives the power to forgive sins (John 20:22-23). The human intermediary, the priest, whom we can see and hear, is our Lord's instrument to mediate his real, concrete, and efficacious grace of forgiveness.

A good confessor can also assist us with individual spiritual direction, either in the context of advice given in Confession or outside the sacrament. Individual spiritual direction, best done by going consistently to the same priest (or a qualified religious or layperson), can be tremendously beneficial for those who are prone to depression. If you also have a psychiatrist or psychotherapist, it is a good idea that you give the spiritual director and therapist permission to communicate with one another from time to time about your progress, treatment goals, and so on. This will better allow for coordinated spiritual and psychological/medical care.

At the Vatican conference on depression, Cardinal Jorge Medina Estevez recommended that depressed individuals receive spiritual direction from a faithful and experienced director. The work of spiritual direction does not compete with, but complements, the work of therapists. A good director can help a suffering person regain a sense of God's goodness and wisdom, of God's desire for each person to be happy. A good director can be an instrument to communicate God the Father's merciful love (demonstrated by the sacrificing of his Son for the salvation of all), his intimate knowledge of every human limitation and sin, and, finally, his desire to forgive. As Cardinal Estevez put it, "One who is living the harsh experience of depression needs, from a spiritual point of view, to recover a profound sense of trust in the God who saves and whose grace is powerful enough to overcome the most rending trials." It is admittedly difficult in these times to find a competent spiritual director who is not already swamped with requests. A decent confessor and good spiritual reading can help in the interim.[63]

The Mass

The most important event that should order our life and orient our days and weeks is the Holy Mass. The Mass is the center and root of our interior life because it is Jesus' once-and-for-all Sacrifice on the Cross, renewed in the present moment for our salvation. The Mass is the time when we can gather up all that has happened or will happen that day and offer it to God. We place everything we have done—our joys, our sorrows, our concerns, our suffering, and our struggles—on the paten with the

---

[63] Thomas Dubay, *Seeking Spiritual Direction: How to Grow the Divine Life Within* (Ann Arbor, Michigan: Servant, 1994).

bread. Then it is taken up, changed, and offered as something pleasing to God in the Sacrifice of the Mass. If he can change bread and wine into his very Body and Blood, imagine what he can do with our lives.

It is in reception of Holy Communion that our union with Christ is most intense. It is important to recall—especially, perhaps, for those suffering from depression—that Christ is there, even when we do not "feel" his presence. If you just show up and try to be present at Mass, Christ will come to meet you there, every time. Thank God that his real presence in the Eucharist is not dependent upon our subjective emotional state. Jesus is always really, truly, substantially present in the Eucharist; his presence is not dependent upon how I feel that day, or even upon the subjectively experienced intensity of my faith. When I receive him, I receive him simply because he gives himself to me, however unworthy I may feel. It matters little whether I am in a state of depression or despair: Christ is still there with me. My union with him is unimaginably close when I receive him in Holy Communion. I should avoid receiving him if I am in a state of serious sin (until I make a good confession), but I should not avoid receiving him simply because I am in a state of depression.

The Mass is not meant to be partitioned off from the rest of life. It is not an event that is foreign to our experience of suffering, to our sorrows or our anguish. We can *extend*, so to speak, the Sacrifice of the Mass throughout the week, indeed throughout each day, by offering up our daily work to God, even offering our perceived failures. St. Josemaría Escrivá was fond of telling students, "Your desk is your altar"—in other words, your ordinary life and work is the place where you offer to God your spiritual sacrifice. He might have said to a taxi driver, "Your dashboard is your altar," or to a cook, "Your stovetop," or to a surgeon, "Your operating table." My wife likes to joke that the diaper-changing table is her altar.

When we are depressed, our daily offerings may perhaps seem paltry—am I supposed to offer to God the effort it takes just to get out of bed in the morning and go to school or to work? Yes, in God's economy, even these seemingly small victories can be taken up and incorporated into that great victory of Christ on Calvary. Perhaps for the depressed person, all that can be offered is the disappointment of not being able to function well, or of trying to engage in treatment and a slow process of recovery. This, too, is pleasing to God. I mention this in the context of talking about the Mass, because it is precisely at Mass, in the Sacrifice of Jesus on Calvary re-presented on the altar, that our daily difficulties or small sacrifices acquire their sanctifying value. In the eucharistic offering, we unite our life and our work to God's work—to Christ's self-offering on the Cross.

Even the suffering that one experiences during depression can be sanctified in this way. Every illness, which God allows for reasons beyond our comprehension, can be spiritually fruitful and a source of personal sanctification. What God does for us even in the midst of depression is most likely going to be hidden from view. Likewise, what happens in the Mass on the supernatural level is largely hidden from view; it is a magnificent reality, but veiled in mystery, as St. Thomas Aquinas wrote in his famous eucharistic hymn:

> Godhead here in hiding
> Whom I do adore
> Masked by these bare shadows
> Shape and nothing more . . .

Sanctifying Ordinary Work and Suffering

But can depression itself be sanctifying, or an occasion for our sanctification? In the thick of depression, this does not seem possible. As with the hidden mysteries of the spiritual life, perhaps only afterwards, on the far side of the experience, will one realize that God was there too, even in the depths and darkness. Author and teacher Parker Palmer responded to the question, "How could depression lead to a richer spiritual life?" In his answer, he discussed his own personal experience with this affliction:

> In the midst of severe clinical depression I have never felt anything redeeming about it, spiritually or otherwise. But when I emerge back into life, several things become clear. One is that the darkness did not kill me, which makes all darknesses more bearable — and since darkness is an inevitable part of the cycle of spiritual life (as it is in the cycle of natural life) this is valuable knowledge. Two, depression has taught me that there is something in me far deeper and stronger and truer than my ego, my emotions, my intellect, or my will. All of these faculties have failed me in depression, and if they were all I had, I do not believe I would still be here to talk about the experience. Deeper down there is a soul ... that helps explain (for me, at least) where the real power of life resides. Three, the experience of emerging from a living hell makes the rest of one's life more precious, no matter how "ordinary" it may be. To know that life is a gift, and to be grateful for that gift, are keys to a spiritual life, keys that one is handed as depression yields to new life.[64]

One of the most common, and most difficult, effects of depression is that it can impair one's ability to engage in ordinary daily work. Appreciating not just the temporal but also the spiritual value of ordinary work can help those who are depressed and who consequently struggle to continue even the most simple daily occupations and tasks. When recovering from a severe case of

[64] Published online at http://www.explorefaith.org.

depression, it may sometimes be necessary, in consultation with one's doctor, to take a leave of absence from professional work in order to rest and reduce stress. But it is typically advisable to gradually get back to work as soon as one is able. For both mental and spiritual health, working is generally better than not working.

While a depressed person's attempts to work may not appear to bear much fruit—perhaps the measurable results are negligible—the spiritual value of the effort remains. If the work is carried out with love for God and for one's neighbor, if it is offered to God, then it is most pleasing in his sight. From God's perspective, it is not the type or amount of work that counts the most, but rather the intention and love with which the work is done, no matter how simple or humble the task. In the midst of a severe depression, when brushing one's teeth may feel like an intolerable chore, learning to offer even this little thing to God with all the love and the good intention a person can summon can assist with recovery and healing. These apparently insignificant things acquire meaning and value in God's eyes.

By virtue of our Baptism, every member of the Church is called to the fullness of Christian life, to authentic sanctity. Holiness is not the sole prerogative of priests and religious, nor is it limited to those who are physically or mentally healthy. It should be the goal for all of us, including those of us who suffer and struggle with various mental disorders such as depression. Since God calls us all to holiness and most of our time is spent doing ordinary professional or domestic work, ordinary work itself must be among the means to holiness. The sanctification of work does not require that we leave our place in the world; it does not mean changing our occupation or state of life. We try to avoid "mystical wishful thinking," which takes us out of the warp and woof of our actual daily existence. We should not set for ourselves unrealistic goals rooted in our own ego or ambition or self-loathing. We simply need to accept the vocation God has given us, no matter how ordinary and mundane it may appear. Sanctifying our ordinary work involves not fleeing from our situation, but doing the very same things with a renewed purpose, with a supernatural outlook, by the moving power of the Holy Spirit.

John Paul II was a man who understood the value of human work from experience, not only from the perspective of his ecclesiastical work as priest, bishop, and Pope, but also from his ordinary work in the world. During the Nazi occupation of Poland, he was forced into arduous manual labor, mining rocks at a chemical plant. Years later he would write in his encyclical on human work that "*the whole person, body and spirit*, participates in [work], whether it is manual or intellectual work."[65] Because of the unity of the human person, work of whatever kind is a spiritual activity. Ordinary work, including even simple activities such as tending a garden or doing the dishes, can be among the things that help elevate our spirit when our mood is trending downward.

The reason work elevates the human spirit is rooted in our original vocation as human beings. From the beginning, man was created by God to work. God placed man in the Garden of Eden to work, "to till the garden and keep it" (Gen. 2:15). This vocation to work was given to us before the sin of our first parents, and it was easy in paradise to live that vocation out. Man worked without toil. So, contrary to some mistaken interpretations of Genesis, work is not a punishment for sin: the commandment to work comes before the account of the Fall. The original vocation to work pointed to the divine image in man, reflecting God's own activity in creating and governing the world. God's punishment of Adam for Original Sin reads, "Cursed is the ground because of you; in toil you shall eat of it all the days of your life" (Gen. 3:17-19), and again, "In the sweat of your face you shall eat bread." But

[65] John Paul II, Encyclical Letter *Laborem excercens* ("On Human Work"), no. 24.

notice that the curse was the toil and hardship (the "sweat of your face") that *accompany* work; *work itself* was not a punishment.

Work was part of God's original plan for humanity: he created us with an intelligent and free nature suited to work as a participation in his providential direction of the world. As it says in the book of Job, "Man is born to work as the birds are born to fly" (Job 5:7). This biblical observation is the deepest reason sustained unemployment is such a significant risk factor for developing depression. It is not just the financial hardship that accompanies unemployment, but the fact that we are deeply unfulfilled without meaningful work. Without work, man feels dislocated in the world, disconnected from his profound purpose. John Paul II points out, "Man, created in the image of God, *shares by his work in the activity of the Creator*," and he quotes Vatican II on this point: "Awareness that man's work is a participation in God's activity ought to permeate ... even '*the most ordinary everyday activities*.'"[66]

Consider the life of Christ in this respect. We sometimes forget that Jesus spent the majority of his earthly life doing very ordinary work — hidden and without fanfare — in the carpenter's workshop in Nazareth. It is true that Scripture says nothing of our Lord's years of ordinary work. The Evangelists record only a few episodes from his infancy and childhood, then skip ahead to his public ministry when he is roughly thirty years old. From this, we might draw the erroneous conclusion that his hidden life as a common craftsman was of little importance, or that his "real work" was his public preaching, his teaching, and his miracles — the big events and grand displays of power.

But to this objection we can reply that Scripture records nothing of his hidden life precisely because there was nothing extraordinary to report. There were likely no miracles or outward signs of

---

[66] Ibid., no. 25.

his divinity during this time. The silence of the Gospels in relation to Christ's hidden life is significant for us: it is an eloquent silence, a silence that speaks volumes. The lesson is this: Jesus' work must have been just like our work—ordinary, everyday, routine. "Jesus ... *was himself a man of work*, a craftsman like Joseph of Nazareth," John Paul II explains. "The eloquence of the life of Christ is unequivocal: he belongs to the 'working world,' he has appreciation and respect for human work ... *He looks with love upon human work.*"[67] He looks with love upon those who struggle in toil and hardship.

One of the apocryphal gospels recounts an incident in Jesus' workshop in which he performed a miracle while working. According to this story, he needed a longer piece of wood than he had on hand to complete a project. So he miraculously fixed this problem by simply "stretching" a short piece of wood to fit his needs. The reason this story is not found in the canonical Gospels is that it almost certainly never happened. Jesus did not use his divine power to skirt the difficulties of ordinary life and work. He encountered all the irritations, pinpricks, annoyances, and setbacks that life entails. With the exception of sin, everything we experience while working—even those elements of work that can be frustrating or demoralizing—Christ also experienced. He experienced work in this way, redeemed it, and sanctified it.

Because he was perfect God and perfect man, each of Christ's human acts had a divine dimension. Every one of his actions was sacramental and redemptive. Of course, his work of redemption culminated on the Cross and was fulfilled in the Resurrection. But even Jesus' smallest and seemingly most insignificant deeds played a role in our salvation. If we work united to Christ, we not only participate in God's creative activity; we also participate

[67] Ibid., no. 26.

in Christ's redemptive activity. The original punishment for sin is changed by Christ into a redemptive opportunity: "By enduring the toil of work in union with Christ crucified for us, man in a way collaborates with the Son of God for the redemption of humanity."[68] This exalted view of human work applies to each of our tasks, from the most prestigious to the most mundane. It applies equally to the work of a street sweeper, to the work of a brain surgeon or a senator, and to the work of a mother managing a household.

It also applies to every heroic effort of the depressed individual in his struggle to accomplish tasks that ordinarily seem simple and effortless. Sanctifying our work involves recognizing the importance of little things, recognizing that in God's sight nothing is little or insignificant if it is done with love. This is the "little way" taught so beautifully by St. Thérèse. Paying attention to little things is not about being obsessive, scrupulous, or nitpicky; the Christian is not a neurotic collector of good behavior reports. Rather, we recognize the importance of little things because of love, because our Lord tells us that he who is faithful in little will be faithful in much.

It is worth mentioning in this context the importance of charitable works in the process of recovery from depression. Helping others in their needs, either temporally or spiritually, and cultivating the virtue of generosity can help with a depressed mood. One should not neglect the works of mercy, even and perhaps especially when experiencing a mental state that tends to turn one's attention toward the self. Works of mercy go hand in hand with contemplation: neither allows for navel-gazing narcissism. The depressed individual can learn to get out of himself and give himself generously to others and, equally important, to receive the assistance offered by others. Parker Palmer writes of the

[68] Ibid., no. 27.

importance of this for his own recovery from depression and links
contemplation to outward acts of love:

> Many of us are contemplatives by catastrophe. We start
> seeing beyond the veil only when it is rent by some crisis,
> personal or societal or both, that reveals things as they are.
> I learned about contemplation in the midst of a personal
> catastrophe called clinical depression. Depressions differ.
> Some are biochemical and can be treated only with drugs.
> Mine was situational, involving the way I was living my
> life, and the only way I could get out alive was to become
> a contemplative. I needed to penetrate the illusions
> about myself and my world that had led me into devastat-
> ing darkness. I needed to touch the realities that might
> return me to the light. Each illusion we lose brings us that
> much closer to reality—and since God is a God of real-
> ity, we are moving in the right direction. Contemplation,
> normally regarded as a private pursuit, needs communal
> support. We are most likely to risk its vulnerabilities and
> be faithful to its implications when we are embedded in a
> community that both evokes and witnesses our truth—a
> rare form of community in which we learn to "be alone
> together," to support one another on a solitary journey.
> We practice being present to others without being inva-
> sive or evasive—neither trying to "fix" them with advice
> nor turning away when they share something distressing.
> Imagine yourself sitting at the bedside of a dying person,
> who is making the most solitary journey of all. Here we
> must lose both the arrogance that makes us think we can
> "fix" the other and the cowardice that tempts us to turn
> away. Since we are all dying all the time, why not prac-
> tice this way of relating before the final hour? Contempla-
> tion, rightly understood, does not plunge us into a pit of

narcissism but returns us to the needs of the world with clarity and commitment.[69]

Sanctifying oneself through work, including works of mercy and generosity, is about becoming a contemplative—a man or woman of prayer. Work is not merely an ascetical remedy for idleness or acedia. An hour of work offered to God can become an hour of prayer. And prayer is healing. When we allow God to unite our work to his work, we grow in faith, hope, and love. The fruits of our work may remain hidden from our view for a time, or perhaps indefinitely. This keeps us humble. Sanctifying our daily life—offering our work and our rest to God—requires constant acts of hope, where the results of our labor are, so to speak, "deposited" with God the Father. In a way, it is not unlike the Divine Son, who deposited his glory with the Father to take the form of a servant (Phil. 2:6-7).

Nothing is ever lost, if it is given over to God and done out of love. In this way we can grow in this highest and most supreme virtue of love, a love that is manifested in deeds and not just in sweet words. If some ordinary activity of ours (e.g., that boring administrative meeting, another load of laundry, another visit to the doctor or therapist) feels lacking in love, follow the advice of St. John of the Cross: "Where there is no love, put love, and there you will find love."

By offering our work to God (perhaps for specific intentions), by remaining aware while working that we are in the presence of God, by persevering in our tasks even when they prove difficult, out of love for God and neighbor—in all this, we are in fact raising our minds and hearts to God, by the prior gracious and loving

[69] Parker Palmer, "Contemplative by Catastrophe," *Spirituality and Health Magazine* (Spring 2012). This passage contains several quotations from the article; ellipses have been omitted for the sake of clarity and flow.

movement of God in our hearts. We are converting our work into prayer, and in this way it is possible to "pray without ceasing," as St. Paul recommends (1 Thess. 5:17).

The letter to the Hebrews describes God's love as a "consuming fire" (Heb. 12:29), a purifying fire that sometimes hurts. Our Lord said that he "came to cast fire upon the earth" (Luke 12:49). Pope Benedict XVI, commenting on these verses, said, "Christianity is great because love is great. It burns, yet this is not a destructive fire, but a fire that makes things bright and pure and free and grand. Being a Christian is daring to entrust oneself to this burning fire."[70] This burning fire of God's love often takes the form of a cross, like depression. But wherever the cross is, there Jesus can be found. The fire of God's love is not destructive; it is healing. If we entrust ourselves to this burning fire while working and while resting, if we unite our heart to the heart of Christ, in whatever environment we find ourselves, we will be a person who spreads this love to others. Even in the midst of suffering, we can raise the spiritual temperature within us and around us. Even if our exterior activity is for a time curtailed by illness, our interior life can still develop. Even in the thick of depression, which tends to turn us in on ourselves, with God's grace we can still become an instrument to bring his joy and peace to others around us.

---

[70] Joseph Ratzinger [Benedict XVI], *God and the World: Believing and Living in Our Time*, trans. Henry Taylor (San Francisco: Ignatius Press, 2002), 222.

Chapter 8

Divine Filiation and the Virtue of Hope

"Christ took all human suffering on himself,
even mental illness. Yes, even this affliction, which
perhaps seems the most absurd and incomprehensible,
configures the sick person to Christ and gives him
a share in his redeeming passion."

Pope John Paul II[71]

↬

Divine Filiation

St. Augustine prayed, "Help me to know myself and to know you, my God." Self-knowledge is one of the central aims of all psychotherapies. But therapy alone is incapable of uncovering the most important and most consequential truths about the human person, truths that can be known only by divine revelation. For baptized persons, the central truth—in cognitive-therapy terms, the most essential and fundamental "core belief"—about oneself is this: I am a child of God. In union with Jesus Christ, the only Son of God by nature, I have become an adopted son of God by grace: every baptized person becomes a "son" in the Son. Jesus himself tells us, "I am ascending to *my* Father, and *your* Father" (John 20:17).

[71] John Paul II, Address to participants in the international conference sponsored by the Pontifical Council for Pastoral Assistance to Health Care Workers, December 11, 1996.

Sacred Scripture teaches this astonishing truth in the First Letter of John: "See what love the Father has bestowed upon us, that we may be called children of God; *and so we are*" (1 John 3:1). God's sanctifying grace does not merely confer a "legal" or "juridical" adopted status on us; it does not merely declare us to be sons of God when in reality we remain wretched; it does not merely cover us outwardly with the merits of Christ. Sanctifying grace, conferred by Baptism and the other sacraments, and strengthened by prayer and good works, has the power to heal, restore, and elevate human nature *from the inside*. Remember that sin and separation from God were never original to human nature. Through the action of the Holy Spirit, we are united with Jesus Christ and we actually participate in the Son of God's divine life, in his eternal relationship with the Father and the Holy Spirit.

God is my Father, literally. He is very near to me, "nearer to me than I am to myself," as St. Augustine put it, in a profound and mysterious formulation. St. Josemaría Escrivá wrote, "We've got to be convinced that God is always near us. We live as though he were far away, in the heavens high above, and we forget that he is also continually by our side. He is there like a loving Father. He loves each one of us more than all the mothers in the world can love their children — helping us, inspiring us, blessing ... and forgiving."[72] This is the central truth of our "divine filiation." For all baptized Christians, this is an objective fact — regardless of how aware of it we are and regardless of how well we live according to this truth. We may be, like the Prodigal Son, an estranged child of God — estranged by our own sins and our refusal to live as a good son or daughter. Or we may be like the older brother in the same parable: the glory and wonder of our divine filiation may be something that we take for granted and fail to appreciate. But it remains an objective fact nonetheless.

[72] St. Josemaría Escrivá, *The Way*, no. 267.

Divine Filiation and the Virtue of Hope

Our task is to subjectively appropriate and live according to this objective reality—to allow it to become the animating theme of our entire existence. The truth of our divine filiation is not one more bare fact among others, not one among a list of features about me. It is not one truth among many about the world that I have committed to memory and could rattle off like a child reciting his lessons. Rather, my divine filiation should be *the* truth through which I see clearly everything else about my life, my circumstances, my emotional state, my vocation, and my destiny—even my depression. Depression, and the sometimes devastating events that may lead to depression, may obscure our awareness of this reality. It can become more difficult to believe that God is really a loving Father when we suffer pain or loss that is incomprehensible to us.

M. Night Shyamalan's film *Signs* can be interpreted as a sort of parable about a man's growing awareness of his divine filiation. On the surface, the film is a familiar science-fiction story about hostile aliens who invade the earth. The protagonist, Graham Hess, is a widower and father of two children. We also learn early in the film that he was formerly an Anglican clergyman who lost his faith after his beloved wife died tragically in a violent accident. He blames God for his wife's death, which he cannot understand. Consequently, he has difficulty believing in the loving fatherhood of God.

In one scene, as the hostile aliens are breaking into his house, Graham hides in the basement with his two children. His son is asthmatic and, in his distress, suffers an asthma attack and is in danger of suffocating. But his inhaler medication is upstairs, where the aliens are, and cannot be retrieved without putting everyone in danger. The boy's father takes his son onto his lap and holds him, speaking in his ear in a calming voice, "Don't be afraid, Morgan; we'll slow this down together. Breathe like me, stay with me; I know it hurts. Be strong, it will pass. Don't be afraid of what's happening. Believe it's going to pass, believe it." The boy clings in terror to his father's pant legs. Although he has supposedly lost his faith, Graham interrupts this dialogue with his son momentarily and tells God, "Don't do this to me again, not again. I hate you, I hate you ..."

Graham then addresses his son again, "The fear is feeding it; don't be afraid of what's happening: believe it's going to pass, believe it. Just wait, don't be afraid, the air is coming ... believe; you don't have to be afraid. Here comes the air ... don't be afraid, Morgan, breathe with me together. The air is going in our lungs ... together ... we're the same, we're the same."

There is an ironic and deep truth revealed in this scene: the protagonist interrupts his words to his son to express his anger directly at God, addressing God as a "you." Graham is praying, and praying very sincerely, whether he wants to or not. God's answer to Graham is contained in the rest of the story. And the answer is precisely what Graham says to his own son: *Don't be afraid, breathe with me together, we are one.*

This scene is a beautiful image of our divine filiation. We cannot see God, but if we are attuned, we can sense him spiritually, holding us, speaking to us in his calm and strong voice when we suffer, when we are in pain, and when we are afraid. Just so, the boy in the film, sitting on his father's lap face forward, cannot see his father's face, but can feel his soothing presence, which calms his fears. He survives the asthma attack. His peace comes when he synchronizes his breathing with his father's. He overcomes his suffering when he unites his will and actions with the will of his father: *we are one.* This scene becomes a metaphor for Graham's own life: even though he cannot see his heavenly Father while he is suffering, the Father is nevertheless present the whole time, holding him and calling to him.

At the end of the film, Graham is given a glimpse of the providential reasons behind his wife's and his son's sufferings: his wife's final dying words help them to defeat the aliens, and his son's asthma—his affliction—ironically *saves* him in the end from the alien's attack (his asthmatic bronchi are closed when the alien sprays him with aerosolized poison). The protagonist is given a glimpse of how God can mysteriously bring good out of suffering. As the story proceeds, the main character comes to realize that God has not abandoned him and that his wife did not die without purpose. He witnesses evil (symbolized by the aliens) defeated by means of water (as through Baptism) and by the providential plan of God, through which God brings good out of the tragedy of his wife's death. This awareness of his divine filiation, of the fact that God is not distant, but a loving and providential Father, allows Graham to regain his faith at the end of the story. Although he could not see God the Father—just as in the scene in which he held his own son—God was really there all along.

This awareness inspires St. Paul to pen such consoling verses as, "I can do all things in him who strengthens me" (Phil. 4:13) and, "Now to him who by the power at work within us is able to do far more abundantly than all that we ask or think to him, be glory" (Eph. 3:20). This modern-day parable on film could be told also through countless stories from the lives of the saints. Blessed Julian of Norwich, through her experience of God the Father's providential grace, could say with confidence, "All will be well, all will be well, all manner of things will be well." Hers was not a naïve or sugarcoated optimism. Her conviction that all will be well grew out of serious trials and experiences of suffering. Like-wise, St. Thérèse was able to say, at the end of her life and on the far side of a protracted period of intense suffering, "Everything is grace." I have treated many depressed individuals who were sus-tained during their periods of darkness by their faith in God the Father's love—although they could not always feel or sense this love affectively, they knew in faith that God would not abandon them to darkness or despair.

Presence of God

What are some ways that we can cultivate a more constant awareness of the presence of God and of our divine filiation? In the midst of depression, the soul may not be able to experience the Lord's presence, at least not in the ways to which it is accustomed. Still, the experience of many patients suggests that an awareness of God's presence need not be restricted to times when one feels mentally healthy and fully vital. Likewise, it need not be restricted to times of prayer or religious observance. Our awareness of God's presence can be cultivated in a thousand ways throughout each day, regardless of our changing moods.

We can use concrete human reminders that help us to be attentive to the presence of God. Simple things such as frequent momentary glances at a picture of our Lady or a small crucifix we keep in our pocket and place on our desk while working. We can cultivate the habit of saying "aspirations," which are brief vocal prayers. These can be attached to various daily routines. For example, when we walk up or down a flight of stairs, we can repeat the words of John the Baptist, "Lord, you must increase, but I must decrease" (cf. John 3:30). When we turn on a light switch, we can repeat the words of Psalm 27, "The Lord is my light and my salvation, whom shall I fear?"

These aspirations can also include frequent acts of thanksgiving. Recent psychological research has confirmed what philosophers from Cicero to Aquinas to G. K. Chesterton have long known about the importance of gratitude in human life. Cicero ranked gratitude as the chief virtue; Aquinas saw it as an essential element of justice; Chesterton claimed, "Gratitude produced the most purely joyful moments that have been known to man."[73] Robert Emmons, a professor of psychology, has researched and

---

[73] G. K. Chesterton, *St. Francis of Assisi*, in *Collected Works*, vol. II (San Francisco: Ignatius Press, 1986), 75.

written extensively on the psychological and social effects of the virtue of gratitude.[74] His work demonstrates remarkable mental health benefits—for the grateful individuals themselves and for others around them—for those who deliberately engage in exercises to improve their sense of gratitude. On the flip side, his research also confirms adverse consequences for ingratitude.

Emmons's research includes this important finding, which is particularly salient for our theme of depression: gratitude is not a warm, fuzzy emotion that prevents the experience of negative emotions. Gratitude is a virtue, and therefore cultivating gratitude can be done even in the context of a depressive episode, although it will obviously be more challenging in these circumstances. As Emmons puts it, "gratefulness does not appear to be a Pollyannish state where suffering and adversity are selectively ignored, but it might induce the requisite psychological resources to successfully weather unpleasant emotional states."[75] Emmons's research suggests that gratitude is incompatible with feelings of victimhood or entitlement. It therefore tends to mitigate or reduce self-pity, on the one hand, and narcissistic tendencies or overweening pride, on the other. His findings suggest that gratitude is supported by the virtue of humility—by the ability to recognize one's shortcomings and to admit that one is not self-sufficient. At the root of such humility is the truth of our divine filiation: I am a child of God who relies on my Father for everything.

The "Little Girl" Hope

In the chapter on suicide, I introduced the central importance of hope. We looked at Beck's research demonstrating a serious

[74] Robert Emmons, *Thanks!: How the New Science of Gratitude Can Make You Happier* (New York: Houghton Mifflin Harcourt, 2007).

[75] Robert Emmons and Charles Shelton, "Gratitude and the Science of Positive Psychology," in *Handbook of Positive Psychology*, eds. C. R. Snyder and Shane Lopez (Oxford: Oxford University Press, 2001), 459-471.

risk of suicide for a person who experiences profound hopelessness. It is my firm belief that man cannot live without hope. This is not just a pious platitude. It is true in a very literal sense. Hope is the ultimate foil against depression. Quite literally, without hope, a person will die.

The well-known psychiatrist Viktor Frankl observed that hope is essential if one is to go on living under difficult circumstances. Frankl was a Jew imprisoned in Auschwitz who years later wrote his most famous work, *Man's Search for Meaning*. There he argued that man's fundamental drive was not the will to power purported by Nietzsche, or the will to pleasure postulated by Freud, but rather what he called the *will to meaning*. Frankl learned this lesson about human nature by observing human beings under the most horrific circumstances of a Nazi concentration camp. While death in Auschwitz appeared random and haphazard—striking any prisoner at any moment for no apparent reason—Frankl argued that survival in such circumstances required that a person find some meaning, some noble end or purpose to his life. In other words, those who survived did so because they maintained hope in a seemingly hopeless situation. (This does not, of course, imply that those who were gassed lacked hope.)

Frankl observed that the death-camp prisoners could tell when another prisoner had abandoned hope. When a prisoner lost hope, the despair could be seen in his eyes, in his face, in the way that he walked. The change was so noticeable that the prisoners had a name for such persons, which roughly translates as "the walking dead." Inevitably, before long, this "walking dead" prisoner would be selected for extermination, or he would fall back in formation and be shot, or he would stop eating or drinking. When the will to meaning was abandoned—when all hope was lost—the person was literally doomed. Man cannot live without hope.

Yet this truth can be stated conversely: even in the cruelest, the most atrocious, the most miserable of circumstances, if man has hope, he has life. If this is true on the natural level, it is much more true on the supernatural level. If a man has *Christian* hope, he has *everlasting* life. We are indeed, in St. Paul's words, *spe salvi*—"saved in hope" (Rom. 8:24). Hope is a virtue that changes everything. It changes the way we think, the way we act, the way we live. In his encyclical letter on hope, Pope Benedict XVI puts it simply, "The one who has hope lives differently."[76] Even if he should be sent to the gas chamber, a man with Christian hope is a man who has been saved. St. Maximilian Kolbe understood this, which is why he sang songs of praise to our Lord even as the Nazis starved him to death.

Returning to Frankl's observations of his fellow death-camp prisoners: in order to face their horrifying present situation, the prisoners needed some sense that a future might await them, a future that promised something better than the present. This insight is congruent with these words of Pope Benedict on hope: "We have been given hope, trustworthy hope, by virtue of which we can face our present: the present, even if it is arduous, can be lived and accepted if it leads towards a goal, if we can be sure of this goal, and if this goal is great enough to justify the effort of the journey."[77] He goes on to say that "a distinguishing mark of Christians [is] the fact that they have a future: it is not that they know the details of what awaits them, but they know in general terms that their life will not end in emptiness. Only when the future is certain as a positive reality does it become possible to live the present as well."[78] This can be applied analogously even to those who are not baptized: although the theological virtue of hope is the ultimate safeguard of human happiness on this earth, natural human hope is the starting point for theological hope and is itself ennobled by the presence of Christian hope in the world.

[76] Benedict XVI, Encyclical letter *Spe salvi*, no. 1.

[77] Ibid., no. 1.

[78] Ibid., no. 2.

The sense of a foreshortened future, of a future that appears only dark, which many experience in the depressed state, is not our true reality; it is merely a trick of the diseased mind. Without hope in the present, man cannot live toward the future. Why, for example, do we see rising rates of depression, as well as rising rates of drug and alcohol abuse, among teenagers today? Because many of them do not sense that they have a future. The present feels unbearable to them, and they have no hope to orient them. In an address to the bishops of Japan, Pope Benedict remarked:

> Young people especially are at risk of being deceived by the glamour of modern secular culture. Yet, like all the greater and lesser hopes that appear on first sight to promise so much (cf. *Spe Salvi*, 30), this turns out to be a false hope—and tragically, disillusion not infrequently leads to depression and despair, even to suicide. If their youthful energy and enthusiasm can be directed towards the things of God, which alone are sufficient to satisfy their deepest longings, more young people will be inspired to commit their lives to Christ.[79]

Hope cannot be merely a nice theoretical idea. It is a virtue that has very practical, everyday consequences for our life. Cultivating and sustaining hope is a central task in the process of recovery from depression, and perhaps the most demanding and challenging. Regarding the practical consequences of living in hope, Pope Benedict teaches that the Christian message of hope does not just *tell* us something: it is not just *informative*; it also changes the way we *live*. It is *performative*: "That means: the Gospel is not merely a communication of things that can be known—it is one that makes things happen and is life-changing."[80] Finding hope

---

[79] Benedict XVI, Address to the Bishops of Japan on their "Ad limina" Visit, December 17, 2007.

[80] Benedict XVI, *Spe salvi*, no. 2.

need not be complicated; it can be remarkably simple. Consider the case of a young father who was struggling with depression because of a debilitating physical condition that kept him from working. As a result he was at home with his youngest daughter. He related later that just seeing the face and constant smile of his joyful girl was enough to instill in him sufficient hope for the day. Our reasons for hope may be right there in front of us, if only we have eyes to see.

While many of us can rattle off the three theological virtues, hope is often the forgotten middle of the three. We hear much preached about faith and about love, but we hear less about the virtue of hope. What exactly is hope? The *Compendium of the Catechism* defines it succinctly: "Hope is the theological virtue by which we desire and await from God eternal life as our happiness, placing our trust in Christ's promises and relying on the help of the grace of the Holy Spirit to merit it and to persevere to the end of our earthly life."[81]

Let us unpack this definition. First, hope involves desiring happiness. This, of course, is not hard for us. In fact, it is impossible not to desire happiness, as we know from our own experience. Aristotle maintains that the desire for happiness lies at the foundation of every human action. The person suffering from depression, of course, wants nothing more than to recover the capacity for happiness, for spiritual joy. But this happiness consists ultimately in only one thing: eternal life with God. Every person, whether he knows it or not, is seeking God, because everyone is seeking perfect happiness and fulfillment, which can be found ultimately in God alone. Our search for happiness can go astray when we mistakenly place our hope in something that cannot deliver. But this fundamental desire for happiness—this desire for God—remains, even when we go astray. As G. K. Chesterton

---

[81] *Compendium of the Catechism*, no. 387.

quipped, "Every man who knocks on the door of a brothel is looking for God."

Hope, according to the definition just cited, involves placing our trust in Christ, relying on the grace of the Holy Spirit, and persevering to the end of our life—all for the sake of *eternal life*, which only God can grant. What are we to make of these words, *eternal life*? Many of our contemporaries wonder: Is eternal life something worth hoping for? The depressed person may have difficulty with the idea of looking for his happiness beyond the present world and placing his definitive hope in the next life. Perhaps this very thought has crossed our minds, especially in times of difficulty or temptation, or during periods of depression or despair: Is the effort toward holiness worthwhile? Is the goal of eternal life worth the sacrifices made in this life? Drawing on the writings of St. Augustine, Pope Benedict responds to this question: "Ultimately we want only one thing ... the life which is simply 'happiness' ... In some way we want life itself, true life, untouched even by death; yet at the same time we do not know the thing towards which we feel driven. We cannot stop reaching out for it, and yet we know that all we can experience or accomplish is not what we yearn for."[82]

The very fact that in this life the human heart remains restless—that it is vulnerable to anxiety, depression, demoralization, and despair—is a clue to the human need for hope and a clue to our ultimate destiny in God. All we can experience in this life falls short of this restless yearning. The man knocking at the brothel door will not find there what his restless heart truly desires. The man downing another bottle of gin will not find at the bottom what his heart thirsts for. The man popping another narcotic pill will not experience what his heart hungers for. God made us for himself, and our hearts are restless until they rest finally in him.

[82] Benedict XVI, *Spe salvi*, no. 12.

Divine Filiation and the Virtue of Hope

We are reaching here beyond what words can adequately express. Benedict XVI observes:

> The term "eternal life" is intended to give a name to this known "unknown." Inevitably it is an inadequate term that creates confusion. "Eternal", in fact, suggests to us the idea of something interminable, and this frightens us; "life" makes us think of the life that we know and love and do not want to lose, even though very often it brings more toil than satisfaction, so that while on the one hand we desire it, on the other hand we do not want it.[83]

To appreciate fully the meaning of *eternal life*, we have to try to get outside our usual ways of thinking and our usual experiences. Pope Benedict says:

> To imagine ourselves outside the temporality that imprisons us and in some way to sense that eternity is not an unending succession of days in the calendar, but something more like the supreme moment of satisfaction, in which totality embraces us and we embrace totality—this we can only attempt.

We simply cannot extrapolate to a vision of eternal life from our typical earthly existence, even on the best of days. Reaching beyond our words and concepts, Pope Benedict takes a stab at expressing what the term *eternal life* might actually signify: "It would be like plunging into the ocean of infinite love, a moment in which time—the before and after—no longer exists. We can only attempt to grasp the idea that such a moment is life in the full sense, a plunging ever anew into the vastness of God, in which we are simply overwhelmed with joy."[84]

[83] Ibid., no. 12.
[84] Ibid.

The Catholic Guide to Depression

The French Catholic layman Charles Péguy wrote a beautiful poem that can make the virtue of hope more tangible for us. The poem opens with the striking line, "The faith that I love the best, says God, is hope."[85] The poem continues:

> Faith doesn't surprise me.
> It's not surprising.
> I am so resplendent in my creation ...
> That in order really not to see me these poor people
> would have to be blind.
> Charity, says God, that doesn't surprise me.
> It's not surprising.
> These poor creatures are so miserable that unless
> they had a heart of stone, how could they not have
> love for each other ...
> But hope, says God, that is something that surprises
> me.
> Even me.
> That is surprising.
> That these poor children see how things are going
> and believe that tomorrow things will go better ...
> That is surprising and it's by far the greatest marvel
> of our grace.
> And I'm surprised by it myself.
> And my grace must indeed be an incredible force.[86]

Péguy employs striking metaphorical and poetical images here to suggest the power of hope, indicating to us how surprising hope can be when we experience degradation, deprivation, suffering, and evil in the world. He depicts hope in the poem as a little girl

---

[85] Charles Péguy, *The Portal of the Mystery of Hope*, trans. David L. Schindler, Jr. (Grand Rapids: Eerdmans, 1996), 3.
[86] Ibid., 3-7.

who has two older sisters, faith and love. Hope is the innocent, wide-eyed, trusting little child:

> What surprises me, says God, is hope.
> And I can't get over it.
> This little hope who seems like nothing at all.
> This little girl hope ...
> Faith is a loyal Wife.
> Charity is a Mother.
> An ardent mother, noble-hearted.
> Or an older sister who is like a mother.
> Hope is a little girl, nothing at all.
> Who came into the world on Christmas day just this
>   past year.
> Who is still playing with her snowman ...
> And yet it's this little girl who will endure worlds.
> This little girl, nothing at all.
> She alone, carrying the others, who will cross worlds
>   past.
> As the star guided the three kings from the deepest
>   Orient.
> Toward the cradle of my son.
> Like a trembling flame.
> She alone will guide the Virtues and Worlds.[87]

Our hope should make us feel every day more and more little—like a small child who relies on God his Father for everything. This life of spiritual childhood has been recommended by many saints, notably St. Thérèse of Lisieux. It is actually indicative of Christian maturity and has nothing to do with childishness. Hope is a child, walking between her two older sisters: wide-eyed and innocent, trusting and joyful. Such should be the

[87] Ibid., 7-8.

shape and character of our own hope. Can a person who is totally imbued with this sort of hope ever be completely overtaken by despair, however terrible the burdens and cares of this life? The depressed person may indeed often feel overwhelmed; but this need not be a cause for final despair. Just as we cannot imagine an innocent little girl giving in to total despair in the face of setbacks or contradictions, so the person with Christian hope can endure even these things with serenity and perseverance.

To understand the power of hope, we can examine the vices that run contrary to the virtue of hope. Regarding these, St. Augustine wrote, "There are two things which kill the soul, despair and presumption." The *Catechism* lists them under the First Commandment as sins against hope:

> By *despair*, man ceases to hope for his personal salvation from God, for help in attaining it or for the forgiveness of his sins. Despair is contrary to God's goodness, to his justice—for the Lord is faithful to his promises—and to his mercy [no. 2091].

> There are two kinds of *presumption*. Either man presumes upon his own capacities (hoping to be able to save himself without help from on high) or he presumes upon God's almighty power or his mercy (hoping to obtain his forgiveness without conversion and glory without merit) [no. 2092].

When we fall into *presumption*, we do not have hope, because we mistakenly assume that we have already arrived at the goal. This is a form of self-satisfied and stagnating pride. The second vice contrary to hope is probably more common, and this is *despair*. Certainly this is the greater temptation for those individuals suffering from depression. We sometimes hear it said that a person has "fallen into" despair. But despair is not actually something we "fall into"; in the end, it is something we choose. To despair means to deny that the Lord wants to or can forgive or assist us. Even the severest depression, however dark, does not entail despair in this sense.

In Dante's *Inferno*, the inscription written over the gates of hell is "Abandon all hope, ye who enter here." Final despair (I refer here not to the difficulties with hope of the depressed person) is the state proper only to the damned, of those who no longer have the possibility of being saved. To be utterly without hope is to be in a hellish state. So you could say that total despair in this life is something of an anticipation of damnation. As St. Isidore put it, "To despair is to descend into hell." Total despair is a sort of hell on earth, where suicide may appear to be the only option. This is why the person who feels utterly hopeless finds it so difficult to summon the will to continue living. Man cannot live without hope.

For example, listening to accounts of addiction given by those who have recovered from drug and alcohol dependence, one can see that the addicted life they describe is simply a state of profound despair—a sort of hell on earth. This is what a person experiences when he places his ultimate hope in a bottle, a needle, or a pill. Depression itself is not equivalent to this kind of despair, although it can predispose and incline a person to despair, as anyone who has experienced it knows too well. It is a great trial of faith to overcome this tendency. But it can be overcome with all the means discussed in this book, and ultimately with God's grace.

St. John Chrysostom wrote, "It is not so much sin as despair which casts us into hell." We may fall into sin, as even the just man sins seven times a day. But in hope, we become a repentant sinner and therefore, through Confession, a forgiven sinner. Sin never has to have the last word. Hope means we do not have to be the people we were. But despair makes our sin the last word about us, even a definitive word, because despair denies the possibility of forgiveness. Every sin is forgivable if we do not despair, if we seek God's merciful forgiveness. Likewise, every addiction, every vice, can be overcome if we do not give in to despair.

This helps us to understand that mysterious Gospel passage which speaks of the sin against the Holy Spirit (Matt. 12:31) that Jesus says cannot be forgiven. This sin is simply the refusal to accept the grace of forgiveness. It is an obstinate despair that refuses God's mercy. As the *Catechism* states, "There are no limits to the mercy of God, but anyone who deliberately refuses to accept his mercy by repenting, rejects the forgiveness of his sins and the salvation offered by the Holy Spirit. Such hardness of heart can lead to final impenitence and eternal loss."[88] The contrast between St. Peter's repentance and Judas's despair illustrates this: both men sinned grievously, but Peter repented with tears of contrition. He did not abandon hope. Peter's repentance led him to become one of the greatest saints. Judas despaired, and this despair led him to take his own life.

To say that hope is a "theological" or "supernatural" virtue is to say that it is fundamentally a gift, the result of grace. To possess this hope, we must be in a state of sanctifying grace, which we can be sure of when we have confessed grave sins we are aware of. But for this hope to grow in our hearts and operate powerfully in our lives, we should pray that our hope will be augmented and strengthened; we should ask God to increase our hope. Our will and our effort do play a role here, since God wants us to cooperate freely with the graces he grants. "Lord, increase my hope" should be an aspiration that comes to us often, especially in times of difficulty.

Let us now try to bring these theological considerations down to a practical level. How does hope help us to manage the stress of life? As suggested by our earlier discussion of cognitive therapy, often it is not so much the external circumstances of life that cause stress but, rather, our distorted and unrealistic thoughts

---

[88] *Catechism of the Catholic Church*, no. 1864.

about those circumstances. If you want to overcome daily difficulties, contradictions, and setbacks, cultivate this virtue of hope. For it will make everything that happens to you appear in a more realistic light. You will see all things not from your limited, earthly perspective, but from the perspective of eternity.

If this life is all we have to live for, then a financial difficulty, a personal loss, or a professional setback can send us into a tailspin. Without hope, we are tempted to reach for inadequate compensation—for the bottle, a sexual fling, a dishonest transaction to pad our pocketbook, and so on. Hope sustains us not just in dealing with major difficulties, but also in the little things that beset us each day. In his encyclical on the virtue of hope, Benedict XVI offers some very sound practical advice about the age-old practice of "offering up" the little difficulties that come to us daily:

> There used to be a form of devotion—perhaps less practiced today but quite widespread not long ago—that included the idea of "offering up" the minor daily hardships that continually strike at us like irritating "jabs," thereby giving them a meaning. Of course, there were some exaggerations and perhaps unhealthy applications of this devotion, but we need to ask ourselves whether there may not after all have been something essential and helpful contained within it.[89]

He goes on to explain how this practice unites us in a deeper way to Jesus Christ, allowing us to participate in his redemptive mission. This suffering, in union with Christ on the Cross, can have sanctifying value:

> What does it mean to offer something up? Those who did so were convinced that they could insert these little annoyances into Christ's great "com-passion" so that they

[89] Benedict XVI, *Spe salvi*, no. 40.

somehow became part of the treasury of compassion so greatly needed by the human race. In this way, even the small inconveniences of daily life could acquire meaning and contribute to the economy of good and of human love. Maybe we should consider whether it might be judicious to revive this practice ourselves.[90]

The virtue of hope can be cultivated in the context of our work, our family life, our leisure, in any honest human activity—and even, mysteriously, in our brokenness. We may sometimes wonder whether our efforts to be a better employee, a better husband or wife, father or mother, priest or religious, friend or colleague are doing any good. Are these efforts worthwhile? Am I contributing anything meaningful to the world or to the Church?

St. Josemaría Escrivá compared us to the donkeys that used to be harnessed to turn waterwheels. Round and round the donkey would go, churning the pump that watered a distant field. This humble beast of burden, with its head down and blinders on, labored in this routine work day after day. He never saw the flowers of the field that bloomed as a result of his efforts. But these flowers were no less real for being hidden from his sight. St. Paul put it this way, "For you have died, and your life is hidden with Christ in God" (Col. 3:3). Our life, our work, the fruits of our labors, our sufferings and pain—all these things are hidden with Christ in God. We persevere whatever the apparent results, whatever the outward successes and failures, because living and working for God is always fruitful.

Christian hope is never individualistic. We hope not just for ourselves, but also for others, for their happiness and salvation. So hope has an apostolic dimension. John Donne wrote the famous line, "No man is an island, sufficient unto himself." Donne, who in his bouts of serious depression was tempted to despair and at times

[90] Ibid., no. 40.

Divine Filiation and the Virtue of Hope

seriously contemplated suicide, understood that to resist despair we cannot struggle alone. Because our life is hidden with Christ in God, we do not know the effects of our smallest acts of love. A few years ago, a man in his thirties committed suicide by jumping off the Golden Gate Bridge. Afterward, his psychiatrist went with the medical examiner to the dead man's apartment, where they found his diary. The last entry, written just hours before his death, said: "I'm going to walk to the bridge. If one person smiles at me on the way, I will not jump." We do not know all that we can be to another person. That smile, that small act of kindness, is hidden with Christ in God.

Sometimes hope may seem like an unrealistic attitude, a luxury of those who do not realize "how bad things are." A cheerful or optimistic outlook may seem ludicrous to the person suffering from depression. But such a person can in fact live in the objective joy, although perhaps at times unfelt, of a life of theological hope. The cheerfulness, the joy, of a Christian is not a naïve and easygoing optimism. It does not involve putting on blinders and ignoring evil in the world. Our joy and peace are rooted in the virtue of hope.

And our hope is grounded in the conviction that the ultimate victory belongs to Christ, a victory that he has already won on the Cross. And he says to us now what he said to his Apostles, "Truly, truly, I say to you, you will weep and lament but the world will rejoice; you will be sorrowful, but your sorrow will turn into joy" (John 16:20), and he assures us, "In the world you will have tribulation, but take courage, for I have overcome the world" (John 16:33).

Appendices

Resources for Further Reading

Internet

The **National Alliance on Mental Illness** (NAMI) is dedicated to improving the lives of individuals and families affected by mental illness. It is the largest grassroots advocacy group of its kind, with chapters in most major cities. Local NAMI chapters have support groups for patients and families struggling with mental illness. The website is a good source for information on various mental illnesses. http://www.nami.org/

NAMI FaithNet is their outreach to faith communities, with some helpful resources on its website, including an excellent article, "Selected Annotated Bibliography on Spirituality and Mental Health," written by Dr. John Peteet, MD.

The **American Foundation for Suicide Prevention** website has helpful educational resources on this difficult topic, including "surviving suicide loss." http://www.afsp.org/

Natural Standard is a reliable evidence-based resource on complementary and alternative medicine, and includes information on alternative treatments for depression. http://www.natural-standard.com/

The **Institute for American Values** published an excellent multi-authored report on adolescent mental health called *Hardwired to Connect*. It assembles an impressive body of research data that supports the thesis that adolescents are "hardwired" for deep and lasting connections to other people, and to transcendent moral and spiritual meaning. It makes a case for the strengthening of "authoritative communities" that foster these connections—the primary authoritative community being the family. The report can be ordered from http://americanvalues.org/.

Books and Articles

Fr. Benedict Groeschel's *Arise from Darkness: What to Do When Life Doesn't Make Sense* (San Francisco: Ignatius Press, 1995) and *Stumbling Blocks or Stepping Stones: Spiritual Answers to Psychological Questions* (Mahwah, New Jersey: Paulist Press, 1987) are practical spiritual guides to overcoming difficulties.

Fr. Timothy Gallagher's *The Discernment of Spirits: An Ignatian Guide for Everyday Living* (New York: Crossroad, 2005) is a solid contemporary explanation and guide through the initial steps in Ignatian discernment in identifying and working with the different movements of consolation and desolation.

Thomas Dubay's *Prayer Primer: Igniting a Fire Within* (San Francisco: Ignatius Press, 2002) and *Deep Conversion, Deep Prayer*, (San Francisco: Ignatius Press, 2006), as well as Peter Kreeft's *Prayer for Beginners* (San Francisco: Ignatius Press, 2000), are excellent introductions to the life of prayer. Peter Thomas Rohrbach's *Conversation with Christ* (Rockford, Illinois: TAN Books, 1980) is an excellent introduction to mental prayer, based on the teachings of St. Teresa of Avila. Also helpful is Eugene Boylan's *Difficulties in Mental Prayer* (London: Scepter Press, 1988).

Harold Koenig's *Faith and Mental Health: Religious Resources for Healing* (West Conshohocken, Pennsylvania: Templeton Foundation, 2005) explores the role that faith-based organizations can play in delivering mental-health and substance-abuse services and is a practical resource for understanding how clergy and healthcare professionals can collaborate.

Robert Enright and Richard Fitzgibbons have written a very helpful book on the healing power of forgiveness: *Helping Clients Forgive: An Empirical Guide for Resolving Anger and Restoring Hope* (Washington, DC: American Psychological Association Press, 2000).

Viktor Frankl's *Man's Search for Meaning* (Boston: Beacon Press, 2006) is widely read and rightly regarded as a classic text in psychology. Frankl's book *The Doctor and the Soul: From Psychotherapy to Logotherapy* (New York: Vintage, 1986) follows up on these themes and applies them to clinical case examples and specific psychiatric disorders.

William Styron's *Darkness Visible: A Memoir of Madness* (New York: Modern Library, 2007) is a powerful personal account of his depression and the best firsthand description of the illness that I have encountered. Styron unfortunately seems to excuse the act of suicide for a depressed individual, taking issue with moral prohibitions against suicide. But otherwise, the book is an excellent account of the illness.

Kay Jamison's *An Unquiet Mind: A Memoir of Moods and Madness* (New York: Vintage, 1997) is a personal account of the author's experiences with bipolar disorder. It is made more compelling by the fact that Jamison is also one of the foremost researchers on bipolar disorder, having co-authored a definitive textbook on the subject, called *Manic Depressive Illness*.

For further reading on the subject of character strengths and virtues, Joseph Pieper's *The Four Cardinal Virtues* (Notre Dame, Indiana: University of Notre Dame Press, 1966) and *Faith, Hope, Love* (San Francisco: Ignatius Press, 1997) are recommended. A shorter treatment is his book A *Brief Reader on the Virtues of the Human Heart* (San Francisco: Ignatius Press, 1991). For more introductory and less philosophical treatments of the virtues, Fr. Benedict Groeschel's *The Virtue Driven Life* (Huntington, Indiana: Our Sunday Visitor, 2006) and Peter Kreeft's *Back to Virtue* (San Francisco: Ignatius Press, 1992) are good primers. For parents raising children, I recommend David Isaacs' *Character Building: A Guide for Parents and Teachers* (Dublin: Four Courts Press, 2001) or the parenting books by James Stenson.

For those interested in psychology and religion, Paul Vitz's excellent article "Psychology in Recovery" can be found on the *First Things* website (firstthings.com). His *Psychology as Religion: The Cult of Self Worship*, second edition (Grand Rapids, Michigan: Eerdmans, 1994) is a cogent critique of so-called humanistic psychology, which was highly influential in the latter half of the twentieth century, and remains influential today.

Prayers in Times of Distress

PSALM 55

Give ear to my prayer, O God;
    and hide not thyself from my supplication!
Attend to me, and answer me;
    I am overcome by my trouble.
I am distraught by the noise of the enemy,
    because of the oppression of the wicked.
For they bring trouble upon me,
    and in anger they cherish enmity
    against me.
My heart is in anguish within me,
    the terrors of death have fallen upon me.
Fear and trembling come upon me,
    and horror overwhelms me.
And I say, "O that I had wings like a dove!
    I would fly away and be at rest;
    yea, I would wander afar,
    I would lodge in the wilderness,
    I would haste to find me a shelter
    from the raging wind and tempest."
Destroy their plans, O Lord, confuse their
    tongues; for I see violence and strife
    in the city.

The Catholic Guide to Depression

Day and night they go around it
    on its walls;
    and mischief and trouble are within it,
    ruin is in its midst;
    oppression and fraud
    do not depart from its market place.
It is not an enemy who taunts me —
    then I could bear it;
it is not an adversary who deals insolently
    with me —
    then I could hide from him.
But it is you, my equal,
    my companion, my familiar friend.
We used to hold sweet converse together;
    within God's house we walked in fellowship.
Let death come upon them;
    let them go down to Sheol alive;
    let them go away in terror into their graves.
But I call upon God;
    and the LORD will save me.
Evening and morning and at noon
    I utter my complaint and moan,
    and he will hear my voice.
He will deliver my soul in safety
    from the battle that I wage,
    for many are arrayed against me.
God will give ear, and humble them,
    he who is enthroned from of old;
    because they keep no law,
    and do not fear God.
My companion stretched out his hand
    against his friends,
    he violated his covenant.

Prayers in Times of Distress

His speech was smoother than butter,
    yet war was in his heart;
    his words were softer than oil,
    yet they were drawn swords.
Cast your burden on the LORD,
    and he will sustain you;
    he will never permit
    the righteous to be moved.
But thou, O God, wilt cast them down
    into the lowest pit;
    men of blood and treachery
    shall not live out half their days.
But I will trust in thee.

PSALM 102

A prayer of one afflicted, when he is faint
    and pours out his complaint before the Lord.
Hear my prayer, O Lord;
    let my cry come to thee!
Do not hide thy face from me
    in the day of my distress!
Incline thy ear to me;
    answer me speedily in the day when I call!
For my days pass away like smoke,
    and my bones burn like a furnace.
My heart is smitten like grass, and withered;
    I forget to eat my bread.
Because of my loud groaning
    my bones cleave to my flesh.
I am like a vulture of the wilderness,
    like an owl of the waste places;

The Catholic Guide to Depression

I lie awake,
   I am like a lonely bird on the housetop.
All the day my enemies taunt me,
   those who deride me use my name for a curse.
For I eat ashes like bread,
   and mingle tears with my drink,
   because of thy indignation and anger;
   for thou hast taken me up and thrown me away.
My days are like an evening shadow;
   I wither away like grass.
But thou, O Lord, art enthroned for ever;
   thy name endures to all generations.
Thou wilt arise and have pity on Zion;
   it is the time to favor her;
   the appointed time has come.
For thy servants hold her stones dear,
   and have pity on her dust.
The nations will fear the name of the Lord,
   and all the kings of the earth thy glory.
For the Lord will build up Zion,
   he will appear in his glory;
   he will regard the prayer of the destitute,
   and will not despise their supplication.
Let this be recorded for a generation to come,
   so that a people yet unborn may praise the Lord:
that he looked down from his holy height,
   from heaven the Lord looked at the earth,
to hear the groans of the prisoners,
   to set free those who were doomed to die;
that men may declare in Zion the name of
   the Lord, and in Jerusalem his praise,
when peoples gather together,
   and kingdoms, to worship the Lord.

Prayers in Times of Distress

He has broken my strength in mid-course;
    he has shortened my days.
"O my God," I say, "take me not hence
    in the midst of my days,
thou whose years endure
    throughout all generations!"
Of old thou didst lay the foundation of the
    earth, and the heavens are the work of thy
    hands.
They will perish, but thou dost endure;
    they will all wear out like a garment.
Thou changest them like raiment, and they pass
    away; but thou art the same, and thy years
    have no end.
The children of thy servants shall dwell secure;
their posterity shall be established before thee.

⁂

PRAYER IN TIMES OF DESPAIR
(ST. IGNATIUS OF LOYOLA)

O Christ Jesus,
when all is darkness
and we feel our weakness and helplessness,
give us the sense of Your presence,
Your love, and Your strength.
Help us to have perfect trust
in Your protecting love
and strengthening power,
so that nothing may frighten or worry us,
for, living close to You,
we shall see Your hand,
Your purpose, Your will through all things.

Anima Christi
(Fourteenth-Century Prayer)

Soul of Christ, sanctify me.
Body of Christ, save me.
Blood of Christ, inebriate me.
Water from the side of Christ, wash me.
Passion of Christ, strengthen me.
O good Jesus, hear me.
Within Thy wounds hide me.
Suffer me not to be separated from Thee.
From the malicious enemy defend me.
In the hour of my death call me.
And bid me come unto Thee.
That I may praise Thee with Thy saints
and with Thy angels
Forever and ever.
Amen.

☞

Act of Abandonment to the Will of God[91]

My Lord and my God: into your hands I abandon
the past and the present and the future, what is small
and what is great, what amounts to a little and what
amounts to a lot, things temporal and things eternal.

☞

Act of Hope

O my God, relying on your almighty power and infinite
mercy and promises, I hope to obtain pardon for my sins,
the help of your grace, and life everlasting, through the
merits of Jesus Christ, my Lord and Redeemer.

---

[91] St. Josemaría Escrivá, *The Way of the Cross*, Station 7, point 3.

Prayers in Times of Distress

PRAYER BEFORE A DAY'S WORK

Direct, we beg you, O Lord,
our actions by your holy inspirations,
and grant that we may carry them out
with your gracious assistance,
that every prayer and work of ours
may begin always with you,
and through you be happily ended.
Amen.

~

LEAD, KINDLY LIGHT
(BL. JOHN HENRY NEWMAN)

Lead, Kindly Light, amidst the encircling gloom,
    Lead Thou me on!
The night is dark, and I am far from home,
    Lead Thou me on!
Keep Thou my feet; I do not ask to see
The distant scene; one step enough for me.

I was not ever thus, nor prayed that Thou
    Shouldst lead me on;
I loved to choose and see my path; but now
    Lead Thou me on!
I loved the garish day, and, spite of fears,
Pride ruled my will. Remember not past years!

So long Thy power hath blest me, sure it still
    Will lead me on.
O'er moor and fen, o'er crag and torrent, till
    The night is gone,
And with the morn those angel faces smile,
Which I have loved long since, and lost awhile!

Meantime, along the narrow rugged path,
　　Thyself hast trod,
Lead, Savior, lead me home in childlike faith,
　　Home to my God.
To rest forever after earthly strife
　　In the calm light of everlasting life.

PRAYER OF ST. BENEDICT JOSEPH LABRE[92]

Eternal Father,
Through the Precious Blood of Jesus,
have Mercy.
Console us in our moment of
need and tribulation,
As You once consoled Job, Hanna,
and Tobias, in their
afflictions.
And Mary,
Comforter of the Afflicted,
pray and placate God for us,
And obtain for us the grace
for which we humbly pray.

---

[92] St. Benedict Joseph Labre (1748-1783) suffered from a severe and persistent mental illness. He felt called to be a monk, but was turned away from one religious community after another in his native France, and later in Italy, on account of his mental illness. He eventually discerned that his vocation was to be a homeless pilgrim who ventured to European sites of Christian devotion. He generously gave to the other poor all that was given to him, and died beloved by the people of the city of Rome, where he spent the last six years of his austere life. He is buried in the church of Santa Maria del Monte near the Coliseum in Rome, and his feast day is April 16.

Prayers in Times of Distress

LITANY OF OUR LADY OF SORROWS

Lord, have mercy on us. Christ, have mercy on us.

Lord, have mercy on us. Christ, hear us. Christ,
 graciously hear us.

God, the Father of heaven, have mercy on us.

God the Son, Redeemer of the world, have
 mercy on us.

God the Holy Ghost, have mercy on us.

Holy Mary, Mother of God, pray for us.

Holy Virgin of virgins, pray for us.

Mother of the Crucified, pray for us.

Sorrowful Mother, pray for us.

Mournful Mother, pray for us.

Sighing Mother, pray for us.

Afflicted Mother, pray for us.

Forsaken Mother, pray for us.

Desolate Mother, pray for us.

Mother most sad, pray for us.

Mother set around with anguish, pray for us.

Mother overwhelmed by grief, pray for us.

Mother transfixed by a sword, pray for us.

Mother crucified in thy heart, pray for us.

Mother bereaved of thy Son, pray for us.

Sighing Dove, pray for us.

Mother of Dolors, pray for us.

Fount of tears, pray for us.

Sea of bitterness, pray for us.

Field of tribulation, pray for us.

Mass of suffering, pray for us.

Mirror of patience, pray for us.

Rock of constancy, pray for us.

Remedy in perplexity, pray for us.

Joy of the afflicted, pray for us.
Ark of the desolate, pray for us.
Refuge of the abandoned, pray for us.
Shield of the oppressed, pray for us.
Conqueror of the incredulous, pray for us.
Solace of the wretched, pray for us.
Medicine of the sick, pray for us.
Help of the faint, pray for us.
Strength of the weak, pray for us.
Protectress of those who fight, pray for us.
Haven of the shipwrecked, pray for us.
Calmer of tempests, pray for us.
Companion of the sorrowful, pray for us.
Retreat of those who groan, pray for us.
Terror of the treacherous, pray for us.
Standard-bearer of the Martyrs, pray for us.
Treasure of the Faithful, pray for us.
Light of Confessors, pray for us.
Pearl of Virgins, pray for us.
Comfort of Widows, pray for us.
Joy of all Saints, pray for us.
Queen of thy Servants, pray for us.
Holy Mary, who alone art unexampled, pray for us.

Pray for us, most Sorrowful Virgin, that we may be made worthy of the promises of Christ.

Let us pray: O God, in whose Passion, according to the prophecy of Simeon, a sword of grief pierced through the most sweet soul of Thy glorious Blessed Virgin Mother Mary: grant that we, who celebrate the memory of her Seven Sorrows, may obtain the happy effect of Thy Passion, who lives and reigns world without end. Amen.

Prayers in Times of Distress

PRAYER OF SURRENDER

(WRITTEN BY A PATIENT WHILE RECOVERING FROM DEPRESSION)

I surrender to you, Lord, the fact that I have many faults and I fall many times a day. I give you all of my sins, deficiencies, and imperfections. Help me to accept everything about myself, help me to know you and to know myself so I may have true interior freedom. Help me to not be surprised when I fall, but to perseveringly get up and try again until I take my last breath.

I desire to be a saint and to reach the degree of holiness you have ordained for me, O Lord. I surrender the impossible task of taking this into my own hands, where I am sure to fail; rather I place all my trust in you, that you will make sure I reach the degree of sanctity you wish me to obtain. I trust you will make me a saint because I desire it, and I know you desire it. I know it is only through your grace that you will somehow transform me, a sinner, into a saint.

Help me to not have disdain for myself as I grow in self knowledge, as I know that will only offend the Holy Spirit within me, as you have created me, God, and know my sins and weaknesses better than I do. Help me to see myself through your eyes so that I may love you within myself; not to be surprised or discouraged when I fall; yet never to remain stagnant in mediocrity. Please give me a deep desire for holiness, and by your unfailing love and grace, guide me there. Help me to be a beacon of light and love to those around me. I pray that I will accept my daily cross and labor cheerfully and always with great love. Help me to make my home a school of love and mercy, not a place of discord, anger, or resentment.

I surrender each day to you, whatever shall come my way—good or bad—that I may never lose my peace or become anxious or discouraged. I pray I will never be afraid or resistant to the cross. I thank you for my crosses, especially this depression and the recent difficulties I have experienced. I accept this cross, knowing it is from your loving hands. I have now grown to somehow find joy in or love this cross, knowing you are consoling me and gently helping me through it. I know my crosses, big or small, are my path to sanctification and to true happiness with you.

I accept everything you give to me because I love you, Jesus, with all my heart. You are my love, my merciful Savior. God the Father, thank you for being my true loving Father. Thank you for creating me, and help me to grow in understanding of your unconditional, merciful love. Help me to grow in the understanding that you love me no matter what I do, that I don't have to worry about being "good enough" for you or earning your love. You already love me no matter how imperfect I am. Thank you for this simple love. You are patient with me, have had mercy upon me always, and have forgiven my most grievous sins, so help me always to show that mercy to others. Holy Spirit, thank you for dwelling in my soul. Help me always to remember and grow in understanding of this awesome gift. Thank you, Jesus, for being present in the Holy Eucharist, so that I can actually receive your Body, Blood, Soul, and Divinity. What a gift!

Your love and gifts are so great that many do not believe we have such a loving God. I pray that every heart may know this truth and choose you. O Holy Trinity, I adore you. Please never let me or my loved ones go. I pray that I may grow in faith, hope, and charity until I take my last breath.

Holy Mary, pray for us now and at the hour of our death
St. Thérèse of Lisieux, teach me your "little way."

Appendix 3

Address of Pope John Paul II on the Theme of Depression[93]

1. I am pleased to meet you on the occasion of the International Conference organized by the Pontifical Council for Health Pastoral Care on the theme of "Depression". I thank Cardinal Javier Lozano Barragán for his kind words on behalf of those present.

I greet the distinguished Specialists, who came to offer the fruit of their research in order to further knowledge of this pathology, so as to improve treatment and provide the right type of assistance to those concerned and to their families.

Likewise, my appreciation goes to those who are dedicated to the service of persons with depression, helping them to retain their trust in life. My thoughts naturally extend to families who are accompanying their loved one with affection and sensitivity.

2. Your work, dear participants in the Congress, has revealed the different, complex aspects of depression: they range from chronic sickness, more or less permanent, to a fleeting state linked to difficult events—conjugal and family conflicts, serious work problems, states of loneliness ...—that involve a crack, or even fracture in social, professional or family relationships. This

---

[93] John Paul II, Address to the Participants in the 18th International Conference Promoted by the Pontifical Council for Health and Pastoral Care on the Theme of "Depression," November 14, 2003.

disease is often accompanied by an existential and spiritual crisis that leads to an inability to perceive the meaning of life.

The spread of depressive states has become disturbing. They reveal human, psychological and spiritual frailties which, at least in part, are induced by society. It is important to become aware of the effect on people of messages conveyed by the *media* which exalt consumerism, the immediate satisfaction of desires and the race for ever greater material well-being. It is necessary to propose new ways so that each person may build his or her own personality by cultivating spiritual life, the foundation of a mature existence. The enthusiastic participation in the World Youth Days shows that the young generations are seeking Someone who can illuminate their daily journey, giving them good reasons for living and helping them to face their difficulties.

3. You have stressed that depression is always a spiritual trial. The role of those who care for depressed persons and who do not have a specifically therapeutic task consists above all in helping them to rediscover their self-esteem, confidence in their own abilities, interest in the future, the desire to live. It is therefore important to stretch out a hand to the sick, to make them perceive the tenderness of God, to integrate them into a community of faith and life in which they can feel accepted, understood, supported, respected; in a word, in which they can love and be loved. For them as for everyone else, contemplating Christ means letting oneself be "looked at" by him, an experience that opens one to hope and convinces one to choose life (cf. Dt 30:19).

In the spiritual process, *reading and meditation on the Psalms*, in which the sacred author expresses his joys and anxieties in prayer, can be of great help. The *recitation of the Rosary* makes it possible to find in Mary a loving Mother who teaches us how to live in Christ.

Participation in the Eucharist is a source of inner peace, because of the effectiveness of the Word and of the Bread of Life, and because of the integration into the ecclesial community that it achieves. Aware of the effort it costs a depressed person to do something which to others appears simple and spontaneous, one must endeavor to help him with patience and sensitivity, remembering the observation of St Theresa of the Child Jesus: "Little ones take little steps".

In his infinite love, God is always close to those who are suffering. Depressive illness can be *a way to discover other aspects of oneself* and new forms of encounter with God. Christ listens to the cry of those whose boat is rocked by the storm (cf. Mk 4:35-41). He is present beside them to help them in the crossing and guide them to the harbor of rediscovered peace.

4. The phenomenon of depression reminds the Church and all society how important it is to provide people, and especially youth, with examples and experiences that can help them to grow on the human, psychological, moral and spiritual levels. In fact, the absence of reference points can only contribute to making persons more fragile, inducing them to believe that all forms of behavior are the same. In this perspective, the role of the family, of school, of youth movements and of parish associations is very important because of the effect that these realities have on the person's formation.

Indeed, the public institutions have a significant role in guaranteeing a dignified standard of living, especially to abandoned, sick and elderly people. Equally necessary are policies for youth aimed at offering the young generations motives for hope to protect them from emptiness or from dangerous fillers.

5. Dear friends, in encouraging you to a renewed commitment in such an important task beside your brothers and sisters who are suffering from depression, I entrust you to the intercession of Mary Most Holy, *Salus infirmorum* (Health of the Sick). May every

individual and every family feel her motherly solicitude in times of difficulty.

To you all, to your collaborators and to your loved ones, I cordially impart my Apostolic Blessing.

About the Authors

Aaron Kheriaty is a psychiatrist and the Director of Residency Training and Medical Education in the Department of Psychiatry at the University of California, Irvine. He also serves as the Co-Director of the Program in Medical Ethics at UC Irvine School of Medicine. He studied philosophy as an undergraduate at the University of Notre Dame, obtained his MD from Georgetown University, and did his residency training in psychiatry at UC, Irvine. Dr. Kheriaty lives with his wife and five boys in San Juan Capistrano, California.

Monsignor John R. Cihak is a priest of the Archdiocese of Portland in Oregon currently working in the Vatican. He teaches a seminar at the Pontifical Gregorian University and is a chaplain and confessor for the Missionaries of Charity in Rome. Monsignor Cihak studied philosophy at the University of Notre Dame and earned his licentiate and doctorate in theology at the Pontifical Gregorian University. He has served as a pastor in western Oregon and as a professor and formator at Mount Angel Seminary.

An Invitation

Reader, the book that you hold in your hands was published by Sophia Institute Press. Sophia Institute seeks to nurture the spiritual, moral, and cultural life of souls and to spread the Gospel of Christ in conformity with the authentic teachings of the Roman Catholic Church.

Our press fulfills this mission by offering translations, reprints, and new publications that afford readers a rich source of the enduring wisdom of mankind.

We also operate two popular online Catholic resources: CrisisMagazine.com and CatholicExchange.com.

Crisis Magazine provides insightful cultural analysis that arms readers with the arguments necessary for navigating the ideological and theological minefields of the day. *Catholic Exchange* provides world news from a Catholic perspective as well as daily devotionals and articles that will help you to grow in holiness and live a life consistent with the teachings of the Church.

Sophia Institute Press also serves as the publisher for the Thomas More College of Liberal Arts and Holy Spirit College. Both colleges provide university-level education under the guiding light of Catholic teaching. If you know a young person seeking a college that takes seriously the adventure of learning and the quest for truth, please bring these institutions to his attention.

www.SophiaInstitute.com
www.CatholicExchange.com
www.CrisisMagazine.com

Sophia Institute Press® is a registered trademark of Sophia Institute.
Sophia Institute is a tax-exempt institution as defined by the
Internal Revenue Code, Section 501(c)(3). Tax I.D. 22-2548708.